D0466057

SEND ME SOMEONE

Send Me Someone

A True Story of Love Here & Hereafter

DIANA VON WELANETZ WENTWORTH

RENAISSANCE BOOKS
Los Angeles

HOUSTON PUBLIC LIBRARY

R01203 86968

Copyright © 2001 by Diana von Welanetz Wentworth

All rights reserved. Reproduction without permission in writing from the publisher is prohibited, except for brief passages in connection with a review. For permission, write: Renaissance Books, 5858 Wilshire Boulevard, Suite 200, Los Angeles, California 90036.

Parts of this work appeared in a slightly different version in *Chicken Soup for the Soul Cookbook* by Jack Canfield, Mark Victor Hansen, and Diana von Welanetz Wentworth, published by Health Communications, Inc. (1995).

Library of Congress Cataloging-in-Publication Data
von Welanetz Wentworth, Diana
    Send me someone : a true story of love here and hereafter / Diana von
    Welanetz Wentworth
       p. cm.
    Includes bibliographical references.
    ISBN 1-58063-200-9
       1. von Welanetz Wentworth, Diana. 2. Spiritualists—United States—Biography.
    3. Love—Miscellanea. I. Title.
BF1283.V66 A3 2001
133.9'092—dc21
[B]   00-069001

10 9 8 7 6 5 4 3 2 1

Design by Lisa-Theresa Lenthall and Susan Shankin

Published by Renaissance Books
Distributed by St. Martin's Press
Manufactured in the United States of America
First edition

You waited until you were alone.
Death is a private thing.
You knew your last act
was to a different audience.

As it entered you—
oh how you must have danced!
curving toward God,
elegant and alone.

Dear one, what is it like?
Tell us! What is death? . . .

ELIAS AMIDON

PART ONE

Paul

ONE

PAUL LAY on the couch, his aching legs comforted by the afghan I'd made the winter we lost everything. Touching the thick stitches, I remembered how—long ago—we'd spent months in a borrowed, snowbound cabin at Lake Arrowhead. To pass the time I'd crocheted remnants of rich woolen fabric together with soft yarn. As I'd laid out the various patterns, Paul and I worried over what direction our lives could take and how we might use our talents to build a future for ourselves and our three-year-old daughter, Lexi.

We'd talked about the milestones of our lives and what had brought us to such a low point. Like those remnants, could it all be combined into something new, more meaningful, and more beautiful? Our answer: *yes.* Our conversations then had helped us realize once again that crisis could offer gifts as well as challenges, and we'd grown from the experience.

But this time, nearly twenty years later, there would be no opportunity to reinvent ourselves. We now had to face the possibility that Paul would not survive the cancer spreading through his body.

He looked plaintively at me. "Are we just fooling ourselves, Kitten?"

It was a good question. Positive thoughts or not, the radiation and chemo didn't seem to be working.

"I can't stand leaving you in a mess." Paul worried out loud about how I'd run our business alone, how I'd manage all of the details he was so good at handling. "Can you get a lawyer on the phone for me? I need to find out about making a will."

Within an hour we'd found an attorney and dictated a simple document. The necessary signatures would be added within a few days, and now there was nothing to be done but hold each other wordlessly. When his breathing deepened, I assumed he was dozing off and rose to step silently toward the kitchen to refill his water glass. He called after me, *"I don't want you to be alone!"*

I didn't stop or even break my stride.

"Then send me someone!" I blurted, surprising myself.

It was an electrifying moment. Something had happened, but I didn't know what.

"I will," he said. Then even more forcefully, "I *will!*"

Lexi and I said goodbye to the last of the hundred or so friends who had come to our home following Paul's memorial service.

She was pale. The stress of the last four months showed in her face, making her appear older than her twenty years. She'd been a trouper during her father's illness, moving home from college, working with our office manager to keep our business, the Inside Edge, running as smoothly as possible. She'd been so busy taking care of her dad and me, she'd had little time to deal with her own feelings.

Kneeling, I arranged photographs of Paul on a small table next to the window, the same ones we'd had on view in front of the altar at the memorial service. There he was, debonair in a tuxedo as he waltzed with Lexi at her debutante ball; there he was, at the helm of a sailboat, the wind blowing in his hair, the pleasure of the moment etched in his handsome face. Among the photos was also a large sepia print of our clasped hands, taken in the hospital only a few days before he died. Alongside the pictures, ashes inside a book-shaped bronze urn were all that remained of his physical form.

Now, with everyone gone, it was just Lexi and me. She sat on the floor next to me and we looked at each other, as though in our silence we might understand something more of all that had happened that day.

Finally, she started sobbing. "You know what's hardest of all for me, Mom? My daddy won't be at my wedding someday. He won't be there to give me away."

All I could do was hold her and rock her until she was quiet again, then she dragged herself off to bed. I snuffed out the candles around the pictures and flowers we'd brought from the service, then changed into my nightgown and went to bed too, waiting for peaceful sleep to overtake me.

But unexpectedly I was alert, sensing Paul in the room just as clearly as I had when he'd been alive. He felt so real that I felt I had to talk to him.

"Why, you're *here*, aren't you?" I whispered aloud.

Yes, he answered in my mind.

A warm sense of release flooded through me.

We'll always be together, you and I. It is our destiny. We were together even before we met . . .

Since his fateful diagnosis only four months earlier, I never anticipated I would actually feel his presence when he was gone. I'd always thought we'd die together somehow. I had even joked about a double coffin. But now I wondered if perhaps those thoughts foreshadowed something else: that we'd simply *be together* . . . as I deeply felt we were now.

This meant I could speak to him anytime—with my thoughts—and he could speak to me.

"Am I just imagining you?" I asked aloud after a moment.

I am as near to you now as I've ever been.

Could I believe any of this? Was my mind just playing tricks? Even if these were mind tricks, I found them comforting. Melting into him as I always had, I fell asleep as if enfolded in his arms.

The following morning I awoke feeling remarkably content. Was this denial? I *knew* denial, knew it because of the optimistic lies I tried to tell myself during Paul's illness. This wasn't denial. This felt like grace.

Yes. I was sure of it! Paul's presence seemed even more real, as if I had his full attention, and to a degree I'd hardly known during his illness, when he withdrew more and more to a private, inner world. But now I felt as if we had truly merged. I was filled with a quiet joy. How many others had experienced these same feelings but kept silent, perhaps for fear of being misunderstood or even of seeming unbalanced?

Love endures, I heard him say. And with that thought, I knew I would find the words to tell this story.

———

I felt Paul's presence with me continually during the next three days. On the fourth, however, I had a fright. As I was falling asleep and tried to feel him, he had—what was I to call it?—he had "disappeared."

"Are you there?" I whispered, as though saying the words aloud would get his attention more effectively than if I simply thought them to myself.

Nothing.

"Where are you?"

I felt myself starting to panic. "Paul?"

He wasn't there. Just as I'd begun to get accustomed to the idea of his being closer than ever, he had vanished. Yet the next morning I felt him with me again. Soon I would find out where he'd been.

Jacob, one of Paul's buddies, phoned that afternoon and said, "We held a kind of wake for Paul last night, and it turned into a real party." He lowered his voice, "It may sound strange to you, but we all felt like he was really there!"

"Oh! So that's where he was!"

"What?"

"Nothing," I said. "I'm just glad he was with friends."

———————

The next morning, a Saturday, I awoke with such a fullness of Paul's presence I reached out instinctively to touch his head of dark hair. Then came the shock of remembering.

I reminded myself, "Breathe, Diana. Feelings are fleeting . . . feelings are fleeting." It was a mantra I'd repeated to myself inwardly over and over during the four months of his cancer treatments.

Golden shafts of sunlight streamed onto the quilt at the foot of the bed, where our calico cat, KC—named for the KCET studio lot where we found her as a stray—sprawled on her back, basking in the warmth and silence. I too could linger as long as I wished. I remembered how Paul often encouraged me to stay in bed on Saturday mornings, even building a fire in the fireplace during the winter and bribing me with a breakfast tray. After straightening my pillows and placing the tray on my lap, he'd watch expectantly to see my delight in the heart-shaped pat of butter he always prepared for me.

No breakfast tray this morning. I wasn't hungry anyway.

I got out of bed only long enough to start my own fire, make a cup of tea, then slip back under the warm covers.

My eyes fell on a paperweight, a sphere of crystal; its clear and opaque surface representing the earth. Paul had given it to me for my forty-eighth birthday a few weeks earlier. Now I realized it would be a touchstone, a memory of that day . . . one touchstone among so many for us. And I wondered what others I might find—things to remind me of the happy times before our world fell apart.

I opened the bottom drawer of my bedside table and took out a large, heart-shaped box that had held an extravagant array of chocolates one long-ago Valentine's Day. In the years since, I'd used it as a repository for my mementos, precious things that wouldn't fit in photo albums—Paul's love letters, my sorority pin, Lexi's letters to the Tooth Fairy. The dark red velvet box was faded now and all the more beautiful for its age.

I lifted the lid and set it aside. My fingers moved to feel the seed pearls stitched into the yellowed lace border of the antique handkerchief I carried at our wedding. Inside its folds rested our wedding rings, two Florentine circles gleaming with a patina of years of daily wearing. They were all we could afford at the time, and served as a symbol of my decision to let go of a life of luxury. Without the graceful spray of tiny diamonds that decorated the front of mine, it would be small enough to fit inside his—just as I so wanted to nestle inside him, forever comforted and safe.

I felt an urge to sift down to the bottom, past the little envelope of baby teeth, past the years of Mother's Day cards and Valentine cards, to the beginning—to the faded blue airmail envelopes with Hong Kong postmarks and a tiny tin of Tiger Balm purchased from a street vendor on the night I first realized I had found my destiny.

I picked up a florist's card. With a fine black artist's pen, Paul had drawn a sketch of a tiger's tail topped with a delicate butterfly and written *I Love You* in Asian-style calligraphy. I arranged the card and the yellowing envelopes with their exotic stamps over the quilt in front of me, laying them out as a treasure map of the journey we'd embarked on together.

October 1962

Our relationship began with a rush of intuition.

Intuition—that subtle sense of suddenly and mysteriously knowing things one has no way of knowing—became something I would understand and trust as the years passed. I remember well my first strong intuitive moment. The event was not earth-shattering for me, but it certainly took me by surprise. I was eighteen years old in the spring of 1959 and had been studying on the pledge porch of my sorority house. Some girls were playing an Elvis Presley song on the radio.

"Can you turn that down?" I asked. One looked at me and said, "We ought to take this somewhere else. Diana doesn't like Elvis Presley." I was overtaken by the strangest of feelings, that to allow the impression to stand uncorrected would make me guilty of disloyalty—to Elvis. Someday I would meet him, I was suddenly sure, even though at the time he was in the army and in Germany, and had obviously never heard of me.

"I don't dislike him," I said, wondering why I was so sure of myself. "In fact, I'm going to date him someday." I was having a moment of prescience, the first of many, and didn't know it.

The following summer my mother took me on my first trip to Europe. We were staying at the Prince de Galles Hotel in Paris. It was June 19, 1959. Bobby, a teenager we'd met, ran toward us to tell me, "Elvis Presley is in the dining room! I'd give anything for his autograph, but I can't get up the nerve to ask!"

I felt a start of memory but concealed it pretty well, I thought. I asked the concierge for paper and pencil and went into the dining room, Bobby trailing behind. Elvis was in uniform, his hair GI short; taking my eyes off him was even harder after my approach caught his attention. Everybody who lived through that era remembers that Elvis was a beautiful guy with a beautiful smile, but when he aimed it at you and pulled the trigger—oh, brother!

"My friend Bobby would like your autograph," I said. He signed and we chatted for a few minutes. That might have been the end of it, but that night my mother and I went to the show at the Folies Bergère and, as it happened, so did Elvis.

His bodyguard recognized me, and when our tour bus returned to the hotel, Elvis was waiting in the lobby. He was very polite, even gallant, and he wanted to speak to my mother. He asked her permission to escort me to the late show at the Lido, the famous Parisian nightclub, that very evening.

It felt wonderful to be on his arm. He was impeccably polite and kind to me even as he was mobbed for autographs. We were shown to a table that was practically on stage where bare-breasted showgirls flirted wildly with Elvis throughout the performance.

The next day I was boarding a bus to leave for the next city on our tour, when Elvis's bodyguard came running up with a note from

Elvis giving me his phone number in Bad Nauheim and asking me to call when our group reached Wiesbaden. I called just after our train arrived, and that evening Elvis and his bodyguard, Lamar Fike, picked me up. We rode for about an hour to the little rented house he was living in off-base.

Lamar put out some dinner for us, then Elvis sang to me for hours in the living room, accompanying himself on both piano and guitar. It was the strangest experience. I couldn't think of a thing to do but smile at him, and after a while my cheeks ached.

I didn't see Elvis again for two years. We stayed in touch through Christmas cards, and I wrote to him the next year when I got engaged. When his time in the army was complete, he returned to Hollywood to make a movie and rented a house in Bel Air. I had just broken my engagement when he called to renew our friendship.

I enjoyed how excited my brother, Gene, and my father were about meeting him, and was actually quite surprised. After all, what did Papa really know of him? Neither wanted to just hang around and stare, so they staged a seemingly natural scenario. It was decided that my brother would answer the door and escort Elvis to the den to meet Papa. Gene would offer him some lemonade, and Mother would then come in to say hello. Finally I would make my entrance.

All went as orchestrated, and I was soon waving goodbye as Elvis and I left in a limousine to ride to his home. There we spent a comfortable evening with the ten or so relatives and bodyguards who lived with him, as well as his father, Vernon, who was visiting.

We watched television and ate pizza, sitting on the couch in his den. One of his buddies, Joe Esposito, took me aside. He handed me a gold record that had arrived that day and kindly gave me the thrill of presenting it to Elvis myself.

19

The next time I saw Elvis, he had moved to an even larger house in Bel Air. He had even more people living with him, as well as a pet chimpanzee who misunderstood and bit me when I took his bowl of potato chips to refill it. Elvis and several of the guys had to pull him off me. The teeth marks lasted for days.

My sorority sisters had never been completely convinced that I was telling the truth about dating Elvis, so one evening after a movie I drove a few of them past his house. As it happened, it was January 8 and there was a huge party going on for his birthday. My friends insisted I ring the doorbell. Joe and Lamar recognized me and welcomed us all.

Elvis and I were friends for years after that. I know he came to a horrible end, but I prefer to remember him in his youth, joyful and full of hope, with the world in his pocket.

———————

It was three years after that, on an afternoon in the fall of 1962, that another sense of clear knowing took me by surprise. I was twenty-one years old and alone in my room in our family home in Beverly Hills, California, when I was struck abruptly with a clear sense of my future. I knew that the man I was expected to marry was wrong for me and that my destiny lay elsewhere.

With this flash of intuition, I felt like I was stepping out of a fog into clear, warm sunlight. I trusted the feeling enough to telephone him then and there. "You don't love me the way I know I will be loved one day," I said. He was surprised, but I could tell by his voice that what I'd said was so. And we ended our relationship.

At that moment my parents were packing to go—by themselves—on a tour of Asia they'd been anticipating for months. But when Mother learned of my canceled engagement plans, she insisted

I accompany them. She stood firm in the face of my father's fury at the last-minute change.

My father——"Papa" to me; Eugene Webb Jr. to the rest of the world——was probably afflicted with what today is called bipolar disorder. We never knew if he would come home from work on a cloud or in a rage. When my father erupted——and it could happen anywhere, public or private——his explosion was terrifying.

My older brother, Gene, and I were shielded in childhood by our mother, who dealt with Papa's sporadic and irrational furies by pretending perfect composure. When his storm passed, however, what remained was something even more frightening to me. She——both of them, in fact——would act as if nothing had happened. And Papa never, ever apologized.

I could have responded in many ways. I might have run to my room, thrown a tantrum, argued with logic, argued with tears. Instead, as children usually do, I did what I'd learned by example. I mirrored my mother and her ability to freeze: don't breathe, don't feel, it will pass.

When my father wasn't around, my mother——Mimi——was very affectionate, always hugging me, always telling me, "I love you with all my heart." And even though she didn't speak up when Gene and I were the subject of his rage, she was still my refuge in that unsafe world, a world in which my father punished us by stinging our legs with a riding crop.

On that day, after Papa's rage had dissipated, he ranted at Mother as if I weren't in the room, "Why do you let her do things like this? I've worked my fingers to the bone to give my family everything! Why in the world doesn't she marry him? He comes from a great family and could provide the kind of life we raised her for. Now that she's dropped out of college, she won't have a chance to meet the right kind of man at all. Diana never finishes anything!"

However, I felt so sure I'd made the right decision that my confidence must have been contagious, and Mother and I weathered the storm easily. The three of us departed only a few days later for Japan.

In Tokyo I had my first taste of a culture that was truly foreign and I was fascinated by its contrasts—the throb of the business districts, the aroma of incense in the ancient temples, the stark simplicity of Japanese homes and meditation gardens.

Trailing behind the other members of our tour group, I was most deeply affected by our visit to the Hiroshima Peace Memorial Museum. Walls lined with graphic pictures and vivid exhibits of the devastation of the A-bomb shocked me with their portrayal of the effects of nuclear weapons. Above the exit, words of entreaty implored us not to cast blame for what happened but to take the steps necessary to assure it will never happen again.

The appeal haunted me, leaving me silent and contemplative during the remaining three weeks of the tour. A yearning began in me that day to do something that would bring people together. Eventually, years later, this same yearning would move me to a midlife career change. Maybe it's no wonder that for much of my life I've worked to create peace and harmony.

Papa was an emotional bomb that could explode at any time. He was even more abusive to Mother, sometimes irrationally accusing her of being unfaithful, knocking her down, kicking her, and leaving her crumpled in her closet.

When I was about sixteen, I silently applauded my mother for settling the battle with Papa's behavior: after years of tolerating his rages, beatings, and threats to leave her penniless and without her children, she filed a restraining order against him and sued him for divorce.

Neither of them left the house though, and after a division of community prop-
erty put half of their holdings in her own personal bank account for keeps, she
dropped the suit. He was much better behaved after that. Much.

Our tour opened new places to me every day—the Japanese countryside, Manila and the jungles of the Philippines, the floating markets of Thailand, the Parisian ambiance of Saigon.

In Singapore we stayed at the sprawling wooden Raffles Hotel,
where so many writers have found inspiration. That's where I tasted
my first Chicken Kiev and slept under a ceiling fan in a bed swathed
in mosquito netting. In Cambodia we hiked through heat and
humidity in the ruins of the recently discovered temple of Ankor
Wat, and our bus was spat upon by people we passed in the villages,
for reasons we didn't understand. Even my father was subdued by all
we were experiencing and only exploded once or twice. In my continuing quiet, receptive frame of mind, I memorized the sights and
sounds and smells.

For the last stop on the tour we were booked into the new,
ultramodern Hong Kong Ambassador Hotel, on the waterfront of
the Kowloon section of Hong Kong. Even though everyone in our
party was ready to drop, the tour guide scheduled an orientation
meeting in the early evening. Afterward, my parents and I dragged
ourselves up to the rooftop restaurant for what we hoped would be
a quick dinner.

Too tired to wait for dessert, I asked to be excused. I didn't
know it then, but as I walked to the elevator, a man who had been
watching me put down his napkin and followed. He reached the elevator door just as it closed behind me.

I awoke very early the next morning and dressed quickly, not wanting to miss a minute of the day. From the street sounds outside, I knew Hong Kong's business day was already beginning. And though my family wouldn't be ready for breakfast for another hour, I hurried downstairs.

The aromas of coffee and sweet rolls were inviting and my first thought was to follow my nose. But something stopped me in the middle of the vast, pillared lobby. I asked myself, *What am I doing here?*

Businessmen in fashionable, narrow-lapeled suits and tourists draped with cameras rushed toward the revolving doors and the tour buses beyond. Suddenly I felt as though the world were going through its paces in slow motion. Self-consciously I headed toward a pillar not far from the elevators, drawn there by a mysterious sense of anticipation.

The doors of one elevator opened and two men with briefcases emerged. The sight of the taller one stunned me. I reeled backward as if I were going to faint and was relieved to feel the support of the column behind my back. The two men, deep in conversation, went by.

A bellboy approached the shorter man, handed him a slip of paper, and pointed toward the telephone. The taller man looked away, minding his own business as I continued to watch him. He looked around, saw me, and—momentarily—our eyes locked. Feeling blood rush to my face, I lost my nerve and looked away. Confused by the intensity of my feelings, I knew even then that I would always remember the moment. I was pleading with myself, *Look at him! Don't let him walk away!* When I looked up again, he was enjoying the situation immensely, his wide gray eyes dancing. He walked up and extended his hand.

"Paul von Welanetz."

"Excuse me?"

"Oh. I'm sorry. My name is Paul . . . von . . . Wel-a-netz."

I shook his hand.

"Diana Webb."

"Easy for you to say."

"What? Oh, a joke." An eon passed. What do I say next? Come on, Diana!

"What brings you to Hong Kong?"

I told him I was on a tour with my parents.

"What countries have you visited? Which did you like most?" He had what seemed to be a faint British accent and a restrained, cultivated air. I don't remember what I said. But at least we were talking—or he was. I was just so relieved that something, anything at all, was happening between us. Somehow I knew him and sensed that later I would come to know him intimately.

I was in a whirlpool of excitement, attraction, and shyness. Out of the corner of my eye I saw his companion hang up the telephone. Paul asked me to have coffee with him that afternoon. I accepted. At breakfast I told my parents I'd met a man I was going to see again later that day. Grumbling, my father wanted to know why I would go out with some guy I'd met in a hotel lobby. But Mother always trusted my judgment and, seeing the light in my eyes, understood right away that this man might be someone special.

After the morning tour, Mother and I separated from the group and she shifted into high gear to help me get ready. We crossed the road to the Peninsula Hotel, where I had my hair done. After, because I hoped my coffee date would become a dinner date, we went shopping. I chose a black velvet A-line dress, a copy of a Valentino—one I have kept all these years wrapped in tissue—along with the parasol that matched the green silk sundress I'd been wearing that morning.

I spent the afternoon in anticipation that tilted beyond anxiety into near terror. I bathed, then wrapped in one of the hotel's thick terry cloth robes, I peered in the mirror, trying to look past my flaws. At nearly 5' 10", with very thick, jet-black hair, I had once been interested in modeling, but even in those years I was a bit too curvy for a big-time career in New York, Paris, or Rome. Paul was also tall—6' 3", I estimated. At least I wouldn't have to wear flat shoes, stoop, or bend my knees.

Attempting to get hold of myself, I curled up in a chair and tried to become involved in an Agatha Christie book. Nothing. Ink on paper. I turned on the black-and-white TV. On the English-language channel was a fuzzy kinescope of a BBC serial, *Coronation Street*. The telephone rang twice, the way English telephones do.

"Hello?"

"Ah, you're there. It's Paul. Let's meet upstairs on the roof in fifteen minutes. Ask for my table, if you can still say my name."

———

Paul von Welanetz rose as soon as he saw me. He had a table by the window. Far below was a panorama of sampans, freighters, cruise ships, and every possible kind of coastal vessel. Around us waiters were delivering trays of drinks. Paul regarded me with amusement.

"What?" I asked.

"You look like you'd prefer a cocktail. Go ahead. I'll join you."

"Why did you invite me for coffee?"

"The way you were dressed this morning, I wasn't sure you were old enough to drink."

"And now?"

"It doesn't matter . . . You're the most beautiful girl in the world."

I sat back, staring into those gray eyes of his.

"You're dressed for dinner. Do you have plans?" he asked.

"None I can't break."

"Consider them broken."

———————

Dinner was a double-date with his partner, Harry, who enjoyed talking business with Paul—the British textbook business, as it turned out. Even if I'd been interested, it wouldn't have mattered, since I didn't understand the business terms they used. Harry's date was no more accessible. A Chinese movie star, she flashed me sullen, contemptuous looks while picking her teeth with an ivory toothpick behind her cupped hand, as is the Chinese custom.

Paul attempted to include me in the conversation, but being with such an obviously sophisticated trio left me afraid to open my mouth. Then there was the age difference. Paul, I had learned, was almost fourteen years my senior, thirty-five years old to my twenty-one. That, plus the fact he was so completely self-assured and at ease, left me limp with insecurity. I felt I was losing all sense of myself.

I was an open, friendly child until I was eight. I loved attending the local grammar school with my best friend, Alice. I felt powerful, and loved to jump and yell and leap off walls. I dreamed of being . . . fabulous.

But Papa's criticism was forever in the background: the reprimands I didn't understand, the sense of being chastised and demeaned. From that I learned things about myself: I never finish anything, I'll never be able to take care of myself.

When I was entering the fourth grade my parents decided both Gene and I should go to boarding schools. Gene was sent to a military school across town and

I went to a girls' school only a few miles away. Just four or five of us from the lower grades boarded there, so our wing of the building was nearly empty. I had a roommate the first few days but she soon left and I had a hall of empty rooms all to myself.

Excruciatingly lonely, I was already good at numbing my feelings, and never realized I could have gone home for good if I had simply asked my mother. Fortunately, I boarded for only a year. I once asked mother why we had been sent away, and she said Papa insisted on it because we children were noisy sometimes and made him nervous.

Because I went to a different school, I didn't really fit in with the other kids in the neighborhood, and I was lonely much of the time. When not in school I spent time in the backyard by myself. I'd climb up into the fig tree to listen to the wind rustle the papery flat leaves, and I'd eat the sticky black figs.

On summer evenings I'd capture moths off the lantana flowers and put them in a glass Mason jar, making holes in the lid with an ice pick so they would have air. My brother told me if I rubbed some of the powder off their fragile wings they couldn't fly away, so I did that, hoping they would stay and keep me company.

One evening, as I lay on the lawn, I could hear a song coming from the radio inside the house, where my parents were listening to The Hit Parade. *"Someone to Watch Over Me." The singer longed for the someone who would one day be her partner, her lover. I felt a tightness in my chest, a feeling I always pushed away. How I yearned to grow up and find that someone.*

Later, Paul escorted me onto the dance floor. I loved being swept into his arms there, but in my nervousness my feet danced every way but his. My legs were shaking so badly, I simply couldn't follow his lead. I stumbled more than once.

Back at the table, he studied me. I tried to hide my trembling as he lit my cigarette, then his own. Increasingly, I felt moments of panic and wanted to bolt. Silent almost all evening, I judged myself a loser and a castoff in Paul's world, but at the door to my room he invited me to dinner again the following evening.

The next day was one of mood-swings and fantasies that left me feeling completely disoriented. At dinnertime I was profoundly disappointed to discover our companions were once again to be the shop-talking Harry and the self-focused movie actress.

The four of us boarded the Star Ferry for the short trip to Hong Kong Island. As we walked along the waterfront to our restaurant, Paul stopped to negotiate the price of a small, paper-wrapped tin of Tiger Balm, which in those days was regarded as a magical cure-all. Not wanting a lump in his suit pocket, he asked me to carry it for him in my purse.

Our restaurant had a glorious view of the harbor, but once again I said almost nothing. On the ferry back to Kowloon, Paul leaned over and whispered, "Don't you ever let your hair down?"

I felt so embarrassed I couldn't answer. I didn't know why I was acting so strangely. I hated him for pointing out my stiffness, and for causing it. Desperate to be back in my room so I could be confused in private, I walked quickly, almost ran, and stayed ahead of him nearly all the way back to the hotel. After an abrupt "Goodnight!" I shut the door firmly in his face, furious with myself for having so obviously lost control.

When I was growing up, I was expected only to be cheerful and decorative. No one knew how much I slept. Sleep was my escape, the way I coped with bouts of heavy, defeating depression that had so darkened my natural exuberance. I woke one afternoon to find my worried brother holding a mirror under my nose to see if I was breathing.

Being Queen of the Beverly Hills Easter Parade in the spring of 1958,
and performing an elaborate curtsy as a debutante in the fall, were a kind of role-
playing that seemed to have nothing at all to do with the real me.

I always just assumed I would be a housewife and mother like my mom, and
had drifted along believing somehow I would find the perfect man for me . . .
someone who would fill my emptiness.

I sat down in front of the makeup mirror and raged at my reflection. "What's wrong with you? He's arrogant! He doesn't care a thing about you! If you ever see him again, you're nuts!"

Moments later, the telephone rang. Against my will, I smiled at the sound of his voice. "You have my Tiger Balm in your purse. May I come and get it?"

"Of course."

Putting the telephone down, I berated myself in the mirror. "Idiot!"

Paul knocked on the door. He leaned casually toward me with one arm against the doorjamb, charisma pouring off him like waves of light. I handed him the little paper-wrapped tin.

"How about having breakfast with me tomorrow morning? It's my day off." His voice was deep, yet sweet at the same time.

"What time?" I asked

"Eight o'clock."

With the door closed again, I hurried back to my reflection. "You are definitely nuts!" I glared. "What in the world are you doing?"

I was irresistibly attracted to him, yet he made me so agitated that I felt paralyzed with confusion. What in the world had happened to my comfortable intuitive sense that I already knew him? And why was he still interested in me?

TWO

IN THE CORNER of my memory box, beneath a yellowed hand-kerchief, lay a tiny faded photograph with a white rippled border.

It showed Paul, a rickshaw and driver behind him, in front of the Ambassador Hotel dressed in a khaki safari shirt, grinning at the miracle of our meeting. He was holding a small paper bag.

November 5, 1962

The next morning I was greeted by a wholly different incarnation of Paul von Welanetz. I'd seen him only in business clothes—light-weight woolens by day; more serious, hard-finish, dark blue suits at night.

I already knew this man had a sense of style, and his idea of casual was also perfect for him. He was wearing a short-sleeved, khaki safari jacket and matching slacks—a look, I was to learn, he would favor the rest of his life. I had on the floral silk dress I'd been wearing when we met, and today I was carrying its matching parasol.

Conversation was far easier for me that morning as we walked along Nathan Road. Away from his business associate and in his cotton safari garb, Paul was relaxed and more accessible. I enjoyed the new sense of ease between us and we chatted and laughed together as if we'd known each other a long time.

We walked for hours up and down narrow alleys, through the Jade Market and the Bird Market, talking about the things we both liked. Among them, books. We entered an English bookstore, and while I browsed, Paul quietly asked for something the clerk slipped into a small paper bag Paul carried as we continued our walk.

Now and then he recited long passages of poetry from memory, in his rich and resonant voice. He said he enjoyed the works of Lin Yutang in *The Art of Living* and the poetry of the East. He was particularly captivated by the rhythm of an Eastern chant: ". . . one hundred thousand years or so."

We began to chant the words together and matched our steps to their rhythm . . . "one *hundred thousand years* or *so*" . . . "one *hundred thousand years* or *so*" . . . as we walked along the Kowloon waterfront and onto a dock jutting into the crowded harbor, where scores of families lived aboard colorful, traditional Chinese junks. A group of ragged children were playing with a ball, which Paul caught just before it would have sailed into the water. For thanks, they asked him for coins. He laughed aloud and knelt down to talk with them in pidgin English, his face on the same level with theirs.

I remember thinking how graceful he was for such a tall man. He moved with the easy elegance of a dancer or an athlete, and I couldn't take my eyes off him. When he stood up again, I knew he could read the expression on my face.

"Have you taken the tram to Victoria Peak yet?"

"No."

"Then let's do it now. It's a wonderful view."

We rode the Star Ferry again across Hong Kong Bay to Hong Kong Central, and this time it seemed a much lovelier, safer place. We walked across Connaught Road and climbed the hill to the Peak Tram Station, from which the funicular railway car pulled us up the side of the mountain at nearly a forty-five-degree angle. From the 2,000-foot peak we had a panoramic view of the entire harbor and the "New Territories" in the distance. It was the most romantic morning of my life.

"What's important to you, Kitten?" Paul asked. When he said "Kitten," I felt as though he'd been calling me that for years.

After a moment, I answered shyly, "Kindness."

We walked—wordlessly, hand-in-hand—along Old Peak Road and past forests of bamboo and fern, until we came to the other side of the island and a view of Macao and the Chinese mainland in the distance. Paul found a small, sharp stone and, standing on a boulder, scratched in the face of a rock:

'62

PW

"Your turn." He handed me the stone, put his hands on my waist, and lifted me high enough so I could scratch my initials beneath his:

DW

A gust of wind blew under and billowed my skirt. As Paul's arm moved down around my legs to hold it from flying upward, I slid down slowly, smiling, turning into his embrace. The move could not have been more natural. Every sight and scent and sacred garden of my journey through Asia had led me to this moment. Paul kissed me and I shuddered like never before. In that moment, I glimpsed a love without any boundaries, a love that would never end.

———

That afternoon I was to join my tour group for a boat ride around the other side of Hong Kong Island and an early dinner at the historic Repulse Bay Hotel. I longed to stay with Paul but I didn't want to disappoint my parents, or tell them what was happening yet. Paul told me he would spend the time rock-climbing and I could look for him somewhere above Victoria Peak.

Hours later I sat alone, in a romantic reverie, on the bow of the sightseeing boat. As it approached the backside of Victoria Peak, I spotted him waving to me from atop the highest point, some five hundred feet above where we'd carved our initials that afternoon. I stood and waved back at his silhouette against the sky.

An eager and smiling Paul von Welanetz was waiting for me at the dock when the tour boat returned that evening. He held a package, a gift for me, the book he'd picked up at the bookshop that lovely morning: *The Rubáiyat of Omar Khayyám*.

On the blue-and-cream paper flyleaf, which he'd removed from the book to insert in his portable typewriter, he'd written:

'62

PW

DW

I feel a great deal more kindness for you than I shall ever have time to speak. And a single page is little space for the troops of gentle thoughts that invest themselves, on every hand, with affection and chosen words.

PAUL

A dreamer, I thought. In his special way, he was just perfect for me. I was just so glad he was alive. As we danced that night in the hotel's intimate little cocktail lounge, our bodies melded together as if we'd always been part of each other.

The next day we rode the tram again and hiked down the backside of Victoria Peak to picnic beside a reservoir. We couldn't take our eyes—or hands—off each other.

He had time that day to tell me tales of his travels, noting that as a result of his wanderlust he'd been around the world four times. He didn't need a book to recite to me, and easily quoted from Don Blanding's poem "Names Are Ships" in his deep, modulated voice:

> *Names! The lure in names of places,*
> *Stirring thoughts of foreign faces,*
> *Ports and palaces and steamers.*
> *Names are ships to carry dreamers.*
> *Pago-pago, Suva, Java,*
> *Languor, lotuses and lava,*
> *Everything a dreamer wishes. . . .*

Paul was not only a dreamer; he'd been an actor too, having attended the American Academy of Dramatic Arts in New York, where he developed the precise way of speaking I'd noticed the morning we met. And he was an artist, trained by the graphic-artist stepfather he loved. He proudly showed me pictures of a mural he'd been commissioned to paint in a church.

He was also an outdoorsman, strong and rugged, yet refined and cultured. He'd hunted white rhino in Africa on the Oomfalozi Game Reserve—not to kill but to tranquilize with a dart gun so the rhino could be safely moved to another location. His more traditional hunting ended the day he killed a mother deer and decided he would never kill again. I was spellbound by stories of his adventures through the jungles of South Africa.

"What do you love to do?" he asked.

Sometimes I'd get very excited about organizing clubs or producing shows for the kids in the neighborhood, or setting up a lemonade or cookie stand. I had two dreams: one of being married to a wonderful man who would cherish me and never get angry, and another of opening a restaurant to serve my mother's spaghetti, a place where families would come to enjoy my food and time together. I never cared much for dolls—my favorite game alone in my room was "short-order cook."

Mimi—my mother—loved cooking. The kitchen was her sanctum, our safe haven, because my father never entered. I loved to sit at the kitchen table and write pretend recipes on index cards for my own wooden recipe-file box, just like Mom's. Sometimes I'd beg to help, and Mimi would tie an apron around me and show me how to do something new, like shelling and chopping walnuts for her chocolate fudge.

More than anything, I loved to help Mimi make her spaghetti sauce. While the tangy tomato mixture simmered and splattered all over the white enamel stove, I would spoon a little into a saucer, open the freezer next to the stove, place it on top of the boxes of frozen vegetables, close the door, and wait restlessly until it was cool enough for a taste. On the days we made sauce, my job was to hold the bundle of dried spaghetti and insert it into the huge kettle of boiling water. I loved how the thin strands opened against the side of the pot like a burst of the sun's rays.

"My passion is cooking," I said. "In fact I've felt an urge to cook and share food with others all my life."

I told him how, as a child, I loved to go to restaurants with my family. I hadn't known my father paid for the food, and I thought waitresses were angels who, out of loving kindness, brought us anything we wanted. Whenever someone asked me what I wanted to be when I grew up, I would say, "Either a movie star or a waitress!"

Concerned Paul might be bored, I looked at his face. It was alive with interest so I continued.

"My favorite toy was an order pad from the dime store. I'd stand by my desk and pretend to take a customer's order, then tear it off and slap it on top of the bookcase I'd moved to separate my room into two parts. After that, I'd dash behind it to my pretend kitchen and break eggs on a pretend griddle and flip some fantasy hash browns. There was always something about nurturing others by serving them food that felt good to me."

After that, Paul told everyone I was a wonderful cook, even though he'd never tasted any of my cooking. How I loved his belief in me.

One of Paul's dreams was to have a sailboat one day and sail around the world. I was ready to follow him . . . anywhere. If he had not been fourteen years my senior, with the maturity that went with it, we would have disappeared from the rest of the world then and there.

But we did have some problems. Big ones. I was leaving in three days, flying back to Los Angeles a week ahead of my parents to be the maid of honor in a friend's wedding. Paul's business was based in London. We lived half a world apart. We would not be able to see each other for weeks. However, considering . . . it was probably good we would have some time to reflect.

"If things were different . . ." he asked me that evening, "and if this stands the test of time, would you be willing to throw in your lot with mine . . . for a hundred thousand years or so?"

I didn't hesitate. "Oh, yes. Definitely, yes!"

It wasn't a standard proposal and that's why I remember the words so precisely. In the look we shared following his question and my reply, we both knew things *would* soon be different and that we were each other's destiny.

———

Neither of us, of course, had forgotten about my parents. Paul was sensitive to their concern about their daughter's sudden romance with an older man.

But I knew everything would be all right. Mother, charmed by Paul from the moment he presented her with roasted chestnuts from a street vendor, could feel my happiness and did not voice whatever concerns she might have had. My father ignored what was happening, mumbling something about "ships that pass in the night."

Those final days in Hong Kong flew by. Paul and I must have walked every street in the city. I began to call him Tiger, because of the Tiger Balm he'd had me carry for him. He continued calling me Kitten, which I loved, for it made me feel vulnerable, innocent, and cherished. He said I was a gentle butterfly and he would be my protector. He sent roses to my room, accompanied by a card on which, in pen and ink, he had drawn a tiger tail disappearing around a corner with a butterfly perched on the end. We shopped for wedding bands and had them engraved inside: *'62 PW DW 100,000 years or so* . . .

On the evening before I would be leaving, I finally brought up the matter of my intuition about him. I said I had always known he would come to me one day. I told him I had been in the strangest mood in the weeks before arriving in Hong Kong—serene, confident I'd done the right thing by breaking off my old relationship before leaving Los Angeles, sure something wonderful was about to happen. And it had.

"Tell me what our future holds!" he said.

"I know we'll always be in love! Is it dangerous for me to wear my heart so much on my sleeve? I don't ever want to hide my feelings from you!"

"I'll not hide mine either. And so I should tell you this. Do you remember when you were having dinner with your parents on your first night here? I must have known you too, because I got up and followed you to the elevator. I would have gotten in with you, but the door closed right in my face."

———

On my last day in Hong Kong, Paul found a coin in the street. He said it was *joss*—an omen (at least in Hong Kong) of forthcoming good fortune. And from that day forward, Paul enjoyed dropping coins now and then from his pockets . . . to spread good fortune to others.

Six days after we met, we said goodbye at Kai Tak Airport. Paul held me close and promised to work hard, save money, and visit me in Beverly Hills in just a few weeks. We would plan our wedding then.

He looked at me intently. "Say 'I promise.'"

"I promise."

We would write each other daily of our love.

———

The flight from Hong Kong to Los Angeles took twenty hours— a night, a day, and part of another night. I stared beyond my reflection in the window and shuffled through memories of the last week. They were like a series of postcards sent to me from another lifetime.

At my friend's wedding, in a small church in Beverly Hills, I listened closely to the solemnity of the vows, eager to make those same vows with Paul, but resigned to waiting however long was necessary. I imagined I would be settling into a routine of writing great outpourings of emotion, counterpointed by mad dashes to the mailbox to get Paul's love notes.

Indeed, his telegrams and letters did begin arriving, several a day—the envelopes and pages covered with romantic quotations, treasure maps, and charming drawings of tigers and kittens. And then the telegram:

Can't sleep. Coming home to you.

He had arranged for some time off in California on his way back to London. He would be in Los Angeles in less than three days!

———

And so it started, really started, fueled by the desperation of separated lovers.

With my parents still in Hong Kong, I drove to meet Paul at Los Angeles International Airport. My friends worried our ecstatic experience together had only been a holiday romance. I even wondered if I wasn't being terribly naïve, but the moment I saw him again I melted. His physical presence was even more masculine and vital than I remembered, his joy and gentleness even more apparent. Again I was sure we could stand the test of time.

We set out immediately in my car, driving north along California's legendary Highway 1, the narrow road that follows the coastline, winding gloriously between the ocean on the left and steep, jagged cliffs on the right. Because it was a weekday in November, we had the highway all to ourselves and stopped often at the turnouts to enjoy the vast ocean views.

When we arrived at Big Sur, with its great coastal redwoods marching toward the sea, it felt for us as undiscovered as it had been when Portuguese explorer Juan Cabrillo first sailed past so long ago. The little hamlet of Carmel was enveloped in fog and scented with smoke from wood fires as we strolled slowly up and down its narrow streets, looking for the perfect place to stay. We settled into a cozy room with a fireplace at Vagabond's House, named for Don Blanding's poem. The owners told us the poet had in fact once lived there.

Rain streaked the windows of our little hideaway for the next three days as we made love and slept and strolled around Carmel, stopping for afternoon tea at the Tuck Box, and visiting galleries where, with Paul's coaching, I began to appreciate art with new eyes. Because we weren't sure when we would be able to see each other again, every moment was precious. Paul quoted Robert Frost:

> *These woods are lovely, dark and deep.*
> *But I have promises to keep,*
> *And miles to go before I sleep.*

He had to leave a week later to settle his complex business matters.

"I haven't any choice, Kitten, but I promise to come back. I can see now the whole purpose of all my vagabond days was to find you and to love you."

———

He was back three weeks later for New Year's Eve, surprising me that first evening with a romantic nosegay he had asked a florist to make especially for the occasion.

It was the epitome of Victorian femininity, artfully constructed of rows of dark red and pale pink baby roses, with lacy sprigs of white baby's breath encircled in a lace ruffle. Multicolored satin ribbons bound the stems and hung down, looping at the ends into love knots. Feeling like a bride, I held his beautiful gift all evening as we welcomed 1963—planning our wedding for the following November 2, one year from the day we met, and dreaming of our future together.

In the twenty-six years that followed, our dream continued, though the future we created was different from anything we imagined that night, different in fact from anything we could have guessed, but even more satisfying . . .

———

I fingered the faded satin ribbons from the nosegay before gathering up the photographs and letters spread on the quilt before me, then closed the lid and put the box back in the drawer for another day. And then I fell asleep.

THREE

WHEN I AWOKE AGAIN, I struggled free of sleep, trying to remember what day it was, what year it was. I hoped for a moment that all of the pain of recent times was somehow far in the past. I looked out the window and saw it was afternoon. A dense fog had moved in along the coast, enveloping my bedroom like a cocoon.

I had hardly eaten for days, and I still wasn't hungry. My meals had been a shared experience with Paul for twenty-five years, and eating alone now was not interesting to me. What did interest me, however, was the notebook next to the armchair where I loved to sit cozily, writing and watching the fire.

Free-form writing (or journaling, as many people call it) is like speaking intimately with a best friend. Even if the friend just sits there and says absolutely nothing, you gain value from simply having heard yourself express your own thoughts to someone who cares.

My old notebook was thus a private place where I'd silently spent countless hours pouring out my confusion and cluttered thoughts without the need to edit them or make them pretty for someone else's eyes. It was mine, only for me to see. Not that it was ever a secret from Paul, because we'd had no secrets from each other.

It was simply a place for my deeply personal thoughts, and he respected that.

My journal writing always seemed to lead me out of extraneous thoughts into a different kind of awareness. Lost in the process, I became receptive to answers I needed, solutions I sought. I began to sense the wisdom of a higher self, a part that sees life as a dispassionate observer and is not caught up in the drama of everyday experience. This part of me always seemed boundless, as boundless as the depths of the night sky with its multitude of stars. It seemed to embrace the realms of the dream-maker, the conjurer of myth, and the artist of the universe that all lie quietly behind the silence of our minds and emerge in beauty, elegance, goodness, and truth.

I remembered with fondness how, ten years earlier, I'd glimpsed the gift it would become as Paul and I sat in a journal writing class at UCLA.

August 1979

Our teacher, psychologist Frances Heussenstamm, explained that journaling is a way we could access our intuition, which would bring us much more information, and a different kind of information, than our intellect could provide. She said we'd use journaling to create "dialogues" with different aspects of our selves and, through intuition, discover things we could learn in no other way.

I was especially interested in her statement that we could converse with an infinitely wise Inner Teacher. Because I already had experience with spontaneous intuitive insights, I was now excited by the possibility of consciously calling on that kind of knowledge and understanding.

In preparation for the journaling experience, Frances told us to close our eyes, slow our breathing, and go "within," where we would find a place of expansive awareness. Then, she said, we may gradually feel the presence of a "wisdom figure"—our Inner Teacher. When we were ready, we would greet the figure and wait. "When it speaks," she said, "record whatever it says, letting the conversation move wherever it may. Take as long as you need."

With the rest of the students, Paul and I left the auditorium and went outdoors into the beauty of the sculpture garden, where we each found a quiet, secluded place to begin our experiment. Then, as Frances suggested, I invited that inner part of me to emerge, to communicate. I waited expectantly.

At last I wrote in my journal: *Hello, my Teacher.*

Then I wrote what I heard in my mind: *Hello . . .*

Diana: I am having a hard time picturing you. Can you help me?

Teacher: Relax, Diana. You don't have to try so hard.

Minutes passed. I felt anxious to see or hear something.

Diana: Describe yourself to me.

Teacher: I am golden.

Diana: Golden? Like an Oscar?

Suddenly, the whole process felt silly. I looked around to see if Paul or the others seemed to feel as foolish as I did. But I realized that what was going on with them didn't matter. *So part of me is skeptical and feels silly,* I told myself. *Who cares? Let's see what's going to happen.*

I slowed down my breathing again. A few moments later, in my mind's eye, I saw an ancient statue of Buddha with circles on its crown. It sat beside a quiet pool. (Later, when I researched that image of Buddha, I learned it was one often seen in Thailand.)

Diana: Can you give me some more images to help me?

I immediately saw the pool was cool and clear. In it was a white rock and green moss. A beautiful bright goldfish darted around the pool.

Teacher: You are a bright goldfish. The sun glints on the white rock, illuminating it. The white rock represents truth; the moss, mystery. Your nature is to move between the two.

I was startled. The Teacher's statement was so simple, yet it summarized something about me I knew was true—though I'd never tried before to capture it in words.

How did my Teacher know that? I wondered silently.

In my mind I heard, *Well, after all, I am your Teacher.*

As the dialogue continued, I was told this part of my mind, of my *self*, could be a place of refuge and reverence and inquiry. I could ask whatever questions I wished, then receive insight and guidance. It was like taking dictation from the highest part of myself, and it would be there whenever I wished to return.

My discovery of an inner place of such grandeur, of such potential, was profound and empowering. I knew with the same intuition that led me to Paul and foreshadowed other turning points in my life that I was being offered something that would have great importance as my life unfolded.

I used to tell Paul that journaling was like climbing to the top of a mountain to a silent place above the clouds of confusion. There, centered—at home—I found I could ask questions that seemed baffling to my conscious mind, then sit quietly listening—intuiting answers. Paul could always see the difference that an hour or so of journaling produced in me. He, too, benefited and he encouraged me to spend time in this quiet inner haven.

Years later, when Paul had asked me to be cheerful for him during his illness, my journaling became something new. In addition to being an opportunity for me to listen, it also became a place where I could pour out my deep grief and despair. On the blank pages I would give private voice to my fears, complain of my exhaustion from running our business by myself, and express my anxiety, the what-ifs, and what-nows that flashed continually through my mind.

―――――――

Now, cross-legged in my chair, wrapped in Paul's afghan, I began as usual with my accustomed routine of lighting a candle and establishing a purpose, which was to open up to the wisest part of myself.

I gently allowed my breathing to slow and imagined that any negativity in me was coursing down through the base of my spine, down through my legs and out my feet, far down into the center of the earth, where it dispersed harmlessly. I then invited the healing energy of the earth to rise through my feet, and the loving energy of God, or Spirit, as I usually referred to the supreme power— I have always been a firm believer—to shower me from above with golden light, comforting me and protecting me from harm.

After meditating quietly for ten or fifteen minutes, I felt what I was waiting for: an impulse to open my journal and begin a new page. Using a favorite pen, I began with the date, then wrote and wrote and wrote—neither judging nor favoring nor disliking nor rejecting any thought or any feeling in any way. I wrote of everything that had happened in the last few days, simply getting it all down. Usually, when that process felt complete, I would ask a question or request guidance and wait quietly for answers.

But on that morning, in response to no plan or intention of my own, I felt an urge to begin a dialogue with Paul. In the past my journaling had included many kinds of exchanges, usually the ones Frances

47

had taught us about. But the idea of a journal dialogue with Paul, the love of my life, whom I had watched live and watched die, worried me.

After a few moments of indecision, not knowing really what I should do, I wrote, *Tell me what it is like where you are.* Then I sat back in the chair, pen in hand, and waited expectantly for . . . I didn't know what.

To my astonishment, I began to sense words. *His* words:

Paul: I felt such freedom when the weight of the body fell away. Everything is lighter now. When you open your consciousness to me, I can flow into you and feel as much oneness as we ever felt together. I now feel no separation at all from you.

I could hardly believe what I was hearing in my mind. He was there with me. Tears of relief slid from my eyes. I wrote:

Diana: I'm so grateful you're not suffering anymore.

Paul: And I'm so grateful you're not having to watch me suffer anymore. Leaving you was worse than the pain, worse than my fear of what I thought would be the end. Now is a completely new beginning for you and for us. Never doubt I am here for you in every moment. Develop an ear and an eye for me. Wrap my love around you as a warm and comforting cloak. We cherish each other even more now because we don't have to deal with the physical world, the illusion of everyday life. Being with you this way is pure and infinite and genuine.

The mirror across the room reflected a woman beaming with love. I was hanging on every word.

Diana: Tell me more.

Paul: We are not our bodies . . . We are not our bodies . . . We are not our bodies . . . (His words ran through my mind as a mantra.) *Death is not at all what I expected. I thought everything would come to a halt, with no more joy, no more sadness, no more sunrises or sunsets, no more being a child. Just a dial tone, then silence forever.*

I asked him what it was like.

Paul: I am experimenting with this new form, just as I loved to experiment with the physical world. I can be anywhere with just a thought. You sensed me immediately on waking this morning. I was with you while you slept. And you were with me, though you don't remember.

Instead of the calmness I usually found in journal writing, my head was spinning. This information was so new I needed time to absorb it. I decided to go for a walk, and try to see things in a more orderly way.

The break helped. During my walk I realized my confusion derived from adjusting to conflicting realities, balancing opposing forces and desires. I wanted to contemplate huge issues of life and death, yet I also needed to focus on small, moment-by-moment matters of survival. I desperately needed the time for my psyche to heal, yet I had an active business to run. Lexi needed to continue her education, yet I wanted her to be with me. I yearned to comfort Lexi, to be her mother, yet I also yearned to have no responsibilities at all.

And then the final paradox was the most difficult one of all. *Paul was gone, yet he was here.* Was I therefore a woman alone or a woman married? It was all so terribly strange, especially because only one other time since I first met Paul in Hong Kong had we ever been separated.

January 1963

After our romantic New Year's celebration we had to face the reality that Paul needed to go abroad again. He worked from his home base in London and from there traveled the world, going almost anywhere a market existed for English-language textbooks. And what would I do while he was gone?

The answer came almost instantly. An old girlfriend with the unlikely but lovely name of Mary Memory called to tell me she wanted to live and work in Paris for the winter. Her parents would allow her to go if I went with her. Did I want to be her roommate?

I needed no time to think that one over. Mary and I had known each other for some ten years, from the time we were in the fourth grade together in private boarding school, and I was sure we'd fit together comfortably. I would be less than two hours from London, Paul's home base. I told him all of this during one of his frequent phone calls and he was delighted. I assured him he could write to me in care of the American Express office in Paris until Mary and I found a permanent address.

Mother, meanwhile, was growing more and more concerned at my developing romance. She'd liked Paul well enough when he was merely the other half of a holiday fling, but now that I was going to *marry* him, her feelings were changing. She worried about his being older than I was. She worried about his having been married before. And she begged me to reconsider. I could understand her concerns, but I also felt very sure of what I was doing. I told her I'd be certain I was doing the right thing. She and Papa no doubt expected my Paris sojourn would make me forget all about him.

Mary and I arrived in Paris later that month. We found a small apartment near the train station, the Gare St. Lazare. The truth was, neither of us adapted to Paris very well. I attended a few demonstration classes at the cooking school Le Cordon Bleu, but they were in French and I wasn't yet that interested in classic French cuisine. The winter was extremely cold and we wound up spending most of the time huddled in the apartment trying to keep warm.

Every day I bundled up and took the ten-minute Métro ride to Place de la Madeleine, then made the short walk to the American Express office, where I waited in a long line for my mail. Almost every day there was a letter from Paul, written (to my considerable surprise) from a hotel in Lagos, Nigeria, though he hadn't received a single piece of mail from me since my arrival in Paris. That meant he had no idea where I was. I knew he'd get my letters soon and know where to find me, but as the days passed his letters grew more concerned, and the tigers in his drawings on the envelopes began to look more and more agitated. "What shall I do?" he wrote. "How will I ever find you?"

Fate stepped in again! Paul had an inspiration to telephone the American Express office in Paris. He asked them to page Diana Webb, hoping against hope I'd be there. I wasn't, but my roommate was—standing in line for her own mail. She took the call. Within minutes Paul and I were reunited by telephone and made plans to meet the following weekend.

During the next several months Paul came to Paris several times, for just a few days each visit. Whispering behind my bedroom door, we wondered if we would ever really have our own private place. We walked everywhere on those gray and frozen days—across all the bridges, even to the top of Montmartre and the Place du Tertre, where artists wrapped in mufflers and warming their hands over glowing charcoal displayed their pictures. Paul soaked it up. He was a combination of everything romance writers create, with one major difference: he was real. With the voice, body, and face of a movie idol, along with the kind and loving heart of a poet, he was irresistible, and the artists loved showing him their works.

———————

When spring arrived, the trees in the Tuileries Gardens burst into green. The window of the flower shop on the Rue Royale held long-stemmed rosebuds the size of a baby's fist.

Paul's visits to Paris always ended too soon, and he would be off to yet another city somewhere in the world. He was working hard to put together some money for our marriage.

In a letter from Greece, he wrote, "I hope you know what you are doing in throwing in your lot with mine. You were expected to marry wealth, to live the life of ease your parents envisioned for you. With me there are no guarantees. But I will love you with a heart and a half." Paul was filled with what he would always say was the most valuable thing of all: hope for the future.

Hope for the future is what inspired him one day in Paris to tell me of his plan to take a trip halfway around the world, to New Zealand, to open a new market. That, he said proudly, could bring about a significant increase in his sales and more income. I shared his pride but was heartbroken that we wouldn't see each other for a long time—many weeks at least.

How could he marry me and settle down in California and be a married man while he was traveling all over the world opening new markets? His romantic nature led him to conclude that anything was possible, but now we both realized that something would have to change.

We agreed that what had to change was his job. He would quit the textbook business and look for work in California after we were married. I was going to be marrying a man who was unemployed.

———

I left Paris after five months and returned home to Beverly Hills. There, the battle for control of the wedding began.

I wanted a small one, my parents wanted a big one. In the end we compromised. The wedding would be small: forty people, only family and close friends. The reception would be large: a gala for three hundred people, to be held some three weeks later after we returned from our honeymoon. Paul and I would be married exactly one year from the day we met, November 2, 1963, in a tiny church I loved in Beverly Hills.

Less than a week before the wedding, Paul finally arrived in Los Angeles. He had lost weight that year and I worried that he was so thin.

Paul's being unemployed did not sit well with Papa, given the vision with which he nurtured me during the years of my childhood. He'd always told me, alluding to the resources he accumulated during his working years, "Diana, you're never going to have to work for a living."

Just days before the wedding he had one of his tantrums. "Paul doesn't fool me with his charming act. He's just a fortune hunter! When the minister gets to that part of the ceremony where he asks if anyone present objects to the wedding, where he says 'speak now or forever hold your peace,' you can bet he'll be hearing from me!"

Don't breathe, Diana, don't feel, it will pass.

Then my brother, who hadn't yet met Paul, flew home from Columbia University, where he was studying for his doctorate. Gene had been always been supportive of me and a great comfort. But now he was in a fit of pique over having to travel so far to be best man at a marriage that "wouldn't last two weeks." I wasn't getting a lot of family support. Even Mother had many moments of doubt as the date approached.

Paul was my only safe harbor and I clung to him.

———

On our wedding day, I did the traditional old, new, borrowed, and blue, and did not see my husband-to-be until I started down the aisle on my father's arm.

Papa looked drawn and pale, but I was radiant and completely sure of the step I was taking. I have a photograph of that moment, an electric moment of my young life that would always remain as an indelible image on a thick page of a leather wedding album.

Paul and I gripped hands tightly and held our breath when the minister asked his question. My father stayed silent.

In his blessing the minister said, "Your marriage will be your ministry." Was it what he said to every couple? I didn't know, but I heard it almost as a pronouncement of destiny.

After a dinner reception, we changed clothes and made our getaway through a shower of rice. We began our honeymoon eighty miles north of Los Angeles at the Santa Barbara Biltmore, where we had driven just the week before to choose the right room for our wedding night. The manager had patiently showed us most of the available rooms before we found the perfect one—Room 230 at the top of the stairs off the lobby. "And how long will you be staying?" he had asked. "Just one night," we beamed.

It was a perfect wedding night. The vows of marriage deepened and sanctified the trust we felt for each other, and I can remember nearly every moment of it, from the pale blue gown and peignoir that spent a lonely night over a chair, to breakfast from room service in front of a crackling fire. I felt safe and cherished and very sure Paul would always treasure me. I also began to experience myself in a whole new, very sensual way.

We drove up Highway 1 again to Carmel, which would always be our favorite vacation spot, and rented a small cottage. It had a cozy little parlor with a fireplace, a kitchen, and a bedroom. There we sated our senses completely with seaside air and sleep and sweet, sweet sex. We also did something else that anyone who'd been peeking in the window at the newlyweds probably would not have understood at all. Paul knew I wanted to learn more about art, so we bought some supplies at a local store and he spent a number of romantic evenings during our honeymoon . . . teaching me the basics of drawing.

And when our time in Carmel was finished, we returned to a little apartment we had rented in the still-bucolic San Fernando Valley, just a few miles over the hills from Hollywood. It was November 21, 1963—the day before our wedding reception.

I was at the hairdresser the next morning when word spread through the salon that President Kennedy had been assassinated in Dallas. In horror and panic, I wanted to cancel the reception, but Mother wouldn't hear of it. Three thousand dollars' worth of flowers had already been paid for to decorate the Bel Air Bay Club.

Nervously, I agreed. But I wondered who would be in the mood for an elegant affair. Would anybody even come?

The afternoon was long, as we sat in front of the television set, switching between Frank McGee and Walter Cronkite, trying to find a coherent reality in the images we saw: Kennedy dead; a balding young man arrested in a theatre; the First Lady, covered in a beloved president's blood, standing beside his successor as he took the oath of office.

But the scheduled party wasn't canceled. Paul and I felt absolutely terrible in the moments before people were due to arrive—if they arrived. Were we asking too much? In her overriding concern for three thousand dollars' worth of decorations, was my mother somehow terribly out of touch with the world of shock, pain, and death we all had suddenly entered?

Everybody came to our party and it was a beautiful evening, in spite of the horror earlier in the day. Perhaps it was our collective way of declaring that life and joy are stronger than death. Regardless, we were all intensely aware of our mortality that night and determined to celebrate the life that was left to us.

The memory of my reception is intertwined with recollections of the national tragedy that happened the same day; it was a coincidence, meaning nothing, but at the time it chilled me to the bone, the tragic end of the young president's life occurring in powerful juxtaposition to this new beginning of our own.

FOUR

"DIANA, we all need to rethink this thing called death . . ."

A friend, Marilyn Ferguson, had said that to me after the memorial service, and my discovery that I could communicate with Paul certainly confirmed it. But now I realized it applied not only to the person who's passed on but also those who are left behind.

My husband of twenty-five years had died only a week before and I was alone, running a business, worried about keeping house and heart together. Who was I without Paul? *What* was I without Paul? He liked to say we were joined at the hip, and I liked hearing it—because in its symbolic way it was true.

To some people marriage means you see each other for a few minutes each night and maybe a couple of hours on the weekend. Paul and I were together virtually every moment, and that's how we liked it. Of course, we didn't sit around all day gazing into each other's eyes. We worked hard. But we worked together, and we enjoyed a division of labor that operated smoothly. Whenever one of us balked at doing a certain job, the other filled in. Occasionally, like any couple who work closely together, we encountered rough spots, but we always got through them.

We'd been an effective, productive team. Paul loved detail work, solving problems in his head, building sound systems. I was more people-oriented and thought in grand concepts. And that had been part of our success, because others could see for themselves how well we fit.

Now that Paul was gone, how would I manage alone? Lexi could help for a while, but she'd promised her dad she would finish college. Delaying her education wouldn't be fair. And how about money? I didn't know what kind of impact Paul's death would have on the Inside Edge membership. We'd refinanced our home, but I would have to sell the house now because the mortgage would be too high for me to carry alone. A most fortunate aspect, however, was that our Inside Edge friend Joe Broderick, who handled the refinancing, had insisted that we take out insurance to cover the mortgage in case anything happened to either Paul or me. I didn't know exactly how that would affect me, but I knew it could be important. Nevertheless, the larger questions loomed. Where would I move? What would I do? Who would I be? How would I reinvent myself now?

On the following Tuesday my alarm clock rang at 3:30 A.M. The middle of the night. A horrid hour for most people but not so for me. I was accustomed to getting out of bed long before sunrise three days a week ever since Paul and I had changed careers in midlife, abandoning book writing in 1985 and launching a new enterprise, the Inside Edge.

At weekly breakfast meetings from 6:30 to 8:30 A.M., the Inside Edge—or as we often called it, simply the "Edge"—met in hotel ballrooms in three Southern California cities: Beverly Hills, Newport Beach, and La Jolla. In each location, individual chapters of the

Inside Edge provided an environment where members heard prominent speakers present forward-thinking ideas about the expansive frontiers of human potential.

I anticipated the high energy of the nearly two hundred members I knew would be present at the Beverly Hills chapter that morning. It was still dark as I drove up the palm-lined driveway of the Beverly Hills Hotel and turned my car over to the parking attendants beneath the famous portico. The attendants had learned in the past few months how to unload the sound equipment from the trunk, load it on a cart, and get it to the hotel's California Room. That job had always been Paul's before.

The lobby was nearly empty at 5:30 A.M., but the large room we rented was already bustling as I approached. I greeted Mary Olsen, my best friend, who was to be host that morning. A vivacious woman bubbling over with a contagious enthusiasm that tended unfailingly to wake everyone up, Mary was in charge of training the emcees at the various chapters. I handed her a copy of the schedule, which included a list of members who would make announcements, the topic for the table discussion, and a list of Edge activities.

Perhaps the simplest description of the Edge's purpose was to encourage each member to recognize his or her capacity for accomplishment, to be accountable, and to take action. The group environment created a situation within which the members rose rapidly to new levels of success in reaching their goals. Numerous well-known and well-respected writers, researchers, psychologists, teachers, and other public figures would also get up very early on those weekday mornings to join us and speak. Among them: Lynn Andrews, Ken Blanchard, Harold Bloomfield, Nathaniel Branden, Steven Halpern, Barbara Marx Hubbard, Shari Lewis,

Dan Millman, Carl Simonton, Patricia Sun, Jeremy Tarcher, Dennis Weaver—and many, many more.

It was also a wondrous environment for what's known popularly today as *networking*. Though members were specifically discouraged from doing business at meetings, the fact was that when a group of smart, ambitious, interesting self-starters assembled in a room, connections were inevitably made. Powerful, meaningful relationships and associations were formed there, many of which still thrive today.

That environment was to stimulate some marvelous accomplishments. Many authors who are well-known today began their careers with a boost from the Inside Edge. Psychologist Susan Jeffers, one of our first Beverly Hills members, had recently moved to Los Angeles with her new husband, Mark Shelmerdine, head of London Films. She got so much encouragement at the Edge for a book idea that she wrote a proposal for it and, to her astonishment, sold it!

Her book *Feel the Fear and Do It Anyway* became an international bestseller, and we were all as proud as if we had written it ourselves! On the day she spoke in a nervous voice to the Edge—it was her first experience as a speaker—we all stood on our chairs and cheered, because she was doing exactly what each of us wanted to do—push our edges outward and live our dreams. By 1991 Susan had written *three* bestsellers. Not long afterward, she spoke at Madison Square Garden, sharing the platform with Deepak Chopra, Louise Hay, and Wayne Dyer.

Louise Hay, bestselling author of *Heal Your Body* and now publisher of a whole library of books—her own and others'—was nearly always at the Beverly Hills meetings as her career got underway.

So was Barbara De Angelis, who would become a national radio host and author of numerous *New York Times* bestsellers.

One effect of the Inside Edge and its powerful environment would become legendary. Our speaker that morning was Jack Canfield, a man Paul and I had long admired for his work building self-esteem among students in the California school system. Keeping his public speaking business funded and running was always a month-to-month challenge, yet he served on our board of advisors and was unfailingly generous with his time.

Another well-known motivational speaker and member of our board from the Orange County chapter, Mark Victor Hansen, had come to hear Jack and was sitting on my left.

After Jack's talk, in the question-and-answer period that followed, someone asked Jack why he didn't write a book of inspiring stories, similar to those he had recounted that morning at the Edge. He responded that he had in fact been gathering stories for such a book and would be working on it soon.

When Jack returned to our table, Mark Victor Hansen leaned across me and said to him, "I'm going to write that book with you!"

"What?" Jack said

"The book you're going to write. I'm going to write it with you."

"You are?"

"Yep!" said Mark.

Later that morning, as I prepared to leave, Jack and Mark were huddled together at that same table, enthusiastically engaged in a conversation I could only imagine involved planning "their" book. Indeed, it did. That conversation led directly to the compilation of *Chicken Soup for the Soul*, the first volume in the phenomenal run of bestselling *Chicken Soup* books—which was subsequently to become the largest-selling book series of all time, with over fifty-five million copies in print.

That was probably the most public of all Edge-based successes, but dozens of other major projects and processes had their start there. And not all of them were in the world of publishing. Friendships and personal relationships that began in those breakfast meetings were to spread out into and across the general population and have an impact that would be literally immeasurable. It's not uncommon even today for individuals to say, "We met at the Inside Edge . . ."

That early morning, as I checked with the staff and put place cards on my own table for the speaker and his guests, a woman who was attending the Edge for the first time approached me with copies of three dilapidated, dog-eared cookbooks Paul and I had written.

"Oh, Mrs. von Welanetz," she said enthusiastically, "I came here today because I wanted to meet you in person. Would you mind signing these books for me? They're just wonderful. I use them all the time. I watched you and Paul every day on your television show and you both are so wonderful." She suddenly stopped, aware of her blunder. "I mean . . . you *were* so . . . I mean . . ."

I smiled. "Thank you. And don't worry. I sometimes get it all mixed up myself."

Relief spread across her face. "What I mean is the real reason I watched your shows was just to watch the two of *you*. You always seemed so much in love, so happy. You had such a wonderful relationship, the way you worked together."

As with so many people I encountered, she wanted to be generous with her praise and gentle with me about my loss, yet she had no idea what to say. I, in turn, wished to be sensitive to her sensitivity, but I didn't want to burden her or anyone else with my grief. Nor did I want to put on a false cheeriness. The best compromise was to simply respond to people's concern as honestly and openly as I could. Being a public widow was not easy, I'd discovered.

When the morning's presentation was over, people stayed and talked with each other for an hour or so after the meeting. These conversations were usually more personal than professional, however, because business networking was not our purpose. We didn't want to turn into an indoor market for self-promoters and job-seekers. In fact, business-card exchanges were discouraged and the staff gently coached new attendees in Inside Edge etiquette: people were there to hear inspiring speakers and to support each other in attaining their dreams.

Mary and I had completed our separate duties simultaneously and now she waited for me to finish talking with everyone. As our staff packed up the equipment, we sat in a corner of the lobby.

"I have some news," she said uneasily. "It's sort of bittersweet. I'm moving to Kauai to be with Don!"

"Don" was Don Kelly, the man she'd come to know in a seminar they both attended in Kauai the previous Thanksgiving. I hadn't met him yet, but knew he was in the black pearl jewelry business and was in love with Mary. As she was with him. They'd made the long trans-Pacific flight several times as they came to know each other better. Now they were going to create something more permanent.

It seemed the perfect solution for Mary. After a painful divorce, she wanted more than anything to meet the right man, someone like Paul, and have what Paul and I had—deep love and full partnership. From what she told me, she'd found it in Don.

I couldn't hide my conflicting emotions about this change in the life of my best friend—my delight in her finding a wonderful new man to love and my disappointment she would no longer be nearby. Especially then.

"I feel awful being so far away. I know it's such a hard time for you . . ." she said.

Mary deserved her turn at happiness, but I wondered why everything had to be changing so quickly for me.

————

Driving along Sunset Boulevard on the way home from the Edge meeting, I went right past the mansion where I'd lived when I met and married Paul. *Still there,* I thought.

Later I changed into some cozy sweats and sat at my desk, wondering where to start with all the mail and telephone messages that had been piling up. But my mind wasn't yet ready to jump back into work.

I couldn't stop thinking about all the changes going on. At what other time in my life had I faced this much upheaval all at once? The afghan I'd made for Paul so long ago lay across a nearby chair. It reminded me of another occasion long ago, when I had struggled to discover who I was.

————

An armchair psychologist who'd known me as a child might have speculated I would grow up and marry a raging, abusive man who regarded me as an armpiece.

After all, that's what so many women do: marry a copy of their father. Why I didn't is something I shall probably never understand. Or maybe I did it in reverse. Knowing all of my father's bad qualities, I selected someone who was, trait for trait, his opposite.

But when I ponder the powerful forces that continually drew Paul and me more strongly together, that deepened our love for each other, I don't think he is someone I simply "chose" to have in my life, someone who fulfilled my dreams.

I think magical forces, cosmic forces, were involved. I believe an extraordinary destiny was somehow being worked out, as two players on the field of time—two souls—were drawn inevitably together because they *belonged* together. I suspect my dreams were a reflection of my destiny, not the other way around.

November 1963

Paul was so different from Papa: even-tempered, stable, always loving and affectionate.

In his safe embrace I learned to trust another person completely, and we shared deep intimacy that felt exactly like what I longed for in childhood. Paul was not only my husband, but he was also the benevolent, protective father I never had. We shared absolutely everything—except the memories of his experiences in the army during the Korean War. He told me that what he had to do there to survive was too painful to remember, and when I pressed him to tell me, he insisted he would never talk about it. And he never did.

As our marriage began, we were both full of hope for our future. Paul knew he'd need to find work soon, probably in sales, and I expected my own fulfillment to come from being the perfect milk-and-cookies mom. Naturally this meant we both needed to learn a few things.

For one, I almost immediately discovered a downside of my privileged upbringing, notably that I had never learned how to clean house.

Paul had to teach me. Discovering that dusting wasn't much fun, I spent most of my time poring over cookbooks, finding that I loved inventing menus in my imagination. On our first Thanksgiving, only a few weeks after we married, I declined an invitation to be with my family, wanting to try my hand at cooking a small turkey dinner just for us. I scorched the gravy and whipped up lumpy mashed potatoes, but it all tasted delicious at our own little kitchen table.

I don't remember exactly when reality first intruded into my perfect world. It may have been when I realized that while Paul did have a salesman's polish, he didn't *want* to be a salesman. What *did* he want to do? He wanted to invent things; his true enthusiasm was reserved for the inventions he wanted to patent. His real occupation, however, was Dreamer. But I wasn't too worried—the full value of my trust fund would come to me within nine years.

Paul had begun job-hunting in earnest, attired impeccably in a Hong Kong dress shirt, suit, and tie. I'd sit on the bathroom sink watching him shave before he left, adoring every minute with him. During the day I found notes he had hidden for me to discover behind a pillow, in my shoes, or under a coffee cup. I still have one in my memory box, a note he wrote often: "I love you with a heart and a half."

He eventually went to work in sales for Herman Miller, a company that designed and manufactured expensive, high-tech office furnishings. Because we now had access through his employee's discount to classic modern furniture, we moved to a townhouse apartment nearby and furnished it beautifully and inexpensively through time payments.

Paul was very talented mechanically. He was skilled at working with his hands and could fix anything. We never had to hire a repairman the whole time we were married. He built Herman Miller desks and bookshelves into the wall in our extra bedroom and, in the evenings, loved to putter there. He also began thinking more seriously about exactly which ideas for inventions he wanted to patent—an electric carving knife and a silk fingernail patch (long before anyone had heard of these things).

Paul loved to discover how things worked. One time I drove him to the dentist's office to have a wisdom tooth extracted. After the surgery the nurse helped him into a small room with a bed where he could rest until the anesthesia wore off. When she went back to check on him after only twenty minutes or so, she was horrified to see that Paul had completely disassembled the intercom system and had the parts laid out neatly on the blanket. She panicked and ran to get the dentist. Paul groggily assured them they shouldn't worry; he'd have it all back together in minutes. And he did.

Another time, he stayed two nights at the UCLA Medical Center for minor surgery. I slept at my parents' house because it was nearby. One morning before I left to be with Paul at the hospital, my father showed me an unusual ship's clock he'd had for over forty years, though he reminded me it didn't work. (He'd taken it to two repair shops but no one could fix it.) Knowing that Paul loved ships (and tinkering), he thought maybe he would enjoy looking at it. I showed it to him when he was just coming out of anesthesia, and within a half-hour he had disassembled it, put it back together, and got it running. Thirty years later, it still works.

One of Paul's most complicated invention ideas was very futuristic. I believe it has actually been made now. It was an elaborate machine that would "carve" or "sculpt" a bust of a person. A holographic picture would first be taken of the subject. Then wood or marble would be placed in the center of the machine and a computer-controlled cutting device, like a router, spinning at high speed, would move automatically toward the material and, matching the outlines of the hologram, carve an exact replica of the original to the desired scale.

We made our own Christmas cards that year. Paul patiently carved an image of Fenwick, our little Yorkshire terrier, into a linoleum block and we used it to stamp the design in black ink on green greeting-card stock.

Just before Christmas, in a shopping mall, we passed a display of sewing machines. I mentioned to him that my mother and grandmother had always loved dressmaking. His mother also loved sewing. He thought it would be great if I could learn, as it was clearly impossible for us otherwise to maintain the wardrobe to which I had been accustomed, considering our overall, very precarious financial condition. We bought the sewing machine with time payments (like everything else), along with some gingham to make my mother an apron for Christmas.

My first attempt didn't go well. I struggled for hours to learn how to baste and quickly became impatient when the thread broke as I tried to gather the material evenly along two rows to fit the waistband. I felt so clumsy and frustrated that I threw the fabric on the floor. "I hate doing this. I'm not going to finish it!" I told him in a fury.

We stared at each other. He clearly didn't know what to say. Finally he asked, "What do you expect from me?"

I blustered, unable to say anything. Then, annoyed, "Some sympathy, maybe. Some understanding."

"Like what? Should I say, 'Okay, don't finish it'? Or tell you that you *should* finish it?"

He looked at me, disappointed, "Diana, I can love you but I can't tell you what you should do. You have to decide that yourself."

I was stunned. I'd wanted to put the responsibility on him and he wouldn't let me. His words were a blow and I sat quietly, waves of hurt reverberating through me. I'd disappointed my hero, my protector, my soul mate. Was that, I later wondered, the first time someone I loved ever believed I would actually accomplish something?

Teachers in high school knew I had a capacity for learning, because my interest in a subject allowed me to do well in it quite effortlessly, but they often reported "Diana isn't living up to her potential." During those years, depression had extinguished anything but short bursts of enthusiasm and I excelled only rarely. "Diana never finishes anything." Those words became a self-fulfilling prophecy, and my unfinished projects were legion.

Now, Paul's obvious disappointment reached a cavernous place in me that gradually filled for the first time with a new-found determination. That same evening I vowed to finish the apron—grudgingly at first, resenting him momentarily for making me look at this part of myself. He sat with me as I awkwardly re-basted, then figured out the pattern directions.

"A man named Mies van der Rohe said, 'God lives in the details,'" he told me. I began that night to enjoy taking fine, even stitches, and felt triumphant when I ironed Mom's apron and wrapped it beautifully in a gift box.

I rediscovered the passion for handwork that I'd had as a child—crocheting, knitting, crewel, and embroidery—and was fascinated by the emergence of patterns as I moved the needles around the yarn, weaving, looping, twisting, commingling. Likewise our souls, Paul's and mine, intertwined as we passed the evenings in our little studio, talking occasionally, basking in the silence of each other's presence when no words were needed. I finished all my handcraft projects.

Paul puttered at his desk, stopping only to light cigarettes for both of us, making technical drawings for his patent applications and developing working models for such things as the carving knife, the silk fingernail patch, and a swivel for an office chair—inventions he hoped would be successful and eventually support us. Ideas flowed and we used what money we had to apply for patents. Would I have preferred, rather than following his heart, that he confine himself to more acceptable and ordinary pursuits? Not really. I was deeply in love with him and just believed everything would work out.

Neither of us, however, had any business or marketing experience, which meant that getting his inventions produced or into the hands of people who could develop them was almost impossible. In our naïveté, we fell for scams in newspaper ads that promised to help inventors develop and market their products.

Except for not being able to sell Paul's inventions, the early years of our marriage were idyllic. I'd become passionate about cooking, trying out new recipes on Paul every evening and, on Monday nights, taking cooking classes from Gregoire Le Balch, head chef at the Escoffier Room in the Beverly Hilton Hotel in Beverly Hills.

Gregoire was French and taught our class of twenty to make classic French dishes. While Paul was at work selling office furniture, I spent much of my time finding just the right veal bones, browning them with vegetables, simmering them slowly for hours, then reducing this stock to use in making a more complicated sauce Espagnole, which I would then use as a base for a multitude of even more complicated sauces. I practiced by making dinners for Paul and me and a few special friends. Everyone loved my cooking—but at that time I had no idea where it would eventually lead us.

———————

Paul went on occasional overnight business trips, and returned from one with a silly gift for me: a bright red fireman's hat with a battery-powered microphone that amplified my voice when I spoke into it.

On our first anniversary I made reservations for dinner at Perino's restaurant, a Los Angeles landmark, and dressed in a very sheer black nightgown for his anticipated arrival home from work. I heard footsteps approaching the front door, so I put on the hat, pulled open the door, and said through the microphone in my sexiest voice, "Hi, handsome!" My face, and the face of the flower delivery man, went white with shock.

Paul arrived a few minutes later and, with my wide-eyed description of the hat fiasco, we began a laughing jag that would last all evening, through our lovemaking, our canceled dinner reservations, and our actual dinner in Chinatown, where we captured our high spirits on a strip of photos in a booth, four for a quarter.

FIVE

TEN DAYS now since Paul died and the house seems to be falling apart . . .
While Paul was alive, even while he was ill, our house behaved
itself. Yet the memorial service was hardly behind us when practically everything mechanical broke.

First the water heater burst and leaked all over the front hall.
I made a phone call and was soon rescued by a "house doctor" who
came by with his toolbox and a new water heater. And that was only
the beginning.

We had electrical problems, plumbing problems, even the vac-
uum cleaner broke. The compressor on the refrigerator decided to
stop working. Pictures dropped off the wall. The shelf over my desk
fell down and books spilled everywhere. My good friend Bobbie
Probstein dropped by one afternoon in the midst of this chaos,
looked over the situation, and diagnosed it immediately. "One of your
planets," she intoned soberly, "is obviously in the house of poo-poo."

Paul had always been the caretaker of the house. Now it seemed
to be going into mourning.

I theorized earnestly along these lines to one of the repairmen,
saying that I felt the house was, in its own way, going through a grief

process. The expression on the repairman's face was exactly what I might have expected after telling him such a thing. His eyes grew wide then narrowed down. His head tilted sideways and he looked at me carefully. He said, "Hmmm . . . interesting . . ."

As I walked away I thought I heard him softly humming the theme from *Twilight Zone*. "Doo-doo-doo-doo . . ."

Not only were mechanical things breaking but I also began to notice all the little ways I had neglected our home during Paul's illness. Cushions on the sofa needed sewing, a hamper was overflowing with mending projects, the drawers were a mess. The place clearly needed a good going-over.

Lexi and Lauren, our office manager, decided that the things in Paul's office could be moved out to make room for Inside Edge records and suggested his tools and drafting supplies be given to charity. We all realized it was far too soon for me to be able to go through his desk and file drawers, so they offered to pack all his very personal things in boxes for me to look through at a later time. But, they said, if I were going to have to sell the house, paying storage on his tools only to sort through them later wouldn't make sense. I agreed, and as I looked over his drafting supplies, each item brought memories of the lovely hours we'd spent side-by-side working on our separate projects.

It would be nearly eleven years before I opened those boxes, to search for more photographs to include in this book. Inside I found a packet of all the love letters I'd ever written—I didn't know he'd saved mine too.

Spring 1967

I continued taking cooking classes from Chef Gregoire weekly, for five years, taking what I learned from him and honing and refining his techniques to my own taste.

As my knowledge of French cuisine expanded, so did our waistlines, Paul's and mine. That problem was solved when Paul and I went on a strict diet regimen; for the first time ever I was as thin as I'd always wanted to be. So I stopped cooking and set about altering my clothes.

Through the simple act of taking in the side seams of my A-line dresses I became more and more proficient at sewing. I soon felt confident enough to buy dress patterns and fabrics and make my own clothes. A year or so later, I graduated to designer patterns and, eventually, to complicated *couturier* styles. Paul would be gone all day and return to find me still in my slip, the sewing machine whirring.

As my interest in sewing developed, my mother gave me the red-lacquered Chinese box in which her mother had kept remnants of fabrics, laces, and trims. It was a treasure. Whenever I noticed it on the shelf next to my sewing machine, I remembered how I'd loved to visit Grammy in the boarding house she ran on Virgil Avenue in Los Angeles next to the trolley tracks, how she'd made all the drapes and curtains out of chintz and polished cotton and ruffled organdy. Whenever I visited she would make ruffled clothes for my dolls out of the scraps in the box.

I begged her to teach me how to knit and crochet, and she was infinitely patient about sitting with me and teaching me to roll a ball from a skein of yarn she rocked back and forth between her hands. I was fascinated by how knitting and crochet begin with only a ball of yarn but quickly become something entirely new. From the void emerges pattern and texture and beauty.

As a child I struggled to keep from dropping stitches, while Grammy would tell me stories of how my mother, when she was a young woman, was a fashion model for Mrs. Goodrich, the proprietress of an exclusive dress salon across the street from the Bullock's

Wilshire department store. Mrs. Goodrich traveled to Paris once a year to buy the newest fashions and copy them for her clients, and her salon was patronized by the wealthy society matrons of Los Angeles. She let my mother take home some of the latest Paris fashions, so that overnight Grammy could draw paper patterns and study the hand-finishing, to make exact copies for Mom.

My mother inherited my grandmother's love of making perfect little stitches, and often on my return from school I would find her in the little sewing room off her bedroom. Fabric of one sort or another would be draped over a dressmaker's dummy. She was so skilled she could use the most elaborate couture patterns and add her own flourishes. One strapless crisp black taffeta evening gown had a bouffant bustle with fuchsia velvet and organza roses peeking from underneath. The gown rustled as she twirled to show it to me, and it remains in my memory the most beautiful dress I've ever seen and she the most gorgeous mother in the world.

Mother and Grammy would sometimes sit and sew for hours together in a comfortable, silent reverie. From these two women I learned an appreciation for creating beauty and for the quiet, almost meditative process of handwork.

It was also from Grammy that I learned to trust love. One day my mother was warning her not to let one of her boarders be late again with the rent. "He may leave in the night without paying you!" she admonished.

"I'll take that chance," Grammy said. "I'd rather believe in the goodness of people than protect myself from them."

———

Paul encouraged my passion for sewing my own clothes. With his artist's sensibility, Paul had an eye for design. He favored dresses with classic and elegant lines, the Audrey Hepburn look, and I trusted his judgment completely. His excellent taste extended to the various gifts he often bought me. A pair of white daisy earrings with yellow centers became my favorites, and his. I wore them every day during those early years and he would repair them whenever they needed it, until they simply wore out.

I now look back on those days as some of our happiest. We had such hope for our future, and our joy in each other kept growing.

My friend Frances Pelham—who, after Lexi's birth, would become her godmother—wanted to learn to sew and wanted me to teach her. A few other friends with whom I helped organize charity fashion shows (shows in which I also modeled) were interested as well, and soon I was giving sewing classes where, almost inevitably, people would ask, "What's that wonderful smell from the kitchen?"

When I described to them whatever was boiling, broiling, toasting, roasting, or baking, I could scarcely have imagined that just over a year later that kind of spontaneous interest would lead to my offering cooking classes as well.

Now, however, it was just the sewing classes. But something of great additional importance was going on. I realized I was a natural teacher. I enjoyed presenting my thoughts and ideas to others and they enjoyed hearing them. My satisfaction was immense, and I heard an inner voice say, "Look, Papa. I not only finish my projects but I'm teaching others as well."

Furthermore, with my dinner parties and sewing classes, I found a recurring theme beginning to develop in my life: whenever I gathered people together around a table, I felt deeply nurtured and fulfilled, as if I were doing what I was born to do. As I would realize more fully during the next few years, the dreams and fantasies of my childhood were slowly taking form in real life around me.

Other new interests were also beginning to emerge. In a stationery store one day, I was fascinated with a beautiful electric typewriter. Paul said, "Why don't we buy it—on the condition that you promise me that one day you'll write a book."

I was shocked. Writing a book seemed an outrageous idea, something *writers* do.

"But I'm not a writer," I said.

"You didn't know how to sew either, Kitten."

I looked at Paul and felt a rush of excitement. Buoyed by that energy and the mystery of what it might mean, I said, "Okay. I promise!"

The following week I had the worst cold of my life and was so groggy I could hardly get out of bed. But during my waking hours I did reactivate my high-school typing skills. After that, the first thing I actually wrote (besides lines and lines of typing exercises) was an entry in a contest sponsored by a beauty magazine. The first prize was a set of electric curlers and, to my absolute astonishment, I won them. I had actually earned something for being *a real writer!*

Still, the best part of the day was when Paul arrived back from work for dinner—either to a home-cooked meal or to Antonio's, our favorite neighborhood Italian restaurant, where a spaghetti dinner for two cost only $2.20.

Then we'd spend those precious hours in our little studio, sometimes staying awake far into the night. I usually wasn't concerned about how late we stayed up—Paul's hours as a furniture salesman were flexible—but Paul liked to keep track of the time. He had his own quirky relationship with it. For instance, he had a benign superstition about digital clocks. If the numbers at the moment he happened to glance up were consecutive, like 12:34 or 1:23, he declared it a good omen—luck was on the way, like the *joss* of finding coins in the street.

Paul encouraged me to pursue anything and everything that intrigued me. His helpful support was a gift from God that allowed me to untangle the knot of my childhood. The grace of his love for me, the undeserved goodness of it, was proof to me of a benevolent universe. Now I was heading in a direction of finding out who I really was and what I loved. I was already dreaming of teaching and writing, of bringing people together to partake of some kind of learning. How different that was from when I was first married, when I had been like a blank slate—prepared only for a life of comfort and unable to clean a house or sew a stitch.

Paul, meanwhile, developed a small space-planning business for offices. Before long he began to bring in corporate clients. The business showed promise and Paul even attracted some attention from a large insurance organization that was interested in buying the company.

————

We'd been married almost five years and the time had come, we both felt, to start a family.

The time had also come when my mother decided she'd finally had enough of Papa's abuse and sued him for divorce. Everything was going her way: she had her youth, her own money—everything except confidence that she would be able to live the rest of her life without being harassed by Papa. But she was willing to give it a try. She rented a small apartment not far from us.

Thrilled that a grandchild was on the way, Mimi helped us with the down payment on a ranch-style house in nearby North

Hollywood. Paul, along with his good friend, an architect named Dave Duplanty, designed a spacious French country kitchen to replace the tiny existing kitchen, breakfast room, and porch.

I now had a dream kitchen. It soon became a place to practice all the cooking skills I'd been acquiring, some of which paid off in surprising ways. For instance, over the years of my studies with Gregoire, the only dish he made that disappointed me was his Grand Marnier soufflé. One day in class, while I was pregnant, I found the courage to tell him so, that I thought his recipe wasn't quite as good as mine. He good-naturedly challenged me to come up in front of the class of thirty and make my recipe while he made his. That was my first experience in front of an actual class, and to my delight, my soufflé was declared the winner.

Soon after the kitchen was finished, we made another major addition to the house—a black standard poodle. We hadn't had a pet in years, not since, at a time when Papa had been desperately lonely, we gave him our little terrier, Fenwick (who had once been his dog anyway). In the meantime, I had fallen in love with a friend's dog, Colette, so for Mother's Day that year Paul and my mother pooled their funds to buy me Colette's sister. (Paul and Mom bickered good-naturedly over who had bought which half.) I named her Misty and loved her inordinately, feeling she was surely the most wonderful pet anyone ever had. She always sensed exactly how I was feeling, leaning against my leg as I sewed, looking up at me with her soulful Barrymore eyes.

Whenever I think of that house in North Hollywood, I picture the huge crepe myrtle tree outside the kitchen door. Bright pink blooms covered it every June, tumbled into my grocery bags on my return from the market, and rained down like blessings on my pregnancy. I felt wonderful, alive, juicy, serene as a Madonna; Paul treated me reverently, with even deeper love and devotion. I was certain that this child would be the first of five, that I'd be filled with maternal feelings when I held my baby, and be forever fully content. I had absolutely no idea of the exhausting reality of parenthood.

Lisa Frances was born July 10, 1968. We would call her Lexi. Labor was hard and swift. Paul stood by the bed during labor with a happy-face pin on his shirt, frantic because he could do nothing to help me. Our little girl had a rough arrival. And I, instead of gushing with maternal feelings, fell into a pit of postpartum depression.

Very little was written or spoken in those days about the dark feelings of new motherhood and just how hard such an adjustment can be. Women's magazines were filled with activities for the happy homemaker and I felt I must be an awful person since I was so overwhelmed. It was all quite a shock.

My postpartum depression was just as debilitating as the depression that had overwhelmed me as a teenager. Further, I was depressed about being depressed—feeling guilty for being unhappy even though I had a husband I adored and the baby I yearned for.

It was also a time of some small but important changes. One day while nursing, I caught a glimpse of myself in the mirror, a cloud of sunlit cigarette smoke wreathing the baby and me. The true harm of cigarette smoking was unknown in those days, though Paul and I cavalierly called cigarettes coffin nails or cancer sticks. I asked myself in sudden shock: *What are you doing endangering this child?* I quit smoking then and there. Paul vowed to quit with me, but the tensions of our simultaneous withdrawals plus adjusting to parenthood led us to snap at each other, so he decided to wait until after I'd gotten through it. He would wait ten more years. It was probably ten years too long.

Quitting smoking was the hardest thing I'd ever done, though I realized I'd truly succeeded at the end of three weeks. Besides feeling great, I experienced a tremendous boost in confidence and, along with it, a wave of nervous energy and a need to keep my hands busy.

So instead of resting while Lexi was napping, I began using some of my newfound energy to make crêpes to store in the freezer for future meals. Three French pans heated on gas burners as I poured batter into one pan, flipped the crêpe in the second, and slid a crêpe out of the third onto the top of a stack and brushed it with butter— a rhythm that left no time to light a cigarette even if I'd wanted one. A more far-reaching consequence, however, was that a friend dropped by and became intrigued by what I was doing. She asked me to teach her. And that, quite simply, was how my cooking classes began.

I let a few people know I would be giving classes in making omelets, soufflés, and crêpes, and women soon gathered around my kitchen table and stove. They loved the classes and told their friends. Soon I began to get telephone calls from strangers all over Los Angeles who had heard about my courses and wanted to enroll. Paul bought folding desk chairs that would fit in the kitchen so I could seat ten people at a time. I was soon offering morning or evening classes four or five times a week, and developed a long waiting list.

After the first series in basics, I began teaching menus for entertaining, including marketing lists and detailed plans for doing everything ahead of time. Entertaining at home during those days was "in" and it was important for hosts to have a handful of menus that could be prepared in advance so they would be able to enjoy their guests.

I thrived on the special camaraderie of those early classes and on the creativity of inventing ethnic menus from around the world.

I only charged between six and ten dollars a class and, in the beginning, spent most of it on cookbooks, groceries for experimentation, and stocking our new kitchen with copper pots, pans, and French cooking paraphernalia that made the classes seem professional.

On Mondays I took the small basket lined with tin from our front door and walked Misty and Lexi in her stroller to the flower stand on the corner. For just two dollars we filled it with daisies and field flowers. Because I loved to set the scene, I'd spend hours at our dining room table establishing the perfect ambiance for the menu I'd be teaching—so the students could appreciate it on their way to the kitchen. Paul was encouraging and loved seeing me alive with passion for what I was doing.

Our daughter thrived too. She loved Mamie, the babysitter I hired to play with her on the mornings I taught my classes. Mamie would bring Lexi to the kitchen door to wave at the women, among whom were Meredith MacRae, who had been a sorority sister of mine, and Linda Evans, who had just married John Derek. The phone rang almost constantly, with people making reservations and asking questions about cooking.

Because the night class was composed of men and women, Paul began to join us, offering advice about wine and demonstrating salad-making techniques. His artistic flair led him to create vegetable garnishes that were truly spectacular. And that was the beginning of the food business for *him*, as he studied and observed and practiced until he was becoming an accomplished teacher on his own. Paul's space-planning business also started off well.

Yet as smooth and untroubled as our lives appeared on the surface, this was the beginning of hard financial times in our marriage. Neither of us had educated ourselves about ways to earn a living, nor had we developed much business savvy. We really knew nothing about how to save money or plan for the future.

Paul put heart and soul into developing the small space-planning business. Then came the recession and suddenly it was foundering. The company that had opened negotiations to buy his fledgling business reconsidered and after six months negotiations broke down.

I began creating one series of classes after another, repeating some I'd already taught, and raising my prices. I gave classes three mornings and two evenings a week, and the money was a big help as Paul's income dwindled. To my great surprise, some television producers even approached us with the idea that Paul and I might do a cooking show together. I loved the idea, but months went by and nothing came of it.

Paul was devastated, not only because his business was failing but also because his inventions were producing no income. My cooking classes, though they were just beginning to pay nicely, could not support us by themselves. We became mired in debt trying to keep the space-planning business afloat until it could be sold. Meanwhile, Papa was involved in a complicated, years-long lawsuit that threatened *all* the family's assets. Not only would the trust funds Papa had created for Gene and me be drained, but Paul and I would also even be liable for any money we'd received over the years from those trust funds.

That's how things were going when we awakened suddenly one morning in 1971 to hear a deafening roar and found ourselves enveloped in blackness, in a house that felt like it was falling apart around us. Instinct drove us both to the place Paul had selected as the safest in the event of an earthquake—the set of three doors just outside Lexi's room.

The floor was snaking like the track of a roller coaster and we could barely hang on to the doorjambs. Lexi's crib was just another three feet away, but the movement was so violent there was no way to reach her, though I could see she was safer staying where she was. Thank God the shaking lasted less than a minute. Lexi slept right through the tumult and awoke smiling and cooing.

The resulting upheaval lasted much longer. Like the time I followed fate and broke up with my old beau, and like the time when Paul found me again by having me paged at the American Express office in Paris—that morning was yet another occasion when destiny shuffled our cards and everything changed. Damage to the house was slight given the violence of the quake. We had broken glass and dishes to deal with, yet the structure held and the pool didn't even crack. But something inside me and Paul did crack. We suddenly felt terribly vulnerable. If such a thing could happen right under our feet, just as our finances were apparently falling apart, what else was in store for us?

We began to question everything we were doing, including the kind of life we were living. How *did* we want to live, really live, now that we'd seen how everything could be taken from us so suddenly?

While we pondered what to do, Paul's business crumbled, along with any certainty about our future.

SIX

TWO WEEKS and two days since Paul died . . . a bleak, chilly morning.

After the Edge meeting was over and I said goodbye to Mary, I waited in front of the hotel for the valet to bring my car and load the equipment in the back. As I did, I saw the tall, slender figure of Tim Piering approaching. Tim was an ex-Marine and a longtime student of the martial arts, who carried himself with an intriguing combination of military reserve and a street fighter's poised alertness. He was married now, with two teenage children—a son and a daughter—and in these, his post-military days, he worked in real estate and as a corporate consultant. He also understood a great deal about motivating people and helping them work free of negative or destructive patterns of behavior. He was the author of several books about developing excellence, and Paul and I thought of him not only as our friend but also as our coach, cheerleader, and confidant.

Tim had visited Paul often during his last days in the hospital, encouraging him to use every bit of focus he had to fight the cancer that was draining away his energy and his life. Tim was very aware of the emotional stress I'd been experiencing.

"How are you feeling?" he called.

"Okay," I said, routinely. Then, realizing who I was talking to, I corrected myself. "Low. Bad. Miserable. Depressed. I guess this is grief. I feel like hell. I miss him so much."

He silently acknowledged my feelings. Then he said, "You know, some physical activity might be good. It can help get the stress out of your body. Do you ever go to a gym to work out?"

"No, never." I sounded so dreary to myself that I thought I'd try some levity. "I'm like Garfield the cat. Whenever I feel the urge to exercise, I lie down until the feeling goes away."

His smile was sympathetic. "You know, this might be a good opportunity to break some old habits."

"Such as?"

"Such as whatever may be holding you back. You might find ways to make yourself feel better. Helping the grief leave your body is one of them. Some physical exercise could help you change gears. I'll go along with you if you want."

I had such faith in Tim that I agreed to try.

"Maybe we could go to a gym together after the Edge meetings on Tuesday, then have lunch. I have some other ideas that I think can help you deal with the really hard feelings."

"Well," I said, "I'm willing to try anything once . . . I guess."

But I wasn't *that* willing. Oddly enough, I wasn't unwilling either. I was just in some kind of nowhere land, a dull, featureless place between Paul's death and the future, following for the moment the lead of someone I trusted. I was, in a sense, ready to go anywhere, to move in any direction I happened to be facing if it seemed halfway reasonable. Or even unreasonable. *Everything*, I realized, was going to be new from now on. *Everything was going to be new.* Paul and I married when I was twenty-two, so walking alone in life was a new adventure for me. I was frightened but also saw it as a noble challenge—at least when I could ease the grief that threatened to overwhelm me at times.

Because of my continuing sense of communion with Paul, various friends and family worried that I was in a state of denial about his death. But I told them I was certain I wasn't. How could I be in denial if the grief I felt was so real, so powerful, on occasion almost more than I could stand? My agony over his illness prepared me for his death and I had been grieving all along. I had watched him waste away, tended him, was with him at the moment he died.

Even as I grieved, letters of condolence continued to arrive daily and were a great comfort. David Whyte, a well-known poet and one of my favorite Inside Edge speakers, sent me one of his published poems:

THE WELL OF GRIEF

Those who will not slip beneath
    the still surface of the well of grief

turning downward through its black water
    to the place we cannot breathe

will never know the source from which we drink,
    the secret water, cold and clear,

nor find in the darkness glimmering
    the small round coins
        thrown by those who wished for something else.

I wrote back, telling him that I was determined to find the win in my loss. And he replied:

Dear Diana,

I understand the spirit behind your expressed desire to make your loss into "a win," but Rilke took this understanding a further step when he said:

> *Winning does not tempt that woman.*
> *This is how she grows:*
> *by being defeated, decisively,*
> *by greater and greater beings.*

ADAPTED BY DAVID WHYTE

I did not immediately grasp the fullness of what David was telling me. I simply was not ready for it then.

Because I was not a person who was inclined to fall to pieces under stress, I had an underlying feeling that I could be *strong* through my grief. I treated it as a problem that could and should be *solved.* I intended to *triumph* over it. I would find the *win.*

David, however, was attempting in his gentle way to say that grief was not a foe to be vanquished but a state of extreme vulnerability that, in service to my own well-being, needed to be honored and appreciated, a very difficult feeling to which I needed to surrender, lest the grief not serve its greater healing and cleansing purpose. His view of my situation was beautiful and well-meant, but I wasn't quite prepared to yield myself up in that way.

Summer 1971

After the earthquake, Paul and I knew something had to be done. Paul decided we needed a buffer, a pause, a way to take a break.

We had heard from friends that people could live very well and very inexpensively in any of several small art colonies in Mexico. It sounded like as good a place as any to make a break for independence and wait out the verdict in Papa's court case.

So we sold our house, packed our Volkswagen van, and drove to a small town in Central Mexico where we were to stay for a year. Two hundred miles northwest of Mexico City, San Miguel de Allende is known for its colony of American artists and writers and its art schools. To Mexicans it has, since 1810, been recognized as the birthplace of their country's independence. We chose it as a fitting birthplace for our own.

"Let's go! To *Mex*-i-co," Paul, Lexi, and I chanted as a sort of battle cry to boost our spirits during our drive south on the dusty summer roads. Misty, head out the side window with ears flying backward, watched the road ahead.

We approached San Miguel from above, stopping at El Mirador, the lookout point, for a panoramic view. Our eyes followed the winding highway as it became paved with cobblestones and led down to the center, to the pink spires of the neo-Gothic church La Parroquia in the heart of the town. Narrow cobblestone streets led away in all directions from the church and the town square, past faded pastel walls overgrown with purple bougainvillea. A patch of green dotted with lavender blossoming jacaranda trees was known as the French Park. The six-foot bell in the church tower was tolling the hour amid the braying of burrows and crowing of roosters.

We looked for a month before finding a newly built, three-story house right on the French Park (furnished, $150 a month) and staffing it with a maid (Anita, $12 a week). I enrolled in two classes—Spanish and macramé—at the Instituto Allende, one of the finest art schools in Mexico. Paul enrolled in a sculpting class at the Bellas Artes and rented a small studio that had once belonged to Jose Mojíca, the famous Mexican opera singer and film star. We enrolled Lexi in kindergarten at the town's bilingual John F. Kennedy School, and Misty waited patiently at the front door for her to come home to play in the afternoons.

Paul became involved in his sculpting, while I developed into the worst macramé artist in a class of thirty women.

I was so untalented that I eventually had to ask myself a very basic question. *Even if I got really good at macramé, what could I do with it?*

The search for an answer led me to examine just exactly where I thought we were going. Or whether we were going anywhere at all. Paul, for example, always had a pattern of moving on to something new if things didn't work out. He seemed so self-assured, but underneath what appeared to be his sense of ambition was an easygoing, gentle man—maybe too easygoing sometimes—who had always floated like a leaf in the wind. I could have seen that trait in him earlier if I'd wanted to, but I hadn't. I preferred to see him as perfect, purposeful, highly motivated, always finishing what he started. Indeed, he taught me how to finish what I started—and did it brilliantly when I was first learning to sew—but I realized that was a case of the student teaching what he had to learn.

Now questions began to come up. *What in the world are we doing here? Don't we need to take steps that will make sense of our future, not just wait for life to happen to us?*

I looked closely at my own life. I had loved teaching my cooking classes, but now I was in Mexico, as much a leaf in the wind as Paul, learning how to make macramé plant hangers.

One evening when I was alone in the house, frustration suddenly exploded inside me. Almost shouting, I asked Spirit aloud, *"What can I do? What am I supposed to be doing?"*

Later I recognized that moment as one in which powerful energies rose in me. I wanted something to change. Not next month or next week or even tomorrow. But *right now!* And as I was to find out whenever I did it, such a plea produced dramatic results.

I let the apparently unanswerable question hang in the air. Within minutes an answer came. *Write a cookbook!* It was a totally unprecedented thought, a wild thought, out of some unexplored part of my brain. But there it was. And I realized it was a great idea! I could write a cookbook made up of menus for entertaining that could be prepared by the hosts before their party.

I was suddenly on fire with the idea. I had all the menus from my classes over the past two years. I still had that electric typewriter, and up the circular staircase on the third floor was a tiny lookout room just big enough for a desk and chair.

Paul loved the idea and he helped me move "my office" upstairs.

I had no idea how to write or format a book. I didn't even know a manuscript should be double-spaced. But that didn't matter, because I was determined. "Diana never finishes anything" was ancient history now. I could *accomplish things* and I knew it. I'd learned to sew and became a sewing teacher. I'd learned to cook and became a cooking teacher. I had a record of accomplishment . . . except, that is, for macramé.

I began writing the book. Through an American woman I met in the town's *mercado,* I was invited to join a group of local women, mostly Americans, who took turns giving cooking classes and donated the proceeds to the local orphanage. On the days I taught there, I remembered why I so enjoyed teaching classes. Camaraderie begins to develop when a group gathers together around a table and, inevitably, the members begin to speak of their hopes and dreams. We all flourish when embraced with the enthusiasm and encouragement of others.

Another significant event occurred on my thirtieth birthday in March, when Paul gave me a copy of *A Gift from the Sea* by Anne Morrow Lindbergh. The author spoke right to my heart.

The setting of this deeply introspective work is Captiva, the north end of Sanabel Island, off the west coast of Florida, where the author went for a seaside stay alone, away from her large family and her role as wife and mother. In a series of essays, she explores the intricacies and the symbolism of the shells she'd find on solitary walks on the beach, relating them to the essence of being a woman and being in a relationship. Her essays encourage women to find the beauty in each step along life's way, and her gentle prodding awakened me more than ever before to my own reflective nature.

Paul encouraged my new introspection, and on an extended visit to a remote beach in Mexico, he took Lexi swimming and fishing in the mornings as I gathered my own shells and thought about what I valued and the kind of life I wanted to live. Using Lindbergh's technique, I began the practice of asking a question over and over in my mind and then releasing any attachment to an answer. Hours or days later, I would be flooded with insight on the subject. I told Paul it was like putting yeasted dough in a warm place to rise—the passage of time cultures and expands our wisdom.

Life was interesting in Mexico. Because we knew we were in some kind of transition, we allowed ourselves the luxury of a certain randomness. We didn't try to structure our lives too stringently, although writing a cookbook soon began imposing a kind of creative order on me, one to which I responded with pleasure. And it was then, for the first time in my life, that I began to wonder exactly what Papa was trying to save me from when he told me I'd "never have to work for a living."

Our odyssey in Mexico came to a sudden end when I got an unexpected phone call from my mother. Papa, she told me, was in the hospital, dying. Within a few hours, I was on an airplane, headed back to Los Angeles to be with him. Paul and I instinctively knew it was time to let go of our idyllic interlude.

———————

When I entered my father's hospital room, he lay in bed in a coma. He was snoring softly, as if he were simply in a restful sleep. I looked at him, feeling sad as I recalled how few tender moments we'd had together, how little kindness he'd ever shown any of us. Papa had believed "security" was the most important thing in the world, and that money could substitute for love.

After Mimi divorced him, he turned into a lonely, unhappy man. When progressive dementia finally caused him to lose even his ability to add a column of figures, he sensed that his life was nearing its end. He had little to live for once his capacity to operate in the intensely cerebral world of finance was gone. He never had much use for human beings.

In spite of his erratic ways, he had, in his own peculiar way, cared about his family and had worked hard all his life to not only provide for us, but also to give us security far into the future. I'd always felt he wanted to be a more loving person but his terrible misfortune was that he was afraid to trust anyone.

Mother had been kind and loving to him after she left him. Papa was always surprised by and appreciative of her help. But nothing about him ever really changed.

———

Three mornings after I arrived, as Mother and I approached his room for the first of our twice-daily visits, a nurse intercepted us and said with compassionate directness, "Mr. Webb expired a few minutes ago."

Expired . . . I guess that means he died.

I tried to feel sad, but was strangely unmoved. I went to his bedside, put my hand on his cheek, and said goodbye. It all seemed very mechanical to me. I was going through motions.

Mother and I made arrangements for delivery of the body to Forest Lawn and used the hospital phone to call my brother. Gene, by then a tenured college professor at the University of Washington in Seattle, arrived the next day; he and Mother went to the funeral home so Gene could say his goodbyes. Alone in Papa's house, I was at the sink washing dishes when I sensed Papa's presence very clearly behind me.

"Forgive me," he said.

I stopped what I was doing but didn't turn around. I almost laughed out loud at myself because I didn't really believe a dead person could communicate with me. While I was sometimes intuitive, I'd had never experienced anything like this.

"Forgive me," he said again, more firmly than before.

I whirled around and saw no one. I wondered at what I was hearing, convinced somehow against the illogic of it that he was really there. A fury rose in me. "Okay! I'll forgive you!" I said bitterly, suddenly sobbing. "But not for your sake! For mine! It hurts me too much to hate you like I do. Just stay away from us forever." I was surprised by my rage, and wondered if I would ever feel at ease with my memories of him.

––––––––––

Being back in the high energy of Los Angeles and away from the sleepy environment that prevailed in our Mexican village stirred me to take action with my book proposal. I left it with a Los Angeles publisher who was recommended by a friend in San Miguel. This, after all, was part of our new beginning.

The head of programming at ABC met with me about a husband-and-wife cooking show. He wasn't encouraging, but our meeting meant that *something* was happening.

After Papa's memorial service, I flew back to Mexico. Three weeks later, Paul, Lexi, Misty, and I drove the old Volkswagen bus back to Beverly Hills. Gene had gone back to the university, leaving me to dismantle Papa's house. And so Paul, Lexi, and I settled into the mansion I'd always hated. Its upkeep would be paid from Papa's estate until it could be sold. Though many people would have envied us for our comfortable circumstances, we could hardly wait to move out of there and get on with our lives. The rooms seemed haunted by his anger.

My mother's long-term unhappiness in the mansion was reflected in the lackluster decor. The kitchen, though dated and old-fashioned, was more than large enough for me to resume my teaching. I planned a new series of classes and sent out invitations to my old mailing list.

So we had a life, a façade really, if not a sufficient cash flow to sustain it. Paul started job-hunting. The mansion, however, was rent-free, the upkeep the responsibility of the estate, which could not be settled while the long-pending suit against my father remained undecided. We registered Lexi in a local nursery school.

In two years, Gene's and my trusts, being entirely separate from the rest of the estate, would be ours to manage. My inheritance would be substantial, enough to invest and provide a base of security, though we still wanted to push forward with my cooking classes and what could be spun off from them—books, perhaps a newspaper column, maybe even a TV show.

Almost as soon as my father died, my mother began dating. Even though they had been divorced for five years, as long as Papa was alive Mimi had remained loyal to him in her own way. But now, she quickly fell in love with a widower named Jack Schneider. Completely caught up in her romance, she was no longer involved in my life. I missed her.

———

In that big house, touching the outside window of my father's closet, was a tiny nest with four eggs, built beneath the shelter of an eave. The mother bird would fly away when I stepped near. I was so enchanted by the promise of new life there that I would check on the birds' progress every day and bring Paul up to date. When, eventually, four tiny babies were hatched and squirmed restlessly for their mother to feed them, I was as thrilled as if I had hatched them myself. Paul and I told each other it was an omen of good things to come.

Then one morning when Paul was taking Lexi to school, something occurred that changed our lives dramatically, casting us into a new level of turmoil that would affect us far into the future.

As I look back on it now, I see it was surpassed in importance only by my first meeting with Paul and the birth of Lexi. But while those two events were life-changing in a wonderful way, this one seemed disastrous. Actually, however, it marked my full emergence from the cocoon of immaturity in which I, the little girl "who would never have to work for a living," had been half-consciously hiding out for my entire adult life. My whole sense of everyday reality would collapse and a new Diana would take form.

The telephone rang and a man asked for Mother. I explained that she was at another address and if he would tell me who he was, I would give him a number where she could be reached.

"Is this her daughter? Diana?"

"Yes."

His tone was foreboding as he identified himself as one of the lawyers to whom my father had paid more than a quarter of a million dollars to defend him in an ongoing lawsuit related to an obscure, complex problem involving various banking statutes.

"I have very bad news for you, I'm afraid. Your father's death made the judge's work easy for him. He's decided against you. He's going to allow your mother to keep her money, but the trusts set up for you and your brother will be revoked to recover the money that was in dispute. I'm sorry."

I nearly doubled over with the impact of the news. Pacing around the bedroom, I tried not to panic. As unkind as my father could be, providing security for his family had always been his top priority. I didn't need to reflect for long to remember all of the opportunities I had squandered thinking a life of luxury lay before me. I realized now, suddenly, that what I had imagined as the mechanism of my salvation—"You will never have to work"—now appeared to be the engine of my destruction.

Frightened, wanting to do anything to change my focus, to find some gentleness and hope, I went to the little window in my father's closet, seeking inspiration and a sense of life. Instead, I found the nest bloodied, ravaged by some predator. It was torn to pieces. I slumped against the wall by the window and, staring blankly, slid slowly to the floor. Our situation seemed hopeless. I sat there, numb and unmoving, for a long time, wondering what words to use to tell Paul. We'd have to think of something fast. The house would soon be sold. How would we make a living?

Distraught, I paced back and forth in the bedroom. For the second time in my life, I found myself pleading aloud, "God, tell me, what can we do? Tell me what to do."

I continued pacing, and moments later I heard an answer, not in my ears, but from the very depths of my being: *"voluntary simplicity."* That phrase was to become widely known years later, after the publication of the book of the same name by Duane Elgin. But I heard it from an inner voice in 1973, fully eight years before the book appeared.

I wrote those two words down, because I sensed they had brought me the answer I needed . . . we both needed. Their full meaning, however, would come to me only gradually.

Paul was wordless with shock when I told him about the judge's decision. We just went through the motions of our daily routine. After a few days though, we decided to dig in our heels. With the money coming in from the cooking classes, we had a few months to make contingency plans. And then my book came back, rejected by the first publisher. I remembered those baby birds. I wondered, What now? What were those two words?

Voluntary simplicity. Far easier said than done. Nevertheless, I sensed that phrase as the answer to every problem we faced. But how would we change a lifetime of habits? It was one of the seminal questions that everyone confronts at some time. *How do I change?* How do I know *what* to change? How do I become different despite the bonds of lifelong habits?

Paul felt he was a failure because he'd had no success in marketing his designs. What *could* we do? We both sensed that my cooking classes would have to be our way out. We mailed the book proposal, unsolicited, to a second publisher.

Mother, head-over-heels in love with Jack, my stepfather-to-be, offered no emotional support at all. Her primary response to the judge's decision was relief that the lawsuit didn't affect her financially. One day she telephoned to tell me she and Jack were in Las Vegas, where they had eloped.

The book proposal came back again, and neither publisher had encouraged me to keep developing it. Nevertheless, there seemed to be more and more interest in cooking and entertaining, and we decided to explore what we might develop out of my classes.

We had no time to waste. We weren't going to realize a penny from the contents of the house until Papa's estate was disbursed and that wouldn't happen until the house itself was sold. In a bold move, we decided to make our way in the world without regard to the house sale. There was little of value to be sold anyway and it would not be central to our salvation.

The house had been on the market for some time, and while there were many lookie-loos in the lingering recession of the early '70s, we got no offers. The trustee of Papa's estate finally had to put the place up for auction. A couple we'd met through cooking classes decided Papa's house was their dream home, so they made a low bid. The offer was good and the house was theirs. Five years later it was appraised at ten times what it sold for. Good timing for them, bad timing for us.

We accepted the offer of Ira and Theresa Kaplan, another couple we'd met through cooking classes, to live in their cabin at Lake Arrowhead that winter while things sorted themselves out for us. All we had to pay were the utility bills. It was the perfect answer, and a kind and generous act on their part.

Clearing out twenty-five years' accumulation of personal possessions in such an enormous house turned out to be a horrible undertaking. Papa, who survived huge losses in the Depression, had seldom thrown anything away. It was August 1973 and blistering hot, especially on our very last day. We were packing and clearing out as fast as we could, running against time. Those last two days found me angry and frantic to escape. Too much heat, too much work, too much pressure, too much emotional baggage, old and new.

Just as we were finishing packing up the kitchen, Paul announced that he was fed up with my nastiness. In that moment I wanted to strangle him and I told him to leave me alone. He asked me why I couldn't just quit pushing my angry mood off on everyone, why I didn't control myself. Why not be reasonable like he was trying to be, so we could finish our work. I snapped at him that I was sorry I wasn't perfect like he was, and if he wanted a cleaning machine instead of a wife, maybe he should go down to the store and buy a robot to help him move. He said he could live without my sarcasm.

That did it! I looked down at the table, at what I'd been packing. Our two favorite champagne glasses, the ones that cost $75 apiece, were right in front of me. I thought, *I wish they'd cost seventy-five thousand apiece*, then in a moment of delicious rage I heaved one of the glasses at the far wall. It shattered. "How's that instead of sarcasm?" I screamed. "How's *that* instead of telling you I hate what's happening? And I *do* hate what's happening. I hate having all this junk bring back the horrible memories of living in this house. I hate that we've lost everything we have, this house is a filthy mess, it's like an oven in here, and now you're being self-righteous. You say you're sick of my mood? Well, I'm sick of yours! So we might as well get rid of these glasses, don't you think?" For emphasis, I heaved our other glass at the wall, harder than the first one, and watched with manic satisfaction as it, too, shattered into pieces.

Lexi watched in horror from the doorway. Paul was frozen to the spot where he stood.

I stalked out of the kitchen and slammed the door.

It was the lowest moment of our marriage.

SEVEN

August 1973

OUR LITTLE borrowed cabin was some eighty miles east of Los Angeles, halfway between the tiny resort towns of Blue Jay and Arrowhead Village. Our drive there was soggy with silence. For the next several days I was in shock. I just lay in a hammock, staring through the trees to the sky.

It had been awful, especially since I was no stranger to such eruptions. I'd grown up around them, around a father who randomly terrorized our home and family. I'd vowed that I'd never be that way myself, that no violent moods of mine would frighten the people I loved. So all of my life I'd controlled my temper if it heated up, restrained any tendency to inflict my emotions and my father's brutality on other people.

Now I had become him. I'd terrorized my own family. I didn't know what to do. My confusion was accompanied by a sense of horror over what losing the inheritance would mean. The strain of handling Papa's house and his endless heaps of possessions had brought me to boiling, to a state of chaos. My mother, always my supporter, was nowhere to be seen. The combination got explosive and I simply blew up.

Paul and Lexi took Misty for walks, made meals, and left me to myself.

I tried to sort through my thoughts and feelings and came up blank. It was as if my mind was protecting itself from itself by simply shutting down. I lay in the hammock, staring through the trees, knowing I would feel better some day, but having no idea when that time would be. The day passed. The next day passed. And the next day . . .

At the end of the third day, Lexi approached me tentatively. She looked at me searchingly, attempting to discover if I was there, behind my eyes. I looked at her. She said carefully, her face controlled, "Look, Mommy. Look. Look what we found on our walk."

That did it. The tears burst forth and I began to sob. Lexi understood and waited there patiently, lovingly. Thank God, I thought, for my wonderful little daughter. I pulled her up on top of me and hugged her close. I cried and cried until my feelings were drained clean, then I rolled out of the hammock and set her on the ground, kneeling to engage her eye to eye.

"Honey, you know I always love you."

"I know," she said.

"I was really angry with Daddy."

She nodded.

"But feelings run through a person like water. You know that. This time they just took a little longer to run through me. I'm better now."

Her trusting little face made a smile.

"Where is Daddy?" I asked.

"He's over there. He's waiting."

I took her hand and let her guide me.

What I told her was true. But of course it was not so simple. Feelings, like water, run through, but in doing so they also cut new channels, overrun banks, and soak into places that previously were dry. The flood always recedes, but afterward the terrain is changed. As I walked with Lexi, the child I loved, to reunite with Paul, the man I loved, I knew we would have to discuss those changes to the terrain. Life would never be quite the same.

———

Paul and I circled around each other for the next several days. Our accustomed spontaneity was not present. We were careful, measured, too polite. Often we communicated through Lexi, speaking with her as though *to* her, but knowing the other heard. Lexi was still wary. Her feelings would go from relaxation to flashes of anger to moody quiet. But she never strayed too far away from either of us physically. That told us both she was okay. Paul and I didn't try to alter or control her behavior. She needed room to feel her inner nature, and we wanted her to have it. Besides, our own plate was full. So Paul and I talked.

"Snow's coming soon."

"I wonder how soon."

"I don't know."

"We probably need chains for the car."

"Probably."

"I wonder if it'll be a cold winter."

"I don't know. We'll have to ask somebody."

We were detouring around the new terrain.

———

I knew Paul was waiting for me to start the discussion. That was usually our way. It was particularly so this time, because I was the one who had changed and we both knew it.

The opportunity came one morning after we put Lexi on the big yellow school bus that stopped at the corner to take her to kindergarten on the other side of the lake. Watching her wave through the window as the bus disappeared around the corner, I said, "I'm sorry for blowing up, Paul. I'm sorry Lexi had to see it."

He nodded.

"I'm sorry for hurting you," I said.

"Maybe I deserved it. I didn't know how upset you were."

"It wasn't really what you think it was. The money. Or the house. Or the heat. It was us. We need to be doing something different."

He was giving me his full attention now. "What do you mean?"

"I'm not sure. But something needs to change."

"Do you know what it is?"

We entered the house and sat on opposite ends of the living room couch.

"I feel like we're stuck. We need to be moving ahead and I don't think we are." I took a breath. "How many of your inventions can bring in money this year?"

"Probably none of them."

"We need to be thinking about income. Our days of waiting for the trust money are over. We need to start doing something ourselves right now. If we don't, it won't get done."

"Okay, the inventions take time. I know that. But you must have something else in mind."

"I do. It's the cooking classes. They're working for me. People like them. And they're producing income."

"That's wonderful, sweetheart. And when the inventions do start making us some money . . ."

"Paul, I'm talking about supporting us—you and me and Lexi. I'm talking about a dependable, regular income."

"Like you can make with the cooking classes?"

"Yes."

"You mean you'd be supporting us?"

I nodded.

He looked straight at me. "But that's my job. It's the job I want. I want to take care of you and Lexi."

I returned his gaze clearly, without challenging him.

"We're headed downhill. We have to face that."

"So we need to make changes. What do you want? Do you want a divorce? Is that what you're saying?"

"No . . . we don't need a divorce. We need a new vision, a different way of doing things."

"What are you thinking?"

"Paul, you know how I am. Some people, when they hit bottom, lose heart and give up. With me, hitting bottom inspires me. It reminds me of how many opportunities there are. I think we need to acknowledge that cooking classes are our future, not your inventions. Not even your jobs in sales."

His face went dark. I knew that even the most forward-thinking man would be devastated to have his wife envision herself as the family breadwinner. Nonetheless, I felt that I had to be honest—no matter how frightening the prospect.

I said, "Paul, do you love me?"

"Of course I do, Kitten. More than anything."

"And I love you. More than anything. And that's what we are and what we have. We're one soul. Haven't you always felt that?"

"Yes."

"So have I. I've felt it since the day we met. And so we can try to fit everybody else's ideas about how a husband and wife are supposed to be. Or we can . . . reinvent ourselves."

For the first time during our conversation, I saw some light in his eyes. "Instead of saying that you've failed or I've failed in playing some kind of role, let's create our own roles and play them out. Instead of giving up, let's look realistically at what each of us is good at and feels passionate about, and then do *that*. That may mean I'm giving cooking classes and you're making sure the details work out right. You love doing that. You know how to make things work. I know how to present ideas to audiences.

"You love researching the history of food and creating garnishes to present my dishes beautifully. I think people would rather watch two people working together and enjoying it, than just one person. I may spend more time in the spotlight than you do, but for all we know, you'll be producing the show. Don't you see?"

He grinned. "It does make sense . . ."

I smiled back. "I wonder if Papa is watching us from somewhere."

"Why?"

"Because he thought you were a fortune-hunter. Well," I laughed, "I don't have any money now. . . What does he think is keeping you around?"

"I think it's the way you throw a champagne glass," he joked.

I hugged him. "Do you think you can keep loving me through all of this, Paul?"

"Oh, maybe for a hundred thousand years . . . or so."

"Me too," I said.

And that's how we began reinventing ourselves. Peace had returned, along with a new creativity in our marriage. We knew changing wouldn't always be easy. It would require surrender of all our standards and expectations about what our life together should look like. We told ourselves there must be moments when a caterpillar is distraught over the dissolution it must go through to become a butterfly.

Lexi was relieved that I was back, that we *both* were back, and she was eager to tell me about a little island she and Paul had spotted only a few hundred feet from shore.

"Pack a picnic!" Paul said. "Lexi will take you to a dock we found. I'll pick you up there."

Paul set off for town where he rented a small boat, then rowed the half-mile back. Meanwhile, Lexi snooped in the refrigerator and started packing the best feast we could assemble from what we had on hand.

We spread a blanket under the pines on the island, then opened a bottle of wine and unwrapped Lexi's peanut butter, crackers, marshmallows, and fruit. Thus we began again—on different terrain, on a different road, with different rules and a different destination, though we couldn't see where the road would lead.

By October it was already cold, a thrill for a California girl who had never experienced the four seasons. A friend Paul met in Arrowhead who was in the haberdashery business gave me stacks of fabric samples of men's clothing, rectangles of rich tweeds and plaids. His wife showed me how to crochet them together with yarn to make an afghan. As I laid out and stitched the pieces, Paul and I put the pieces of our life back together.

We walked hand-in-hand every day through the woods on a carpet of pine needles to get our mail at the post office. We could hardly have lived more simply. I kept working on my book and sending it out randomly to publishers, but it kept coming back, rejected. Each time it came back I lost heart . . . temporarily. Nevertheless, I was feeling a new sense of strength and responsibility.

Still, weeks would pass before I could muster the courage to think about revisions and sending it out again. I mused that I could wallpaper a den—if we only had one—with my rejection letters. Paul was helping me add finishing touches to the book now, researching which publishers might be interested in it.

Sometimes on weekends the three of us would go skating at the Ice Chalet in the nearby village of Blue Jay. Paul had taught figure skating as a youth at Rockefeller Center in New York and his form was nearly perfect. Lexi and I were fascinated, watching him glide and speed skate and spin. Just as he loved to lead me around a dance floor in a waltz, he now crossed arms with me and held both my hands in front of us, leading me in a swaying motion around the rink. Then it was Lexi's turn, as she struggled to stay upright while holding her dad's strong hands, and she was triumphant when she got it right.

The beauty of his form reminded me that he had a myriad of talents, not the least of which were his flair and showmanship. Both were qualities that would become vital to our cooking career, and in fact would identify our style.

It snowed lightly the day before Thanksgiving, a magical event for us. Christmas would be very simple that year, and as it approached I sewed remnants of calico and trims I found in my grandmother's sewing baskets—treasures I had been unable to part with—to make our Christmas tree ornaments. I drew patterns and sewed hearts of varying sizes that I'd stuff and decorate with lace and ribbon and buttons. Using a remnant of red flannel, I sewed matching old-fashioned nightgowns for Lexi and me, trimmed with white cotton ruffles. I found a box and wrapped the finished afghan as my present to Paul. We spent almost nothing that holiday season, but it was one of our richest holidays ever. If that's what voluntary simplicity was all about, I found little fault with it.

There was no snow after Thanksgiving, and the ground stayed dry and barren until New Year's. The day before New Year's, our landlords, Theresa and Ira, arrived. Ira offered Paul a job with a small salary designing new products for the gallery and art print business he owned in Los Angeles.

A cause for celebration! We broke out a bottle of champagne we'd been saving for a special occasion and playfully improvised a little snow dance in front of the house. Let it snow for the benefit of the local resorts! Give Lexi the thrill of seeing falling snow!

Snow began to fall almost immediately and continued for the next eight days. At first it was glorious, and we taught Lexi to lie on her back and move her arms up and down to make "angels in the snow." Our boots squeaked in the white powder that blanketed the lakeshore on our way to the post office. But before the storms stopped, the entire lower floor of our cabin was buried and the path from the front door to the driveway was mounded by drifts piled twelve feet high on either side. Paul shoveled the path to the road daily.

Since a national gasoline shortage was in full force, Paul left the house each morning at 5:00 to search for gas in nearby San Bernardino before starting the two-hour drive from there to Los

Angeles. Once or twice a week, to save money, he spent the night in Los Angeles at Ira's gallery.

But the severe weather made life unpredictable. For instance, early one morning an avalanche of snow from our roof severed the power lines. The roads were impassable. Paul built a roaring fire and we huddled close together in front of it for warmth. That night Paul, Lexi, Misty, and I slept in a pile. So much snow fell on Lake Arrowhead during January that it was declared a disaster area, and finally we were evacuated until the roads could be cleared and the power restored. So much for playful snow dances and wanting to experience real seasons.

Spring arrived and the snows melted. Paul was gone during the days, driving the four-hour round trip to L.A., and after Lexi boarded the school bus in the mornings, I'd work on the book until she came home for lunch. In the afternoons I planned new classes to teach in the future.

In May, Papa's estate finally closed. It would be months before everything was completely settled, but we were grateful to find we would have a small income from the estate for a short time. With Paul working in Los Angeles, we recognized that the time had come to go back.

EIGHT

THREE WEEKS since Paul died. Feeling overwhelmed . . .

Facing the challenges of being newly widowed meant, whether I liked it or not, dealing with some hard realities—such as my precarious financial situation. I knew that some big changes would be required, like selling our cozy little house and moving for the first time in fourteen years. It would also require some small changes, like learning how to do something with an automobile other than just drive it.

That matter arose when Lexi, who would soon be returning to college, told me she was worried that I hadn't a clue about how to take care of my car. The very thought of learning anything mechanical about the car evoked in me a desperate need to take a nap.

When she'd been in high school, Lexi asked her dad to teach her enough so she could get a job pumping gas at the local Chevron station. Paul and I both suspected she wanted to be near one of the boys who worked there, but that didn't matter. Her approach was creative, and for her to learn how to deal with an automobile seemed like a good idea to us.

So she knew what she was doing around cars, and her determination to teach me became more urgent one morning when I was to be the host at the San Diego chapter of the Edge. Lexi had promised to get up at 3:00 A.M. to accompany me.

Just before leaving the house, I had an intuition to take a change of clothes and shoes with us.

"What are those for?" she asked.

I told her it was my intuition, something I couldn't explain, and added that I'd learned to pay attention to such feelings.

Rain began to come down just as we left the house, and about two-thirds of the way to San Diego we suddenly had a flat tire. We were on a stretch of highway that was part of Camp Pendleton Marine Base, where there were no gas stations or other businesses for thirty miles. We had no car phone. But my precious Lexi knew how to change the tire—in the pouring rain!

When we were underway again, she put on the dry clothes I'd brought and we got to the meeting just in time.

The next day Lexi made me drive to a gas station. She told me to get out of the car and showed me how to fill it with gas, wash the windows, and check the oil. She demonstrated the basics of changing a tire.

So much for little things. The big one was getting serious about selling the house and preparing it to be put on the market. When I had done that, I would know I was starting to meet life on its own terms.

Lexi volunteered to help me rid the clutter, but the house itself badly needed some fresh decorating touches. I invited my dear friend Candace to come and have a look, to help me brainstorm.

A beautiful and engaging woman, Candace and I first met when she was the line producer on a television pilot Paul and I had taped in 1980. She had an attitude of wonderment about life, and I felt an instant connection with her, an immediate trust. It was one of those times when you meet a stranger and have a flash of mutual recognition, when your hearts open so quickly to each other that the mind has no time to edit the experience. *Oh yes, I know you!*

I told her that day, "You and I are going to become very good friends." And we did, forging a friendship I still cherish.

Candace, full of enthusiasm and affordable ideas, now kindly agreed to help me. I'd always left the visual decisions of the house to Paul—he'd been the designated artist in the family. Now I welcomed Candace as an artistic teammate. She brought me paint samples and swatches of fabric. I attacked the clutter.

In the corner of Paul's office upstairs I found boxes and boxes of photographs and clippings from the years in our cooking career. They deserved organizing, so I went to an art store and bought a huge scrapbook to hold them.

May 1974

After that winter in Arrowhead, Paul and I needed to find a house in Los Angeles with a gracious kitchen for cooking classes, a house near Ira's gallery. Paul was still working on his design for the sculpting machine and other ideas, but he was no longer expecting that the inventions would be the basis of our financial security. We had such faith that once the book was sold we would both find many new opportunities.

Paul soon discovered a modern furnished house for lease near the coast. It was ten miles west of Beverly Hills, close to the intersection of Sunset and the Pacific Coast Highway. From the balcony of the master bedroom we could see waves breaking on the beach below—a real white-water view. What a contrast to the homey little cabin where we'd holed up for the winter.

We moved there in May and life lightened up enormously. Lexi attended summer school at nearby Marquez Elementary while we settled in. Paul bought a bicycle and pedaled her to school on the back. Her new best friend was a freckle-faced, high-spirited redhead named Michelle Friedlander. She knew every joke and riddle of the day and had us all giggling every time she visited. After school we loved to take Misty for a walk on the beach, watching her run back and forth, playing tag with the waves.

Paul and I designed invitations to a new series of cooking classes, which we had no trouble filling. As the holidays approached, I had the idea of doing a class on "With Love from Your Kitchen," for which I created nearly thirty new recipes packaged as gifts. I taught the class five times that year. It was a triumph and created a lot of word-of-mouth about my regular, year-round classes.

We were barely through the holidays when Paul came home to say that, due to changes in the business, Ira didn't need him anymore. He was out of a job and justifiably dejected. It seemed to me, however, that it was a perfect time for Paul to join me in a cooking career—full time. Paul hadn't really found his niche yet, and I can't say that cooking was what he truly wanted to do at first, but it seemed the ideal solution and we were excited at the prospect of really being a team. Paul even planned a class of his own, "The Taming of the Stew."

For once our timing was impeccable, and the end of Paul's job at the gallery is what would finally transform everything for us— our relationship, our careers, our lives.

With the burgeoning interest in home entertaining nationwide, our first order of business was to get my book, now *our* book, published. I had sent it to twenty publishers with nary a nibble. By March we were so disheartened, our friend Theresa insisted we make an appointment with her psychic to ask when the book would be published.

"I see a circle around the month of June," Ed Hindes told us. "But not just one book! There are two!"

Driving home afterward, Paul and I laughed about what he'd said. Two books, indeed. It had taken three years to write one!

A new friend from my cooking classes, Mary Erpelding, helped us do a final polish on the prose. Paul decided we needed an agent, someone who could tell us what the book needed and then get it to the right publisher. He found one, Carol Schild, who was just starting out in the agenting business. She had *chutzpa*—nerve and self-confidence—in the publishing world, exactly the qualities we still lacked.

Carol tried to get Los Angeles publisher Jeremy Tarcher interested in the book and he rejected it. But to our tremendous surprise, he gave us a $6,500 advance for a book he *did* want, based on a small volume Paul had printed of the recipes from my holiday class: *With Love from Your Kitchen.* We had six months to write it and felt we were, if not on top of the world, well on our way up one of its more promising slopes.

Carol next headed for New York with the original manuscript, the one Tarcher didn't want. She visited publishers in alphabetical order starting with Abrams (an art publisher, we found out later), which rejected the book out of hand. She next met with Atheneum, and negotiated a $10,000 advance. Just as the psychic had predicted, two books sold in June. We were ecstatic! We had a career together and it was taking off! Who needed an inheritance?

Paul was wonderful at helping plan menus and classes, and I loved sharing the work with him. He quickly developed an aptitude for being in charge of wine selection, advertising, and how the food looked; I was in charge of cooking techniques, developing menus, and how the food tasted. On Carol's advice we hired a talented publicist who arranged to have my next holiday class photographed for *House and Garden* magazine. The spread was on a page facing a matching story about Martha Stewart. Martha and I were presented as "Entertaining Experts, East and West."

Atheneum wanted us to add six more menus to our book, so Paul took care of Lexi, proofread my text, fed us, and kept me supplied with correction fluid while I stayed attached to the typewriter. In those days before computers, I had to type and retype each page and each recipe until it was perfect. But those were just pesky details. What really mattered was that we were now on our way to sharing a career as chefs and as writers.

————————

Our lease was soon to run out, so with two book advances and great hope, we began looking for a house we could lease and eventually buy.

A realtor drove us down a narrow tree-lined street in Pacific Palisades that led to a cul-de-sac, where we saw a very small, lovely house perched on the edge of a cliff that overlooked the ocean. The minute we saw it, Paul was elaborately enthusiastic about what we would come to name "The Treehouse." And though I knew intuitively that it would become our home, some sort of new survival mechanism helped me stay cool about everything during the complicated lease-option negotiations—until we closed the deal.

On September 7, 1975, we moved into our new home. The Treehouse. Center front was a huge, old sycamore tree around which the architect had built the entry. There was a feeling that the house was part of the tree, and from the front windows we would watch its graceful limbs through the California seasons. Paul and I named the tree Seymour.

On the opposite side of the house, past the living room, was an expansive redwood deck and dining patio overlooking a canyon that fanned open to the Pacific Ocean. On most days we could see the island of Catalina, twenty-six miles off the coast.

Lexi loved the house. And since she had moved so many times in her seven years, she said, "If we ever have to move from this house, I want to be given five years' notice." However, to be able to afford it when the lease was up, we knew we would have to be very successful in our cooking career, so I had to tell Lexi we'd do our best but we were now serving notice, just in case.

Our small, cozy bedroom with its high, slanted ceiling was always my favorite room. It had a corner fireplace and sliding glass doors that opened onto a deck with a tree-covered spa area. Though there were other homes far across the canyon, we had no window coverings anywhere on the canyon side—distance was our curtain. The only eyes that watched us belonged to squirrels, raccoons, a possum, a red fox, and a small family of deer.

The raccoons claimed the spa as their own and we had no choice but to share it. Late at night they would wash their food and playfully shove each other out of the hammock into the water. Sometimes they were so boisterous we would waken, turning on the deck light to watch. Brazen little creatures, raccoons. They would put their noses to the screen door and peer back at us. We wished they would be less rowdy, yet we couldn't help but laugh at their antics.

Our other wildlife was "Bert," a blue scrub jay that was tame enough to take peanuts right out of our hands. We often ate lunch at the umbrella table on our deck and Bert swiped spaghetti right off my plate, thinking it a special delicacy, perhaps an albino worm. He was every bit as daring as the raccoons and sometimes flew right in the open kitchen window to pilfer kibble out of Misty's dish.

Our out-of-town guests were always surprised that we could live in such a huge city as Los Angeles and still enjoy such an uncrowded country feeling. It was the Los Angeles that tourists never see.

Because our Treehouse was small and had no lawn, it was low maintenance and we did our own housework. We were very happy taking care of it, and on Saturday mornings the three of us threw ourselves into the task. Our house was to be a generous parent to us, protecting and nurturing us as our love continued to grow, giving us a sense of roots and an identity we appreciated.

The kitchen didn't work well at all for cooking classes but we taught there anyway, until our neighbor, tired of cars parked in the street, reported us for running a business in our home. The kindly inspector who showed up at the door one day clearly didn't want to hurt us. "Tell me you don't run a business here," he said. "You just have a few friends in for cooking classes from time to time, don't you?" We appreciated his attempts to go easy on us, but we also understood the concern of our neighbors. The time had come, we realized, to think about finding a professional kitchen.

Things were also beginning to fall into place with our publications. The book for J. P. Tarcher, the expanded version of *With Love from Your Kitchen,* was chosen as the featured book of the month for the *Better Homes and Gardens* Book Club. In the absence of an actual finished product, the club had made its choice on the basis of only three mock-up recipes and illustrations.

In May 1976 a package arrived with the presentation copy of our first book, now retitled *The Pleasure of Your Company.* What a feeling, after five years of working on it, to actually hold it in our hands! Cookware stores and department stores asked us to appear in person to do cooking demonstrations and sign books. We were guests on the popular morning TV show *AM Los Angeles.*

With Love from Your Kitchen was released three months later, in September. We went on a ten-city book tour and did many newspaper interviews and radio and television appearances, ending with *Good Morning America.* That's when Paul and I, strolling down Fifth Avenue in New York City, went by Rizzoli's, the great bookstore. Near the door were huge stacks of both of our books. I jumped for joy. *Look, Papa, at the girl who never finished anything. I did it!*

As traveling cookbook writers, we had to carry various kinds of food with us for our demonstrations. Included were many bunches of parsley that Paul used to create a centerpiece of a green holiday tree studded with cherry tomatoes. That tour, one of the most exhausting, dizzying experiences of our lives, was also a time during which Paul and I had to laugh at ourselves. There we were, "author-celebrities," in the middle of a frenzied media whirlwind—just reeking from of the foul aroma of mildewed parsley.

Three years earlier I had been haunted by the prospect of a "lost" inheritance. Now Paul and I had something even better than that kind of money: our own name and our own money which we had made ourselves. We were in our own house with a nine-month lease and an option to buy.

Then, after so many years of economic slump, something astounding happened in California. The real estate market took off! In the nine months of our occupancy, our house appreciated by fifty percent! We had to buy it. We were so excited when the house belonged to us . . . and the bank.

Our momentum continued. We sold a concept to Jeremy Tarcher for a book on buffet-style entertaining and now we had to write it. It turned out to be a great experience, writing a cookbook and enjoying friends at the same time.

The momentum also included low points, such as the time we catered a boutique opening on the Sunset Strip and learned just how poorly some guests treat people in service. As a result, we never wanted to cater again. But what fun it all was when, on that same day, we also learned that *The Pleasure of Your Company* had been given the Cookbook of the Year award. The book that had taken five years to complete and was rejected by at least twenty publishers had been voted by food editors nationally as the best book in the category of entertaining.

I thought the news of the award was a proclamation that what we were doing was valuable and worthwhile. We were on a roll now and could finally leave our desperate past.

Two decades later, I know better. There was a far deeper, yet unseen, current to our lives and it was not going in the direction we were trying to take through our teaching, cooking, and writing. We had no idea then that any of our activities would lead us beyond food to bringing people together in an entirely different way—not just so they could enjoy "the pleasure of their company," but also so they could discover and realize their most profound dreams.

NINE

A FEW WEEKS after Paul died, Lexi and Lauren announced they were kidnapping me for a drive up the coast to a beautiful spot they could hardly wait to show me. I sat in the backseat next to an ice chest full of refreshments.

Everything I looked at seemed eerily sharp, in an almost crystalline focus—not so much because I was seeing it anew but because I felt it was reaching out for me as it never had before. From the highway in Malibu we saw whales leaping out of the deep blue water and I couldn't help but wonder if Paul had figured out a way to put on a show for me.

In one of my early talks with him in my journal, he'd mentioned a desire to experiment with influencing certain life forms. I recalled stories I'd heard of how the world of nature apparently is sometimes affected by the will of those on the "other side," who often seem either to be sending messages or offering reminders of their presence. I'd heard about roses that suddenly bloomed through the snow in the coldest months of winter, and of birds and animals that appeared as though from nowhere and behaved in unusual ways. Perhaps, I thought, just as certain people believe angelic spirits can enter the world of humans for particular reasons, the soul of someone now departed might be able to move into the realm of nature and exert an influence. Why not?

Was Paul's soul somehow mingling with those whales, offering me a bright, leaping, fun-filled greeting, or maybe a little cheerleading? He did seem still to be there for me, still talking to me, rooting for me, praising my effort to put one foot in front of the other, saying, "Look! Accept! Appreciate!"

When we finally arrived, the girls were excited to show me the beach they'd found. Amazingly, it turned out to be the very spot where Paul and I had walked, arms around each other, while producer Sharon Lindsey took photographs for our TV pilot—only five months earlier. Was that coincidence? I didn't think so.

It was not the first time that Paul showed up in startling ways. On April 1 (April Fool's Day, no less), two weeks after his passing, I was driving to Beverly Hills to get my hair cut. Suddenly I sensed Paul in the passenger seat beside me.

Turn in there! he said.

Sloane's furniture store? I'd never been in the place. I laughed and said "Oh, sure," and drove on past. I could sense his frustration.

Please, just do it. Do it for me! Go into Sloanes!

"What for?"

You'll see!

I felt really crazy but drove around the block and parked. As I walked in the door, the first thing I saw was a glass dining table and six chairs—exactly what the two of us had been looking for—marked down from $1799 to only $299. I would have purchased it eventually anyway, but at that enormous 83 percent discount, I didn't hesitate even a moment. I bought it and regarded it as a gift from him.

Paul had always been in charge of decor—that was part of our division of labor—and I had no doubt he had chosen the table and chairs. At the same time, I was aware of a new responsibility emerging: I needed to learn to "see" on my own and not just depend unthinkingly on Paul's guidance.

Fall 1977

Paul and I—now the celebrity chefs and co-authors of two published books—embarked on the first of many cruises on which we were the guests of the cruise line in return for giving cooking demonstrations. We had just finished the book on buffet entertaining and signed a deal with The Cookstore to open a cooking school in its Sunset Strip demonstration kitchen. A large red-and-white sign on Sunset Boulevard read *The von Welanetz Cooking Workshop.*

We were ready for show biz in our new commercial kitchen, and our timing was excellent. Julia Child had been on the cover of *Time* magazine ten years earlier, and the momentum behind the art and craft of home cooking was still growing. We hired various teachers such as Wolfgang Puck, who was then the up-and-coming chef at the wildly popular Ma Maison, a restaurant that prided itself on having an unlisted telephone number. And we hired other rising stars, such as Jean Bertranou of L'Ermitage Restaurant; Milton Williams, L.A.'s most outrageous and popular caterer; and Michel Stroot of the Golden Door Spa, to give classes at our school while we were out making a name for ourselves nationally.

Our latest success came as *The Art of Buffet Entertaining* was published by J. P. Tarcher and was picked up as the main selection of the *Better Homes and Gardens* Book Club in the fall of 1978. Another big book tour.

As our career expanded, we moved further away from the small, intimate classes around our kitchen table that had lured me into the cooking world in the first place. Now more and more people were coming to larger and larger classes, wherever we held them. We were a great team, often referred to in the press as "The Lunt and Fontanne of the Kitchen," and our talents and skills wove together like a graceful dance. The best moments though were when we were more like the Abbott and Costello of the kitchen, when we made mistakes and cracked up laughing at ourselves. It was all such fun and I loved the shared adventure our lives had become.

The school brought us a lot of publicity over the next year. We involved ourselves with another publicist named Judi Skalsky. Thanks to her, Robinson's, an upscale department store chain in Southern California, invited us early in 1979 to become their gourmet spokespersons. We would do a series of large-scale demonstrations in their six biggest stores, and appear in all their housewares advertising. Robinson's threw a gala press party to announce *The von Welanetz Cooking Workshop.* Beaming with pride, among the guests was my dear mentor and cooking teacher, Chef Gregoire Le Balch.

The classes became popular beyond anyone's expectations. *Entrée* magazine, a national trade publication for the housewares industry, included us near the top of their annual list titled "Who's Hot, and Who's Not." We spoke at store openings. Videos of our demonstrations appeared on small monitors in the housewares departments of all the stores. On the mornings of our classes, mobs of women waited outside the store so they could rush inside when the doors opened and find seats near the front. Our friend Jennifer Edwards assisted us in packing everything we needed and preparing small servings of each class's recipes for two hundred people to taste.

We loved our work. On only two occasions did I want to take a break, though our schedule simply did not permit it: when my mom required emergency heart surgery, from which she recovered beautifully, and when our precious black standard poodle, Misty, then fourteen years old, was diagnosed with leukemia. She'd been such a great family companion, encouraging Lexi to take her first baby steps, traveling with us to Mexico and Lake Arrowhead, sitting quietly next to my feet as I sewed or tested recipes. We were all grief-stricken when she died. Paul arranged to have her cremated and we held a ceremony to bury her ashes beneath Seymour, the sycamore tree in front of our house.

Life, meanwhile, went onward—and upward. One day after a class at the Robinson's in Beverly Hills, we were approached by a former ABC television executive we had met a year before, who said, "It's time for us to do a pilot."

That's all we needed to hear. We were off and running. We were going to have a TV show! Maybe.

When we weren't working on the television pilot or teaching classes, Paul and I were putting on cooking demonstrations from one end of the country to the other. Huge food fairs sponsored by major newspapers were our favorites. As the stars of the *Toledo Blade* Food Fair, we performed in front of more than 18,000 people— 4,500 at a time. A huge marquee in front of the auditorium read:

Unexpected events and spontaneous mishaps were abundant. We were at the *Milwaukee Sentinel* Food Fair playing to a very large audience one night when Paul simply disappeared from the stage. I had my head in the oven, and when it was his turn to speak and he didn't, I turned to where he was supposed to be. "Where'd he go?" I asked the thousands in the audience. Then a huge sneeze erupted through Paul's wireless mike from behind the curtain. Thousands cheered! The food editor was prompted to write in her column that Paul deserved a "Gesundheit" from the city of Milwaukee, and printed our home address. He received hundreds of postcards.

At that time we began our long association with Princess Cruises. The company's executives didn't classify us as lecturers but as the headliners for their gourmet travel packages. Our pictures were in every stateroom and we were treated like royalty. Over the next three years we made several trips through the Panama Canal, another up to Alaska, and still another through the Mediterranean. We invited and hosted James Beard, Craig Claiborne, and Wolfgang Puck on some of the sailings. Lexi always came along too.

We had an idea for a new book. It would be a reference work on ingredients used in the cuisines of all the major cultures around the world, offering descriptions of all the foods found on the shelves of ethnic markets, how to store them, and how to use them. The encyclopedia of ingredients turned out to be a major nightmare.

I worked on it for ten months, often spending fourteen hours a day at our new word processor. My eyesight began to suffer; my back and shoulders hurt almost all of the time. Paul ran the errands, did the grocery shopping, and picked up Lexi after school so I could stay glued to the project. He did invaluable research on the history of the foods and wrote the chapter openings. Together we gathered information about culinary traditions throughout the world. The idea had sprung from our passion for the communal experience of people dining and being together. The whole project turned out to be much bigger than we'd intended, and the final manuscript of *The von Welanetz Guide to Ethnic Ingredients* ran 1,500 manuscript pages.

The book took so long to write that we neglected to market our services as chefs. Two years had passed since we made our television pilot but nothing was happening. One of Hollywood's top agents approached us about doing segments on the evening news and was trying to make arrangements with one of the networks, but it was taking forever. I really, really wanted us to have our own show, particularly because money was getting scarce and we had to generate some income. Paul was even consulting the want ads when he thought I wasn't looking. Our situation got so bad that one day in great frustration I demanded to know what was going on. Looking skyward and opening my arms, I hollered, "Why is this taking so long? We've paid our dues, worked hard. Give us our show *now!*"

That statement—coming in a sudden burst of emotional energy when *I really wanted some results and I wanted them now*—became one of the clearest examples of what I later came to call "spiritual alchemy." Because within twenty-four hours everything changed. The ABC executive called and a new cable network called. We were offered two shows on the same day!

The weeks that followed were as crazy a time as we ever had. Our television agent wouldn't let us sign a contract offered by the new

Cable Health Network (CHN), which was the deal we preferred, because he insisted we shouldn't be on cable at all. We should be on network TV! He had the unsigned CHN contract on his desk, but stopped taking our calls or returning those of the producers.

The day before the CHN taping was to begin at KCET—the public television outlet in Los Angeles—was pure frenzy. CHN still didn't have a signed contract from us. Our show, *The New Way Gourmet*, had a crew of forty standing by and they were all depending on us. For almost a week, the stress had caused my stomach to tie up in such a knot I couldn't eat. Paul and I decided to do the show whether the agent approved or not. CHN produced another copy of the contract, which we signed. We were ready to go.

Our first guest was Richard Simmons, who told us before we went on the air that the only way we would succeed on television was if we fought with each other, a sort of Battling (but still Baking) Bickersons. Thanks but no thanks, Richard. Television, we discovered quickly, was difficult enough without turning ourselves into something we weren't.

All that summer we taped new episodes of our show at KCET, sharing a soundstage with Regis Philbin, who had his own one-hour daily show on CHN. In the beginning, Paul and I found the silence of cameras and our large crew intimidating, since we'd gotten used to live audiences and their spontaneous laughter and applause. Nevertheless, we did sometimes get to enjoy a sense of spontaneity—largely springing from the directive to never stop the flow of what we were doing. The people in the control booth would decide if and when to halt the taping.

On one show, things went from bad to worse. I was given a crêpe pan that hadn't been seasoned and the batter stuck to it like cheese to a griddle. I kept going. Then Paul tried something that didn't work either. I said, "Wow, we're getting into deep Bandini." I crossed to the oven and orange flames shot up from the stove. Now I started laughing and said, "Nice little fire we've got going there." The director never did stop the tape and the show turned out to be one of our most popular. And I gained the reputation for being unflappable.

Our contract was renewed after thirteen shows, and we went on to finish a total of thirty-nine. Paul didn't much enjoy doing television but I loved it, probably because I was more naturally extroverted than he was.

The Cable Health Network was pioneering what everyone thought would be an explosion of cable success. One of the owners, a physician and media personality, Dr. Art Ulene, assured us that our show was one of the network's most popular worldwide and that we would have a new contract and be taping more shows soon. He begged us not to talk to the other networks.

What followed was another long, antsy waiting period—for nothing. We felt completely betrayed when our patience and the loyalty went unnoticed and no new contract was offered. In the meantime, CHN was benefiting from the work we had already done. They had the right to run our original shows for three years and so they did, eight times a week, even after CHN became the Lifetime Cable Network and shook off, like something stuck to its shoe, its commitment to health. Of course we made appearances when we were asked, but no new contract or remuneration was forthcoming.

Nevertheless, we did start a nice little cottage industry that provided us with some cash flow. A blurb at the end of our television show invited viewers to send in one dollar for each show's recipes. In response, envelopes containing dollar bills began arriving from all over the Western Hemisphere. Lexi's job was to mail back the correct recipes and enclose order forms for our books.

Overall, however, we were discouraged. We felt like we were always waiting for the phone to ring to bring us work. We longed to have more control over our lives.

———————

It was during this interim period in our career that Paul and I took the first of the journaling workshops taught by Frances Heussenstamm and based on the book *At a Journal Workshop* by Ira Progoff (Dialogue House Library, 1975). There, five years after Papa's death, I had a remarkable experience in which I began to confront my feelings about him more clearly than ever before.

My relationship with him had never, obviously, been good. As time passed, however, and I reflected on his life and how he affected mine, I found myself wondering if I could ever look at him dispassionately. Could I see him with neutrality, free of judgment or criticism?

Frances described exactly how we might converse with persons in our lives—from the present or the past, living or dead. I chose to have a dialogue with Papa. Just the thought of doing it created fluttery feelings inside. I still felt anger and resentment toward him, though I hoped I might finally be able to clear those feelings away.

Frances gave us the instructions. "First, before you begin the actual dialogue, write the ten or twelve major *Steppingstones* in the person's life."

I wrote of my father:

He was born in Vicksburg, Mississippi, in 1891.

He quit school in the eighth grade when his father died, because he had to support his mother, younger brother, and sisters.

He moved his family to Los Angeles.

He was ambitious, worked in a bank, as a traffic court judge, and experienced
some success.

He married Katherine.

He lost everything during the crash of '29, got divorced, had to begin again.

He married Mother, became determined to hold on to security at all costs.

He started a savings and loan company that would earn him millions.

He fathered two children when he was 48 and 50.

He grew old, contracted diabetes, worried about a lawsuit.

Mother divorced him.

He died alone and afraid.

As I reviewed the list, it seemed filled with striving and with sadness. For the first time, I noticed in myself a budding feeling of compassion for him.

As the final step before starting, Frances told us to write a "focusing statement," a reason for beginning the dialogue. I wrote, *You have been dead since Labor Day 1972. I know I have emotions to deal with that are deep and covered.*

Frances then told us to begin.

I knew my intention wasn't literally to communicate with my father. Rather, I would probe into deep realms of my own mind that I did not ordinarily visit. Using my lifetime of knowledge about my father, I would try to see things from his point of view and perhaps understand them from a wider perspective than usual. One part of me, though, did consider that Papa could somehow actually speak to me—and I left my mind open to hear what he might say. This is what I wrote:

Diana: Hello, Papa. I think you would be proud of me now. Perhaps you always were. Why were you so critical, why couldn't you show any affection to me?

I sat quietly, almost trembling, for what seemed a long time. Eventually I began to sense what he would say.

Papa: I was in pain. I always hurt. I was afraid for you.

Diana: Afraid of what?

There was a long silence. I waited, focusing on keeping my heart open, not wanting to fail at establishing a deep communication. Eventually "he" began again.

Papa: I was afraid that you would be hurt as I was hurt. Money became an insulation no one could penetrate. But you always could, my family always could. It was my pain. Why did all of you hate me so when I was the one in pain?

That truly surprised me. And I realized it was true that he'd had so little joy. He continued:

I worry about you and Mimi. Yes, I am proud of you. I'm surprised you are so strong. I always wanted you to have a glamorous life, and I wanted you to have a safe life, but didn't know how to give it to you.

Diana: Sometimes I wish you were here.

I hadn't been aware of any such wish until that moment. I continued:

I want to hold you, feel your silvery whiskers, clean your glasses . . . I am so grateful for what money you left us. It gave us the opportunity, more than once, to find our niche in the world. But why didn't you try to give me confidence, help me become self-motivated? Your only demand was that I be a pretty, shallow façade of a girl having "a good time."

There was a long silence and I thought perhaps the communication would end there, but I decided to stay with the feelings that were circulating through me. Finally I began writing again:

Diana: Is there anything you want to tell me now?

Papa: Yes. Appreciate your life, what you have. Don't worry! Have as much joy in your work as you can. Make it fun, stimulating, but don't bury yourself in it. It's not all there is . . .

Diana: Why were you never loving and affectionate toward us?

Papa: I would feel weak and helpless to depend on someone else. I needed to be in control.

Diana: Poor Papa. I love you. I wish you could be peaceful. Can I help you now?

Papa: Yes. Let go of your resentment of me for your own sake. I did the best I could do at the time; feel kindness for that. Let me go in peace.

Diana: I do. I really do. Thank you.

I sat quietly in my seat, surprised by all that had just happened. With this fresh perspective I felt much freer, lighter, and more forgiving of my father. How hard it must have been to have his father die and be only thirteen, and know that the welfare of a family of five now depended on *him*. How hard it must have been to have a very cold mother who probably never praised him; even as a grandmother she'd certainly never shown my brother and me any love, as my other grandmother had.

Clearly my father had succeeded far beyond his own parents' abilities to care for a family. He'd wanted to give us all the things he'd never had, and he had needed us to appreciate those things.

As I considered my exchange with Papa, I realized that I'd turned away from so many opportunities my life had offered me, including schooling, as a way of scorning him. I had done it all unconsciously, of course, but now I understood. That's why I banged up one new car he bought me and had eight other auto accidents. That's why I continually lost my coats and sweaters—to show my disdain for what he provided. That's why I left the lights on, to show him that for me money *did* grow on trees and was about as valuable. What he so revered, worked so hard for—*security*, the most important thing in the world to him—was beneath my contempt. Thwarting him felt good, but I saw then that it was a lose-lose game.

Sometimes I wonder what would have become of me had I been raised by a loving, caring father, one who prepared me to live confidently and authentically in the real world. Would I have been the same person? Surely not. Would I then have missed out on meeting and knowing Paul? Would I have missed out on the most wonderful, loving, intimate relationship I could imagine? Probably. Would I, then, prefer to have been a different person with a different father?

It's a strange and powerful question, but the answer comes to me quickly. Not for anything would I have missed out on doing what I have been able to do in my life, most especially the opportunity to know and live with Paul and to have borne and raised Lexi.

And that, of course, is the burden of forgiveness. In forgiving those who have brought difficulty—difficulty that has defined a life and led to worthy, deeply fulfilling outcomes—we must accept the difficulty as a gift.

———

The von Welanetz Guide to Ethnic Ingredients was published in February 1983 to critical acclaim. Newspaper food writers raved about it as an excellent reference work, and *Bon Appétit Magazine* sang its praises. Every library and test kitchen in the country bought one. Unfortunately, few consumers did, so the sales were disappointing.

Maybe that was some kind of sign of things to come. The cooking world was already changing dramatically. Michel Guerard's Nouvelle Cuisine from France and Alice Waters' California Cuisine had arrived. At the same time there was a rush of women into the labor force, gourmet markets and take-out places were appearing everywhere, and more people than ever were eating out. Cooking itself was becoming even less an art and a craft, less a form of creativity and self-expression for all, and more and more a showcase for superchefs. Life was being lived faster. There seemed to be less time to eat, less time for preparing good food.

I wanted to get out. We both did. The cooking world had stopped being fun. The spirit of gathering people around the table as they had gathered around a campfire in ancient times is what had drawn me into cooking. I loved the ritual of breaking bread, the camaraderie of sharing heirloom recipes for holidays or for a school bake sale. I enjoyed preparing someone's favorite food as an expression of love, evoking in others a sense of belonging, a sense of home. What did that have to do with the competitiveness that was developing around serving food as modern art, and microwaving prepared foods that substituted for home-cooked meals?

We didn't want to be glitzy media chefs. Nor did we want to become an international conglomerate or be front-persons for a food company. We just wanted to help people perform the primal need of nourishing their families and communities. The changing focus away from home cooking was causing our career to crumble around us.

We'd done so well, attained so many of our dreams. Were we now going to have to reinvent ourselves again?

TEN

NINE WEEKS since Paul died. Mondays are hardest because I miss the fun we had getting ready for the week ahead.

Physically I remained healthy, and my career as founder of the Inside Edge was one of the reasons why. The work I did there and its incessant demands on me were frequently a strain, but also a blessing. Had the Edge not asked so much of me, grounding me in the realities of the everyday world, I feared I might fall into an unfathomable well of grief.

Intuitively, I knew that focusing all my energy on myself would be destructive—in the same way that sunlight focused through a magnifying glass ignites a piece of paper and then consumes it. The alternative, sending love and caring through myself to others, offered so much more. I remembered the pleasure, a deep maternal pleasure that came to me from being completely in service to Paul, loving him through his illness.

Be involved in giving, he now told me through my journal. *The Edge is our garden—your garden now. Serve the roses.*

After the Tuesday morning meetings at the Inside Edge, Tim Piering and I had been getting together at a gym, where he coached me on how I could gradually build up my muscles and my stamina through weight training. Then we would have lunch somewhere nearby and talk and talk and talk. Other men, Edge members and visiting speakers, often invited me to lunch as well.

This was something new in my life. I had always liked men and enjoyed being with them, but when Paul was alive I was usually with him. I simply never saw any reason to spend time with other men, except perhaps for an occasional business lunch or dinner, and even then Paul was usually along. And why not? He was my husband, my best friend, and my business partner. Paul and I had plenty to talk about and plenty to do all the time, and we preferred each other's company. But after his death I had to reevaluate my whole attitude toward men.

The reevaluation started with my old friends, who were usually Paul's old friends too, the men with whom I had longstanding personal relationships. They would not ordinarily have sought out my company, simply because they knew Paul was the focus of my attention.

But in the first few days after Paul's death, they were in touch with me. They let both Lexi and me know they were available if we needed them for anything at all, from grocery shopping to having the car washed to just talking. They dropped by the house just to check in, and also invited me out now and then for lunch or dinner. These were not suitors, nor would suitors have been welcome at that time. These were male friends, who could offer their masculine presence in a way that I found immensely valuable. Without exception they were gracious, unselfish, caring, and generous.

Once, not long after Paul died, at a women's writing class I'd enrolled in at UCLA, one of the women asked if I missed having male energy around. I told the group I hadn't had much chance to miss it. The previous week, I said, I had actually shared meals with five different men—four lunches and a tea. These were men like Tim Piering; Larry Probstein, who with his wife Bobbie had founded the Business Edge; Joe Broderick, who had helped us refinance our home; Michael Coleman, a favorite Inside Edge speaker and my investment advisor. I told these women I was grateful for having such good male friends, men I could trust and whose company I could enjoy without sexual overtones getting in the way. I said they had been extremely helpful in the difficult times since Paul's death.

I was startled by their strong reaction, by their scoffing at what they called my naïveté. *"You* may not be feeling sexual energy, but you can bet that it is running *them!"* they insisted. "That's why they're with you!"

"Whoa!" I said. "I know the difference between a suitor and a friend. These are friends, good friends. They've been wonderful to me and their interest is *not* sexual!"

One woman smiled at me patronizingly. "There's no such thing as a man whose interest isn't sexual! Just wait, and you'll see. They'll make their moves." Most of the others agreed.

I rankled at their vehemence. Nothing I could say made any inroads into their beliefs, and I was sure I *and* my male friends were being misjudged. During subsequent classes I began to develop a theory about why these women felt as they did. Listening to them share their writings, I realized most of them had histories of only unsatisfying relationships with men. My sense of it was that these were women who basically didn't like men, women who didn't tend to give men the benefit of the doubt, who judged them quickly and harshly and dismissively. Wouldn't it be natural that the men who showed up in their lives would unconsciously respond to what was expected of them? Or perhaps these women wouldn't even have been interested in a man who didn't fit their grim expectations. "Loving, caring, sincere men not wanted here. Apply elsewhere."

In thinking more on the matter, I began to realize I not only didn't regard men harshly and judgmentally, but I also held a core belief that differed from theirs. Somehow I had always believed I would attract men who would be good to me, and kind and trustworthy. Where did this belief come from?

My father had been a terror. Yet my brother, Gene, had been my stalwart supporter through my teenage years and treated me with respect and genuine compassion. Perhaps, thanks to him, I treasured men as friends. Of course, I met scores of boys and men who were attracted to me only physically, who had their own direct, uncomplicated agenda, but their intention was obvious. I knew they'd offer me only temporary, conditional attention—a dangerous detour.

As I further pondered this disagreement with my women classmates, I marveled at how the universe does seem to provide us with what we expect. Even as the twenty-one-year-old woman I was when I met Paul, I not only liked men but I also knew I deserved nothing less than to be loved purely, passionately, permanently. I knew I would settle for nothing less than being completely devoted to my partner, and he to me, exclusively. Maybe that's because my father had been so difficult, and by knowing what I didn't want, I was able to define what I did want. Regardless of where it came from, I had known what I wanted.

As a twenty-one-year-old woman, I'd believed when that man finally arrived there would be a sense of inevitability about our being together. I expected us to be interested in the same things and to grow together, and that's the way it turned out.

September 1984

Paul and I didn't know it, but things were already beginning to change. We needed the change, too. We felt as though we were stuck in life's "green room," the television-studio term for where you wait until the producers tell you they're ready for you to go onstage.

The passion for expanding our cooking career had disappeared. Being media chefs had become a sort of dog-and-pony show. We were in a rut and felt we were hiding behind masks that were hardening into place.

Our focus for so long had been either on our relationship or on financial survival. Now, however, riding atop multiple waves of success as book writers, television presenters, and food-show stars, we were dealing with a larger world. Our perspective was widening and we were contemplating the greater issues around us.

We began thinking in terms of doing some sort of work that would feel more valuable than what we were currently involved in, that would contribute somehow to society's becoming more nurturing and supportive. We grew concerned as we heard everyday news about the buildup of nuclear arms in the world and the growing violence permeating television, movies, and the print media. These were matters to which I had not given much attention since the time twenty-two years earlier when I had visited the Hiroshima Peace Memorial Museum in Japan.

While we went through the paces of our cooking career, I spent my free time exploring those larger concerns in my journal, searching for ways that ordinary citizens could more deeply affect the political process and the world. I was studying books and audiotapes on self-discovery and human potential, and would discuss them all with Paul, who loved the time we spent considering the many positive, inspiring ideas I encountered.

At the same time, I became very involved in my continuing friendship with Candace. She had an upbeat, childlike sense of wonder and I loved to be around her. She believed in the *possibilities* of things. Candace started a meditation and discussion group on personal growth, which met in her home on Monday evenings. Paul liked to attend as much as I, and that's where we met a wonderfully zany character named Tom Sewell. He was a photojournalist and landlord of many of the art studios in Venice, California, a quirky beach community that an early developer had modeled after its Italian namesake, canals and all. Venice, even years after it lost the flavor of being a facsimile, still retained a charming individuality that set it apart from other nearby beach areas.

Tom was enthusiastic about his involvement with a motivational seminar called Impact, which met from 6:00 A.M. to 8:00 A.M. every weekday in Hollywood. Paul and I were intrigued that a seminar could motivate people to get out of bed long before sunrise nearly every day. Tom insisted we attend a morning meeting with him, and when he promised to pick us up and drive us there, we finally agreed.

Impact, I learned, was an offshoot of Erhard Seminars Training, known universally as "est." It was founded by a woman named Tracy Goss, who would later write *The Last Word on Power: Executive Re-invention for Leaders Who Must Make the Impossible Happen* (Currency/ Doubleday, January 1996). She was bringing a vision of a radically transformative "possibility thinking" into the entertainment industry.

Though her goals may have sounded grandiose, the results Impact achieved through the many who attended provided ample evidence of its effectiveness. It is where we would meet Tim Piering, Jack Canfield, and Mary Olsen, the woman who would later become my closest friend.

Participation required our agreement to attend every weekday morning for three weeks, plus a weekend at the beginning of the program and another at the end. It was quite a commitment. Nevertheless, it didn't deter hundreds of the industry's most ambitious people from showing up promptly at 6:00 every morning during those three weeks.

At Impact we learned some of the most important lessons of our lives.

One: *Be accountable and always do what you say you will do.*

Two: *All that makes a difference in your life is the action you actually take—all your considerations, excuses, reasons why things can't work, resistance, and avoidance simply don't count or make any difference.*

And three: *We were personally capable of accomplishing so much more than we had ever dreamed we could.*

We felt we'd found the genie in Aladdin's Lamp who could make *all* our wishes come true. Of course, the genie *was* in ourselves—it was ourselves—just a part of us we didn't usually use.

We learned those things through actual experience, not from studying abstractions or hearing lectures about theory. For instance, during our introductory weekend we were told to come up with a measurable goal that would, in our own estimation, be "a huge stretch" for us to accomplish.

Paul and I decided that whatever our goal was it would have to raise some cash. As our cooking career was crumbling, we were getting nervous about paying our bills. We decided our goal would be to secure a $100,000 contract as spokespersons for a cookware company. We would produce a video that the company could show in retail outlets, one in which we would be demonstrating their line. Paul and I were paired up with separate partners to whom we had to be accountable for our stated goals and timelines every day.

Our energy levels—supplemented by the power of the group—rose so high that we barely slept. At first we pitched our project to a large company we were familiar with from our work at Robinson's. We set up a meeting with their sales reps and were greeted with great enthusiasm. Because getting all of the necessary approvals (or the actual go-ahead) would take time, the people running Impact declared that we had reached our goal and had us set another one, which we had to accomplish in the two weeks that remained in the original three-week period.

For the next goal, Paul and I decided to focus on a project we had already begun. We were involved in a huge New York department store promotion called "The Spirit of L.A." We'd been hired to bring California Cuisine to New York City, which included choosing L.A.'s six top chefs and taking them with us to the Big Apple. Among others, Paul and I chose Wolfgang Puck of Spago; Piero Selvaggio of Valentino; and John Sedlar, then of St. Estephe.

Our contract also called for us to write the companion book—half cookbook, half restaurant guide—which would be called *L.A. Cuisine* and would be published by J. P. Tarcher. It was to be designed by the same team that had just designed the graphics and logo for the very successful 1984 Olympics in Los Angeles.

So for our next goal, we decided to complete the first draft of the book in the two weeks we still had left—and once we decided that, we realized that we already *had* the recipes—items we judged too exotic and Californian for inclusion in our other books. The rest was easy. We were excited to whiz right through a project that, had we not tapped into our new "just-do-it-now" skills, would have taken us many months longer.

Whenever someone at Impact reached a goal, that success would be announced in front of the whole group, which led in turn to a standing ovation. Often one of the leaders would say to the person, "Look what happened. All of this . . . *just because you said so!*"

Just because you said so! And that's when I finally understood something I'd known about for a long time but never had examined with much care. I'd seen it happen in Mexico when I cried out to Spirit to show me what I was supposed to be doing with my life. It happened again when I finally got terminally impatient with waiting for the television show to materialize and said, "Give us our show *now!*" And again, here at Impact.

These moments seem to come out of the blue. I'll be plodding along passively, not having things work out the way I want them to but not doing much to change them either. I may even seek help through dabbling in solutions or appealing to the Almighty with weak, submissive little prayers like, "Oh, please help me with this," or "I sure would like help with that." But not until authentic frustration arises within me, not until the feeling of being sick and tired of a current situation hits me, not until I know that things must change *now*, do things actually change. That's when the prayer sounds more like, "Okay, God, let's get this *done*, and let's do it *now!*"

I've learned that this spiritual alchemy is the very essence of the process of creation. I can see now that our coaches at Impact guided us skillfully to that place of frustration within ourselves, then moved us to the point of transforming it. Instead of allowing us just to set vague goals such as, "I think I might want to be a writer [actor/rock star/gymnast/CEO/world traveler] someday," they helped us change our indecision or our frustration or our stuck energy into measurable goals, goals we could envision in terms of the success we actually desired.

That *measurable* goal, by being present in our lives, confronted and challenged us. It also presented us with a deadline. *We had to do it, and do it by a certain time.* We had no acceptable way out. Our partners were checking on us daily (and we were checking on them), and we discovered that all of the barriers to what we wanted to achieve just fell away in the force of that kind of commitment.

———————

As this work was underway, Paul and I found ourselves grappling with something new about working together. More and more as our marriage matured—for reasons he and I thoroughly understood since our breakthrough conversations at Arrowhead—I had become the take-charge partner in our relationship.

This had now begun to cause problems. Though both of us were creatively stimulated by the intensity and immediacy of the environment of Impact, Paul said I was getting bossy. He said, "You're always saying something like, 'I just had this great idea . . . let's do so-and-so,' and you expect that I'll just follow along. It leaves me no room to add my own thoughts."

"You can *always* add your ideas," I protested. "I've *never* thought they weren't valuable."

"That's not the point," he continued. "I know my ideas are good. But a lot of the time you rush ahead so fast that you're putting things in action before you even know if I have something to contribute. If we're going to be a team, we have to agree that *we're* going to move ahead before *you* move ahead by yourself. Otherwise I'm always following behind you, asking you to wait."

Reluctantly, I saw what he meant. I realized I'd begun to think that I, in my role as the primary idea-person, also had all the power and authority in the relationship.

"I'm sorry, Paul," I said. "How do you think we ought to handle this?"

"I don't know. But there has to be a way for each of us to do our best and to still have a partnership that works."

"That's the way we saw it in Arrowhead, wasn't it?"

He looked at me a long time, then finally said, "I think it's pretty simple. If we were two little kids on the sidewalk with a red wagon, we'd have to decide whether we want to share it and ride together, or if one of us would just take off without the other and ride alone."

"Paul, I don't want to ride alone. I never have. You know that."

"And neither do I, Kitten. So, how about this? If we always remember that the partnership comes first, it's simple. When one of us comes up with an idea, we can just say, '*What if* we do such-and-such?' That way we'll include each other every time."

It was a great solution and we put it into practice immediately. The *what-if* technique would become very important in days to come.

———

We completed the first draft of the book that would be called *L.A. Cuisine* and notified Impact that we had achieved our second goal one day before the end of the three weeks.

"And what are you going to do with that extra day?" our group leader asked.

Paul and I looked at each other blankly. We were exhausted and we knew we should have kept our mouths shut. I whispered, "Oops, we're in trouble." Paul, with an accent and a leer on his face, quoted Zorba the Greek, "Trouble? Life is trouble!"

"You can set a third goal," the leader said, not missing a beat. "That's the idea. Not 'what's the least we can accomplish' but 'what's the most?' You've got another day, so set a goal you can meet in a day."

What are the possibilities? Within a few moments Paul said excitedly, "Here's what we'll do." He stopped. "I mean, *what if* we do this? We've been looking for a retirement home in L.A. for my mother, right?"

I nodded. We both knew his recently widowed mother was unhappy living back East. Paul had been looking casually for a month or two but hadn't been impressed by any of the places he'd seen.

He said, "What if we find her a place out here? By tomorrow."

That was it! I got on the telephone immediately and spoke to a retirement home recommended by a friend. We checked it out that afternoon, phoned Paul's mother with the details, and signed her up. We assumed the monthly cost ourselves. We knew we could do it. After all, with everything we'd accomplished in the last three weeks, we were certain we could do anything! And we decided we didn't have to tell the tyrants at Impact we'd achieved the goal so quickly, because there were a few hours left . . .

———

At our very first Impact meeting, my attention had been drawn to a blond woman, a producer for the popular prime time show *P.M. Magazine*. I was so immediately taken with her lively personality that I whispered to Paul, "Go get that woman. Wouldn't she be great for our group?" Paul worked his way around the room and, with a wry smile, took the woman by the arm and said, "My wife wants you. Come with me." And she did, for who could resist that charming man I was married to? Her name, we learned, was Mary Olsen. And that is how I met the woman who would become and remain my closest friend.

After the three-week course was over, we signed up for a nine-month Impact program, meeting three mornings a week and one weekend a month. It was expensive and required a major commitment of time, but we were continuing to learn new things and the facilitator's coaching and perspective were invaluable. We considered it an investment in our career, and our training there continued to produce results that amazed us.

We used brainstorming sessions to come up with ways to produce income, and doing so was paying off. Pauline Kelbly, a friend with whom we had once worked, hired us to write a book of recipes for a plasticware company and to provide twenty color pictures of our menus—using the company's product line but without actually mentioning the company.

Paul and I planned the book that we titled *Celebrations,* using our new what-if strategy to perfection. The result was that we decided everything together, did our separate jobs, then came back together with a sense of full participation and mutual satisfaction in what we had completed. Paul did all the food styling for the photographs while I completed plans for the New York promotion.

We took ten days off from Impact that year to host James Beard and Craig Claiborne on a Princess Cruise to Alaska, taking Lexi and Paul's mom along with us. But both of us could hardly wait to get back to the stimulation and forward thrust of Impact.

———————

Even though our cooking career was thriving, we began once again to feel the call of a different kind of work, a deeper work. We wanted a career *we* were in charge of, one that didn't depend on our waiting for the phone to ring. And, most important, we wanted to do something with real value, something that mattered! What we'd learned at Impact over the previous year was that when people are encouraged and kept accountable, they can create miracles.

One afternoon I came right out and said it to Paul. "I don't care at all about being a superstar chef," I told him. "What matters is what we've just learned, that gathering together with others to listen to and encourage each other's dreams may be the only thing that *does* matter."

"What does that have to do with us? We're not in that business."

"Now, there's a what-if question," I said. "What if we were? What if we quit cooking? What then?"

It was a really *good* question.

———

At one of our last Impact meetings we were working in a small group with Tracy Goss, the leader. She had been telling us the benefits of creating an imaginary observation point ten years in the future, from which we would be able to look back at the steps we had taken to get there.

Suddenly, she turned to me. "Diana, picture it now! You're *there!* What do you see?"

It was as though a window opened—then instantly slammed shut. I'd had another flash of intuitive knowing. I struggled to find words for what I'd seen. "I don't know what it is. I saw a large room full of people. It's some kind of human potential organization we've created. It isn't a church though. There are people from all different cultures and faiths, and there's appreciation for that diversity. Everyone is excited about attending it and grateful we created it."

I could see no more than that. But the vision left me with an insatiable hunger for whatever that next work would be.

ELEVEN

TEN WEEKS since Paul died. All I want to do is sleep . . . really deep sleep with no alarm before dawn to awaken me.

Now, with all the deep grief-related changes occurring in me, I needed to snooze and nap and rest. Like an animal in a cave, I needed a season of hibernation. In the slow passing of those days, all I wanted was an end to my pain and emptiness.

My eating habits were changing dramatically. Dinner had always been a team decision. Lunch too. Our conversation in restaurants usually consisted of, "What are you going to have?" or "Let's ask the waiter what's good," or "Want to order two things and share them?" And so on, for years. Now I was thinking just for me. I was "grazing"—munching a little of this, a little of that. I began losing the comfort weight of marriage.

I seemed composed on the surface, but frightening questions arose when I didn't expect them. Could the Edge support Lexi and me financially without Paul helping us run it? Would I ever again feel as close to someone, feel cherished? Most frightening of all—the grief. I was terrified that if I surrendered to my grief, let myself really feel it, I would be sucked downward into darkness, a bottomless emotional spiral from which I may never return. I knew I had to do something. And I had a pretty good idea where I could start.

I decided to make an appointment with Tim Piering, our ex-Marine friend with whom I'd been going to the gym on Tuesdays. He had said he wanted to try some new techniques with me, some new processes that had just recently been developed to help heal inner wounds.

At his office in Sierra Madre, in the foothills of the San Gabriel Mountains outside of Los Angeles, Tim asked me how I was doing. When I told him I was doing fine most of the time but had days of absolutely paralyzing lethargy, he asked me if Paul would want me to grieve for him.

I thought about it. "No, I can't imagine he would," I answered finally. "In fact, he'd strongly object."

Tim said, "I think we can work through some of the grief you're feeling, and lessen it. Would you like to try?"

"Yes," I said tentatively. Nevertheless, I felt as though I also wanted to hold on to my grief out of loyalty to Paul, despite knowing he would scold me for doing so. "Yes," I repeated. "Yes."

Tim said grief is a natural process that shouldn't be inhibited but could be speeded up significantly. He had me close my eyes and bring up all my saddest feelings until they were overwhelming. Tears ran down my cheeks and then became a torrent. My body heaved and twisted as I felt the pain of losing my husband. Next, Tim had me imagine being in future time one month later and told me to feel the grief. Then he had me cast my imagination out three months and six months and one year. He suggested I could do most of my future grieving right then and there. It was as though my grieving timeline had been pulled into the present. We then went out as far as two years and, to my surprise, my grieving was greatly diminishing, as it would have been in real time. For half an hour I sobbed and wailed, and then it was over.

To end the session, Tim told me to tap areas around my eyes with my fingertips, opening and closing my eyes while trying to keep my sad feelings prominent and in the center of my awareness. The technique made my feelings subside even more.

I was amazed that after only an hour or so, I felt as if a huge weight had been lifted from me. But I was dubious whether the effects would last.

"That's only one technique I think will help. There's more." He led me to his truck and drove us along a rising, winding road into the mountains, navigating among the steep canyons, high cliffs, and treacherous drop-offs. Finally, he pulled onto a shoulder and stepped out of the vehicle, dragging an assortment of coiled ropes and pulleys out of the truck's bed with him.

He hadn't said anything about what we were doing, but clearly the ropes were part of it. I began to suspect these forbidding mountain heights and canyon deeps were part of it also.

We came upon a bridge that spanned a dry wash a hundred feet below. I watched as Tim attached the ropes and a pulley to the bridge railing and finally to himself. Then he calmly climbed over the railing, swung into empty space, and let himself down slowly to the bottom of the canyon.

Cautiously, I leaned over the railing and looked down.

He called up to me, "Want to try it yourself?"

I was struck with fear at the thought. "Are you nuts?" I called. "Not on your life!"

Tim climbed back up the side of the ravine carrying the tangle of ropes, then crawled over the side of the bridge once again, showing me how he could maneuver down and how a safety rope was in place just in case. Once more, after reaching the bottom, he climbed back up the rocky terrain to the top.

I had to admit he made it look safe, but the thought of doing what he had just done made me feel queasy.

"I might try that someday."

With that small crack showing in my armor of fear, Tim wasted no time. "You know," he said wryly, "someday is always on the way and will never ever come. I love what Helen Keller said, 'Avoiding danger is no safer in the long run than outright exposure. Life is either a daring adventure or nothing.'"

He strapped the gear on me and attached the rope to what he identified as my "rappelling ring." He showed me how to slide the rope through the ring gradually and how, if I wanted to, I could come to a complete stop during the descent. Then he attached the safety rope.

"Okay, now just step over the railing."

Trying not to seem as though I had no courage at all, I leaned against the railing. And I made the mistake of looking down. Ancient survival reflexes programmed over millions of years turned my insides to jelly. Streams of stark fear coursed through me.

"I can't do this, Tim."

"That's exactly what your body wants you to believe. You can overcome that. Your body doesn't know it's safe yet. Your mind does, from watching me. Your body doesn't."

He waited, looking at me with casual confidence. He was, in his gentle way, challenging me. I could either do it or not. It was up to me.

"It's a metaphor, Diana. Aren't you ready to go for what you want in your life?"

That did it. I couldn't remember ever being more terrified. I trembled at the mere thought of standing on the outside of the railing. For years I'd had a recurring nightmare of teetering on a window ledge. But as a child I played at being afraid. "Boo!" was a great game, full of thrills and a profound glee when it ended. I realized this was a game too, and the only way for it to end was to just do it.

Very, very slowly I eased one leg over.

"Oh, my God, I am so scared!"

"I know," he said.

Tim held both of my hands firmly on the railing as I lifted the other leg over, nevertheless leaning as far toward him as I could.

"Maybe we should just forget the whole thing!" I protested, even as I was preparing to do it.

"It's your decision, Diana. You don't have to."

Was I going to look back on this experience and remember I chickened out? That we'd driven all the way up here only to have me prove to myself I was gutless? Where was all of my Impact training when I needed it?

"Okay, what now?"

"Let go with one hand. Hold the rope tightly so you won't start moving until you're ready."

I was nearly whimpering with fear. But I finally did what Tim said. That was the crucial moment: letting go with one hand. Then the other. And there I was, swinging free in small arcs over the canyon. Swinging. Swinging in the air.

My God! I was breathless, wide-eyed, but my fear had vanished. It was transformed to excitement. I was really excited, not terrified.

Tim's comforting voice came to me. "Now—very slowly—inch your way down, just a little . . . then a little more."

I did. I took a long time lowering myself to the bottom, relishing the view and the victory over the fear. When I felt my feet touch the ground, my body was electrified with a feeling of accomplishment.

Tim ran down to meet me.

I was sure that my eyes were as wide as dinner plates. "I did it!" I shouted. *"I did it!"*

Tim said, "That you did!"

And so I had. Exactly like a U.S. Marine! If I could do that, I could do anything! I felt elated, more powerful than I ever had felt before.

Afterward, Tim drove us to a nearby firing range and, after some basic instruction, had me put on ear protectors and fire a semi-automatic pistol over and over again at a target fifty feet away—another thing I would never have dreamed of doing. Again my body was electrified with a primal kind of thrill.

Tim's intention, I realized, was simple. The grief was powerfully *emotional* and had turned me profoundly inward so I could heal and recover from my loss. Rappelling off the bridge and firing a gun, on the other hand, were powerfully *physical.* They turned me outward, producing a balancing effect that modulated the grief. Only two months after Paul's death, there I was, blasting away. I could feel my life beginning again.

March 1985

Just a week or two after Tracy asked us to look back at our lives from an observation point ten years in the future, a group of television producers we'd met at Impact approached us.

They invited us as media personalities to be part of a documentary they would be making in the Soviet Union in May 1985. Their idea was to film American "citizen diplomats" who despaired about the arms buildup between the Soviet Union and the United States, and to show them talking with Soviet citizens on the streets about what would be required to end the Cold War. They had already gathered an impressive group of people from various fields to make the long journey.

I was eager to go, and when I learned that many in the group were the authors of books or audiotapes I'd studied and celebrities I admired, I was even more determined. I told Paul I had a strong intuition that the journey might somehow lead to the career move we were looking for, the one that had nothing to do with cooking. Paul was skeptical and not nearly as eager to travel to Russia as I was, but he was supportive of my enthusiasm—and keenly aware that my intuition often brought valuable guidance.

So, we accepted and soon found ourselves participants at a press conference with actor Dennis Weaver, husband and wife actors Mike Farrell (from *M.A.S.H.*) and Shelley Fabares, futurist Barbara Marx Hubbard, lecturer Patricia Sun, author Alan Cohen, philosopher and spiritual teacher Swami Satchidananda, Dr. Patch Adams (whose life story was later made into a Robin Williams film), photojournalist Tom Sewell (our Impact friend), and others who were also going.

Later, a reporter from NBC came to our house to interview us about why we would want to do something so radical—even dangerous—as going behind the Iron Curtain. Good question.

"What if," we responded, "Russian and American citizens begin speaking to each other, opening dialogues to understand each other and resolve conflicts? It may seem hopeless, but it might begin a new kind of peace process." The reporters and even some of our friends looked at us as if we were a little mad. But my friend Mary cheered us on. And the evening before we left, when Candace called to say goodbye, I began to weep and just couldn't stop.

"What's going on?" she asked softly.

My words came from deep within me. "I know Paul and I will be forever changed."

On Mother's Day 1985, after having arrived on long flights from all over the United States, eighty of us convened at a hotel in the Finnish countryside, an hour from Helsinki. There, before crossing the border by rail into Russia and reaching our first stop, we would spend three days being briefed on Soviet protocol by our group's leaders.

One of the leaders, Rama Vernon, was a beautiful, visionary woman, founder of the magazine *Yoga Journal*, and an expert on conflict resolution, who had already made several trips into Russia. She radiated a strong, maternal quality that comforted us all. A model of receptivity, she taught us to listen deeply to the people we would be meeting, to let them pour out all their confusion and concerns. "Until you do that, there is no room, no space for something new."

Rama told us, "The best way to meet Soviet citizens is to change your money into *kopeks*, get purposely lost on the Moscow subway, then ask for directions. Or you might go to nightclubs where there is dancing, because barriers are usually down in that environment. With luck, you'll even be invited into someone's home."

Rama said that Russians, like most people worldwide, know at least the basics of English as a result of intensive study in grammar school. Not surprisingly, however, the members of our group were unfamiliar with the Russian language. So we had some catching up to do. She taught us a few basic phrases. The ones I remember were *mir i druzhbah,* which means "peace and brotherhood," and *pozhaluista,* a combination of "please" and "you're welcome." *Pozhaluista.*

Rama told us that we would be watched closely and that our hotel rooms were sure to be bugged. She added that Soviet citizens were not allowed to gather in groups and were always careful not to do things that would get them noticed—so we should likewise be careful not do things that would call attention to those we spoke with.

I kept my notes of all these things in a small, black-and-white speckled composition book that I carried with me through Russia. As I open it now to remind myself of Rama's words, I am startled to find a yellow sticky note on the very first page, the kind Paul would post around the house, in my shoe, or on my computer monitor. The message is in Paul's writing: I love you. He stuck it there in Russia, consoling me, knowing how homesick I was and how strange we were finding every moment of this trip. At the most curious times, Paul comes back to me.

We were soon to be foreigners in a strange culture of suspicious, fearful people; a closed society, a police state. It was a totalitarian culture where citizens could be, and over the years in huge numbers had been, hauled away to freeze and starve in the gulag without anything even approaching the due process that we Americans staunchly claim as a constitutional right. What was it like to live in that kind of fear? Did Paul and I have any idea at all?

Further, the modern history of Russia and the Soviet Union had included cataclysmic losses in WWII followed by forty continuous years of Cold War. To the Russian people, we Americans were the enemy, and the ever-looming possibility of nuclear annihilation cast us as the nation to be feared. Did we have even the slightest concept of how these people regarded us?

————————

After arriving in Leningrad, on our first afternoon there, Paul and I decided to find our courage and try the subway ploy.

How would we start a conversation? We got an idea. Our hotel room was full of handmade dolls—eighty of them—provided by church groups in the U.S. Each of our group had carried one doll across the border, and once we were all assembled at our first plenary meeting, Paul and I volunteered to be the doll caretakers because their little faces would cheer our stark hotel room.

So, the first move was obvious. Armed with a blue-and-white, gingham-clad doll, we headed for a Metro entrance. Riding an escalator down, we saw the station was as it had been described to us: spotless, with gleaming chandeliers. The people were polite and reserved.

Boarding the subway car, we saw the passengers on two long benches that ran the length of the car and faced each other across a single, narrow, center aisle. We sat down, ready to be ambassadors of goodwill.

The few people who had spoken to us on the streets did so furtively—obviously afraid to be seen talking to us. Now, no one would even make eye contact. I wondered about our clothing. I had on a white vinyl raincoat; Paul wore a rich tweed jacket and a lavender muffler around his neck. Everyone in the subway car, by contrast, was dressed only in endlessly repeating tones of gray and black. Our more expensive clothing marked us as foreigners. This was my first deeply felt awareness that, in this very different culture, we were the outsiders.

Then a couple with a little girl boarded the train and sat oppo-site us. We all exchanged polite smiles but said nothing. The child seemed fascinated by the doll I held.

Paul said, "This may be our chance. What if we get off at the next stop? You can give her the doll on the way out."

The train slowed and halted and we stood up. Smiling, I held out the doll.

"*Pozhaluista!*" I said softly. The little girl, frightened, dove behind her mother's back.

What now? I thought, wondering if in my naïveté I was going to create trouble instead of promoting peace.

Looking into the mother's eyes, thrusting the doll toward her, I again murmured, "*Pozhaluista!*"

She and her husband rose to their feet to face us, regarding us with warm, welling eyes. They held their hands over their hearts and bowed slightly in the universally recognized gesture of appreciation and thanks.

"*Pozhaluista,*" they whispered, as we stepped through the closing subway doors.

———

With that quiet encounter, everything we'd seen and felt about Russia abruptly crystallized into new, irrevocable understanding.

When we entered that subway we had, quite unknowingly, still regarded Russia as though we were watching it on television. The preparation, the flight over, even the talk by Rama—it had all been interesting, but also abstract, intellectual, uninvolving, a school exer-cise about a distant land about which we might later have a pop quiz.

Now, the reality of what we were experiencing had suddenly altered. We were two Americans who had come here with the vague idea of bringing peace to the world. But, due to a random encounter in a subway car in a place so far distant from our everyday lives that we were not really able to comprehend the distance in any meaningful sense, we had suddenly changed. We were suddenly alive, beautifully and disturbingly alive, to a world that was real and full with human feeling.

Paul and I walked silently along the platform. I felt shaken and very moved by the strange encounter, for it seemed to epitomize everything we were there to understand and explore. People, strangers who essentially lacked the ability to communicate with each other and were on opposite sides of an enormous cultural gap, had nevertheless communicated with perfect, almost incandescent clarity by using the language of the heart.

I wondered how those people would describe us to their family and friends later. Paul seemed to read my thoughts. He said, "They will call you the Madonna of the Metro."

We met many Russians in our subsequent forays into the subways. Some invited us to their homes, and we followed them down dark streets not knowing where they were leading us, trusting in Rama's assurances that city streets were crime-free and that we would be safe.

Experiencing the humanity of the Russians, these strangers, in this way, was astonishing. Behind the despair and hopelessness that seemed prevalent on the subway and that we saw on faces in the streets were open, passionate, and very vulnerable people—certainly the opposite of the cold and humorless Bolsheviks in the cartoons with which we'd grown up.

Others in our group had strikingly similar experiences. One night in our plenary meeting, three people said they met a woman on the street who invited them to her home. There they all talked until 3:30 in the morning. When the three left, accompanied to the street by their hostess, they realized they were in a residential area. One of them remarked, "I don't think there is any way in the world we're going to find a taxi at this hour in the suburbs."

The Russian woman suggested that they hug a tree.

"What?" the visitors asked.

"Let the tree relax you," she said, "When you relax and allow things to happen, life provides exactly what you need."

They told us that they held back their skepticism, hugged a tree, and a taxi soon appeared.

One man in the plenary group said, "I came here a little self-righteously, as an ambassador of peace, prepared to teach these people something. What I'm finding is not at all what I expected to find."

Another in the group observed, "I feel like the cartoon figure Pogo, when he said, 'I have met the enemy, and he is us.'"

During the days that followed, our group met with Soviet peace committees where we presented quilts and the remaining seventy-nine dolls, and visited museums and other cultural landmarks.

We visited an enormous grave, where the bodies of 475,000 Russians lay buried, and we listened to how Leningrad had endured nine hundred straight days of bombing by the Nazis during World War II. All outside supplies had been cut off from the city and more than a million of its citizens died of injuries or starvation.

A number of the Soviet people we met said they knew we Americans hadn't experienced war on our own soil in our own lifetimes and asked why the U.S. was building up so many arms. At first

I started to cite some history and raise a few issues of international politics, but I realized quickly that I was just parroting the propaganda I'd been raised on. These people wanted to be heard, to be understood. I listened carefully and acknowledged that these were profound issues, worthy of our attention—which was the major reason for our presence.

We also had some odd moments. For instance, Boyd Willat, the man who invented the Day Runner, a sophisticated personal organizer and meeting planner, brought eighty shiny, silver-vinyl date books that he had carefully translated into Russian to give away to Soviets he met. I still smile when I remember the puzzled faces of the people to whom we presented them. Why? Because the Soviet people hadn't the *slightest concept* of the purpose of a meeting planner. A meeting planner? Nobody plans meetings! They couldn't imagine such a thing, since having meetings was illegal in Russia.

Boyd's good-hearted miscalculation was a good example to me of how international differences show up even when one has the very kindest of intentions.

———

After four days in Leningrad, we boarded a train to Moscow. We arrived in pouring rain and inched along a platform blocked by an ocean of umbrellas and Soviets who were waving flags to greet a visiting diplomat.

The parks we passed later in our tourist bus all glistened in the rain. Lilacs and apple trees were in bloom, and the orderly rows of red tulips that were clenched tight in Leningrad were open in all the parks of Moscow.

Our hotel room, however, was bleak. Paul and I were afraid even to speak about what we were doing there, knowing that microphones were hidden in the room and that something innocent we said might be misconstrued and cause trouble for our group. It brought us an interesting awareness of how fear can lead to fear, and widen the distance between people.

As Paul and I wandered alone around Red Square, admiring the domed structures of the Kremlin, we saw one of our group, Michael Killigrew, who had been born in Nazi-occupied Holland, talking to some elderly veterans. He touched the medals that were pinned on their uniforms and said *Spasibo*—thank you. The old men hugged him. An old woman nearby was in tears at the sight, and kept repeating, *Mir, mir.* Peace, peace.

The day before we were to begin our long journey home, our entire group attended Moscow's large Baptist church. There we had what was, in my view, the most remarkable experience of our entire Russian journey.

We already knew that religion in Russia was, at best, controversial. It was tolerated but not encouraged. We also learned that the people who attended church regularly were mostly old *babushkas*, the grandmothers who had seen too much wartime pain and lost too many loved ones to care about their own safety. But what we were not prepared for were the gentle passions that accompanied a religious observance in the Soviet Union.

As the service was about to begin, all eighty of us, looking colorful compared to the Soviets in their dreary garb, climbed up a creaky, winding staircase into the balcony. (Patch Adams, as usual, extended the whole concept of "colorful" by wearing his ever-present clown suit and red rubber-ball nose.) Our ascent took a long time, and finally, awkwardly, we found places in the ancient wooden pews. A sea of faces below, somber and resigned, stared straight ahead.

In his opening words, which our interpreter translated into English for us, the pastor told the congregation that something unusual would be happening.

"Today," said the pastor, "instead of our usual service, we have a guest speaker from America. The people in the pews above are *Amerikanski* who have come all this way on a mission of citizen diplomacy, to be a presence of peace between our two countries."

At that, most of the congregation looked upward, apparently curious to realize that we had an agenda different perhaps from those who might just have visited their church to sightsee, to gawk.

Swami Satchidananda was to be the speaker. He was an elegant man, bearded, white-haired, and dressed in the long coral robes he had worn throughout the entire trip. He walked forward, took his place, and began speaking to the congregation through an interpreter. We could see the citizens below looking up and becoming even more open, more curious.

He spoke of the hope that our countries would learn to resolve conflict without the use of arms. "Our governments are both saying that disarmament will lead to the loss of jobs. I would ask the governments, 'So, should we agitate for crime so policemen won't be out of work?'"

He continued for some ten minutes, in a talk that ranged from expressing his belief that we must all hold a vision of peace in our hearts to his certainty that compassion could become an international language. Could anything at all be done when the terrible armaments and enormous economic forces of the superpowers were poised for war? Could everyday people, such as those who were today in this congregation, have any impact on this perilous world situation? He observed that the very fact of asking such a question implied that people were insignificant and powerless, whereas, he said, people with passion and commitment and energy could accomplish anything at all. He closed by noting that change comes by drops, but drops make an ocean.

The pastor asked for divine blessing for our group of citizen ambassadors and wished us Godspeed. We then sang to them a Russian song we'd learned while riding around Moscow in our buses. They were delighted, and sang back to us in glorious harmony.

The sense that we were all somehow representing the possibility for a peaceful world permeated the sanctuary. Every person in the balcony, as well as those in the pews below, was in tears. I saw eyes glistening, shirtsleeves furtively raised to the faces of the very few hardened old men, and old women openly wiping tears from their eyes. The women in the congregation, some nearly toothless, smiled broadly, waved, and blew kisses at us.

The congregation sang another song of goodbye as we filed back down the rickety circular staircase to find ourselves enthusiastically surrounded. There was much waving and clasping of hands. *Mir i druzhba*—peace and brotherhood—we promised each other.

As we slowly worked our way through and past those who stood around us, an old woman took one end of Paul's lavender muffler and reached up to his face to gently wipe his eyes. In one smooth motion and without even a moment for thought, he lifted the scarf from around his neck and put it gently around hers—a gift. She nodded, eyes closed, and touched her hand to his heart.

We did return from the Soviet Union forever changed. Friends phoned to find out what we'd done there, but we had no words to express all we'd seen and felt. Nothing would ever again seem the same.

TWELVE

THREE MONTHS since Paul died. Mary will move to Hawaii in a few days and I'm going to miss her terribly.

Mary insisted on hosting a tea in my honor before she left and inviting my closest women friends. She reminded me of the day, years earlier, when she and Paul and I had been having lunch on our patio. I said that day I wouldn't be able to bear losing Paul, that I wished he and I would die together. Paul had been visibly upset, admonishing me, "Don't say that!" Later he'd approached Mary alone in the kitchen and said, "If anything ever happens to me, promise you'll be there for her!"

Now she told me, "This party is a way I can keep my promise to Paul. You two were together so much, you didn't really need your girlfriends. But I want you to discover how wonderful and supportive they can be. So, I'm not inviting Tim or Joe. This is just for the girls."

A harpist was playing as I entered the elegant salon of the Westwood Marquis Hotel to see the women Mary had assembled: my old friends Candace and Bobbie; Sharon Lindsey, producer of Paul's and my television pilot; Margaret, the manager of the San Diego Edge; Lauren, my office manager; and Lexi.

At Mary's request all were wearing tea attire, including hats and gloves. Mary was right—I felt celebrated and deeply comforted. We had a grand time as we sipped tea and nibbled on exotic little pastries, feeling frivolous, like schoolgirls playing dress-up.

Candace and I, as it happened, were sitting in chairs that faced the lobby of the hotel. Suddenly, out of the corner of my eye, I noticed an odd shape in a long flowered dress dart past the lobby door. It looked like an imposingly large bag lady. Candace asked, "Did you see what I just saw?"

Raised voices came from the lobby and all conversation in the large room stopped. Even the harpist stopped playing. The grotesque creature entered with security men trailing behind, looked around the room, then headed straight for our group. She plopped into a chair that she unceremoniously hauled over next to me. Our visitor's wig was askew, and stockings with seams in the back were slipping down very muscular hairy legs into high-topped Granny Yoakum boots.

"Hiya, honey!" she said to me in a croaking falsetto.

Mouth open, I just stared at her . . . no, him. Ohmygod, it was Tim! Bridge-jumping pal, author, ex-Marine. In a dress, with lipstick, bright circles of rouge on her cheeks—his cheeks—and a small wicker purse over his arm. No men allowed, remember?

The security guards left reluctantly when they saw that the bizarre apparition belonged to our party.

"I brought you a present, honey!" he squeaked at me in that hideous voice. "It's here somewhere . . ." Tim rifled through his purse, spilling the contents, which included a number of feminine napkins, makeup and perfume, until he located something he'd torn out of the food section of the *Los Angeles Times*. "Here's a recipe for you, honey." Then he winked. The bag lady was giving the food lady a recipe.

I hadn't really laughed out loud in a long time and I honestly didn't know I could laugh that hard. Then in a falsetto voice he began to lecture us on what to watch out for in men. He said that they were all just after our bodies and we should get a commitment before letting them put their grimy paws on us. Women at the other tables were gawking.

The hilarity returned and even rose another notch a short while later when he decided he wanted to use the restroom. We ladies trailed behind as he darted back into the lobby and down a hall to . . . the men's room. We waited outside.

Seconds later a gentleman with a horrified expression rushed out, zipping his trousers as he ran.

Then Tim emerged, calling out to the fleeing man in his falsetto voice, "See ya later, honey."

Tim returned to the table and stayed with us until we all left, remaining in character as the bag lady, at what was probably one of the strangest ladies' afternoon teas ever to be held at the Westwood Marquis.

Later, as we stood at the curb waiting for our cars, I asked Tim where he'd found such a large dress and that pair of boots. Slipping out of his bag-lady character for the first time that afternoon, he told me he had shopped for the clothes in a thrift shop. His daughter had helped apply his makeup, complete with pink lipstick drawn way above his lip line.

"How did you ever get the nerve to do it?"

"I make myself do something absolutely terrifying as often as possible," he replied. "It's good for the soul!" Then he laughed and confided, "The worst part was on the hour's drive here. Officers in two Highway Patrol cars were really eyeing me. I just stared straight ahead, stiff as a board. If they had pulled me over, I would have had a hard time explaining!"

Tim's wacky joke that afternoon was good for my soul too. In fact, I often wondered if I would be doing anywhere near as well as I was doing now if I'd not had my friends from the Inside Edge.

June 1985
"One must have chaos within, to give birth to a dancing star."

FRIEDRICH NIETZSCHE

We were emotionally and physically spent when we returned from Russia. The culture shock of arriving back in America was jolting. Its effect was to drive us inward, into quiet and introspection. Paul and I had little to say, even to each other. The prayer of St. Francis of Assisi kept running through my mind, and I repeated it over and over, "Lord, make me an instrument of Thy peace . . ."

We felt even more strongly that we were ready to take a new step in our lives, yet hadn't a clue as to what the next one would be. So we did the usual. We taught a few classes. After we'd been home about a month, we were scheduled to go on a Mediterranean trip for Princess Cruises—payment for having headlined at the Scottsdale Culinary Festival the previous February. Three shipboard cooking demonstrations in two weeks—nothing to it! Our demonstrations felt hollow though. The food was the same, but we'd changed.

Contemplating the Soviets' lack of wealth and comforts, we began to question our own, and our society's quest for material things. As a culture we have become complacent, accustomed to a standard of living that people in many countries would regard as a reflection of fabulous wealth, yet frequently we either don't appreciate what we have or we don't recognize its worth. We were uncomfortable with that awareness, yet didn't know what we might do about it. I called out to Spirit over and over, "Please give us valuable work to do. We promise to do whatever it takes!"

———————

Meanwhile, since Paul and I had developed the habit of waking up early during our time with Impact, we kept doing it. We liked it—the stimulation of being out of bed as the energies of the day began to hum.

So . . . *what if,* we asked ourselves one day, what if we were to start an organization of our own? We'd read about something in New York called "Power Breakfasts." What if we were to start an organization whose members could gather weekly for an early breakfast to hear inspiring, popular speakers in fields such as psychology, personal development, and human potential? We imagined that the kinds of creative speakers we'd invite—who might have busy schedules and even sky-high lecture fees during the evening hours—would very likely be available at 7:00 in the morning.

The concept seemed brilliant! Not only could we present visionary speakers to our members, but we could also provide a space for them to create new friendships, new dreams, and new possibilities. It would be a forum for personal expansion as well as for the creative exploration of such vital issues as environmental awareness and world peace—as we had done in Russia. Further, as Paul pointed out enthusiastically, we were perfectly well qualified to do it, for we had a proven ability, demonstrated convincingly over the years, to bring people together productively in an environment of joy and comfort.

What if? became *That's it!* That's what we had both been waiting for. Paul reminded me of the vision I had when Tracy had taken me to an imagined observation point, years in the future.

Elated, we literally danced around the living room. Spirit had surely answered our prayers and given us a big job to do.

One of our first important decisions was to ask a number of people we knew through Impact and from our trip to Russia to join a board of advisors. That would not only provide us with access to their enormous creativity but it would also give our fledgling organization immediate credibility.

What would we call our group? Its name arrived during a brainstorming session with Mary and Tim, as I was scanning various periodicals and my eye fell on a recent issue of the highly regarded *Brain-Mind Bulletin.* Edited by Marilyn Ferguson, internationally known author of *The Aquarian Conspiracy*, the *Brain-Mind Bulletin* gathered the popular writing of innovators in both the hard and soft sciences. When my eyes fell on the title of a column in that issue—"The Inside Edge"—I knew I'd found what we were looking for.

"That's it!" I cried, and the others agreed. To me, that phrase succinctly described the part of everyone that is always learning and growing, willing to be at risk in moving toward accomplishment. Mary said it suggested to her the feeling of being on the inside track. Paul told us that the "inside edge" for a skater is where one finds balance.

At the same time, in my mind, I saw the logo we could use: the outline of a heart superimposed over a stylized drawing of planet Earth.

Soon we were on our way! With our years of experience producing programs and hiring outside talent, we had all the skills to do what was necessary. We found a restaurant on the outskirts of Beverly Hills with the right ambiance: futuristic, artsy, elegant. Paul handled all of the finances, which included negotiations with the restaurant, developing and maintaining an audiotape duplicating and sales business, and handling the actual logistics of the meetings, which included setting up a sound system and getting all of the printing and other marketing tasks handled. Tim helped us word the invitations. I searched for guest speakers, entertainers, and potential members.

We sent out 150 invitations for the opening morning and seventy-five people showed up, including Tim, Mary, Jack Canfield, and Barbara De Angelis (all of whom were friends from Impact). They stood with us in front of the assembled attendees and spoke of what the group could become. Only a few people signed up for membership that first week, but on the next, when the speaker was futurist Barbara Marx Hubbard, many more came aboard.

The Inside Edge had been launched!

For Paul and me, those first meetings held a deeply rewarding sense of fulfillment and of promise. Our lives, individually and together, had again intersected with destiny.

On the day after Thanksgiving 1985, Paul and I gave the first nonbreakfast Edge gathering, a party in our home. The members brought their best leftovers and we spent an evening with what we called our "extended family of choice." I was good at inventing various processes—shared interactions around specified themes. In this case, we all spoke about what we were grateful for. Happily for us, everyone was especially thankful for the Edge. In fact, gratitude became a major component of everyone's experience of the Inside Edge, and people started saying that their weeks began not on Monday but on Tuesday mornings, with the joy and thankfulness of those meetings.

The time was 5:45 A.M. Our new business was just a few weeks old. When Paul and I pulled into the parking lot of the restaurant where the Inside Edge meeting would convene in less than an hour, the sky was obsidian blue-black, glowing with threads of pale yellow.

A parking lot that ordinarily would have been deserted was beginning to fill. People were getting out of their cars and striding toward the restaurant. One of our volunteer staff members saw us and waved when he passed in front of our headlights. Candace grinned as she crossed behind him, lugging her special sound equipment. Pert, blonde, and effervescent, she was later to become another Inside Edge success story, gaining popularity as a singer in clubs and musical theater. This morning, though, she was simply the soloist who would close our meeting with the song "Somewhere," from *West Side Story*.

Paul turned off the engine and we looked at each other, simultaneously aware of how far we'd come, how much we had changed, and how decisions and plans we'd made were affecting so many lives. All of these people were here on this early Southern California morning in response to action we had taken. The words of the Impact leaders came back to us. In unison, we said, ". . . just because we said so!"

The Edge became so successful so quickly that we opened a second chapter in Newport Beach, fifty miles south of Beverly Hills, just two and a half months after convening the first one.

The work was stimulating and fun. Every day brought new opportunities and challenges. For its Valentine's issue in 1986, *Los Angeles Magazine* featured Paul and me as one of L.A.'s "most romantic couples." We had been married for twenty-three years by then and had a reputation for still being wildly in love and devoted to each other.

Word-of-mouth was the only advertising the Inside Edge ever needed, and both chapters thrived almost from the start. The Beverly Hills chapter already required more room to grow, so we moved it to the more spacious and convenient Beverly Hills Hotel.

That same month we received a phone call from a Sharon Huffman in San Diego, who had heard about the Edge and thought we needed to start one in her area. We knew instantly that we would be able to do so, with her help and with the help of a local board of advisors. In April we opened another chapter in La Jolla, in San Diego county.

The three chapters grew and we soon had nearly a thousand paying members, providing enough income for us to live on modestly.

Also in 1986, we hosted at Candace's home the first of what would become one of our most outrageous parties. Paul and I invited the members to arrive dressed and acting as who they would be five years in the future. We told them they would speak as if all their goals had been achieved and their dreams had already come true. We suggested that visualizing and experiencing their dreams so vividly could bring about powerful changes in the future.

Members would be videotaped as they arrived, and they were requested to bring any suitable "future props"—such as bestselling books they planned to have written by then, magazine covers they'd been on, awards they'd won. We would spend the evening applauding and celebrating each other's successes.

The partygoers really stretched their imaginations. One woman brought a mock *Time* magazine, with her own face on the cover in recognition of advances she made in international peace. One man showed up as a multimillionaire beach bum and handed out lottery tickets (real ones) to all the other guests. Dr. Susan Jeffers, who was just embarking on her career as a writer, arrived with her husband in a (real) limousine. She held three mock books for everyone to see and was congratulated by the others for her appearances on various national television talk shows with her future *New York Times* bestsellers.

By the end of the evening, all the celebration and support had people really believing they might accomplish what had seemed like outlandish goals before they joined the Edge. And, indeed, Susan did produce those three bestsellers within five years.

Early in 1988 the Edge was still growing. Paul and I were very happy and nearly always exhausted. Our alarm was set for 3:00 A.M. three days a week for us to be on the road long before sunrise.

We felt as if all our talents—as hosts, as masters of ceremonies, as producers, as talent scouts, and as party planners—were being used to support others in going for their dreams. And we were further developing our own talents all the time. Paul continued to be in charge of the finances, various negotiations, and marketing the tapes of our morning speakers, while I networked with authors, publishers, and motivational speakers all over the world to spread the word of the Edge's success in Southern California. Our old, tired superchef masks were cracking. We had found, individually and together, our authentic paths, and each day was a labor of love.

Money was tight because we were stretching and growing in every direction. We refinanced our home and used the proceeds to lease office space and hire a young redheaded woman by the name of Lauren as an assistant to help us run the organization. Joe Broderick, one of our Orange County members, arranged the loan, insisting that we take out mortgage insurance in case anything happened to either one of us. Mary Olsen was in charge of public relations and acted as host and host trainer for all three chapters.

Each of the chapters had many subgroups, or "sub-Edges," but those were run by the members themselves in their private homes. For example, the Business Edge, created by Larry and Bobbie Probstein, held brainstorming groups for members on how to succeed in their businesses. The Film Edge, headed by Mark Shelmerdine (owner of London Films), held showings of thought-provoking films at the old Paramount Studio lot, films dealing with human potential. The Razor's Edge was the men's discussion group.

A few months earlier, Sharon Lindsey, a television producer and member of the Beverly Hills chapter, took the idea of doing an Inside Edge television show, with us as the hosts, to Vin DiBona. Vin was enjoying enormous success as the producer of the hit series *America's Funniest Home Videos*. He came to several Edge meetings and was enthused by their positive focus. He wanted to do something different on morning network television, and soon we were taping a pilot that he hoped to sell to one of the networks or major syndicates.

One morning a camera crew shot a typically upbeat breakfast meeting at the Beverly Hills Hotel. Two hundred people sat at tables of ten as Paul and I previewed the morning with our customary informal repartee. There were, as usual, hugs among the members during the greeting process and cheers and standing ovations for the morning's speaker, who happened to be Martin Rutte, a successful business coach. We always had brilliant entertainers to end the meetings—singers, mimes, and musicians. That morning it was piano-playing songwriter Dale Gonyea.

Vin used some of the footage from our old television cooking shows to demonstrate how easily Paul and I worked together, alone and with guests. For something more current, Vin and his camera crew focused on me, lying in the hammock next to our deck at home, the very hammock in which the raccoons played at night. He asked Paul to hand me a glass of champagne as the two of us looked into each other's eyes. Paul quoted Robert Browning for the camera:

Grow old along with me.
The best is yet to be . . .

The pilot for the TV show was nearly complete when Vin asked that we provide him with still color photographs of us walking on the beach. It was a gorgeous afternoon at an isolated beach near Point Dume in Malibu when Sharon Lindsey shot those photographs.

Both of us were barefoot. Me in a long white skirt and pink silk shirt blowing in the breeze. Paul in the Ralph Lauren Polo whites he loved to wear, his arm around me. We were so happy that day. It was the culmination of all our dreams—we were fulfilled in our work and had great hope for the future. Later that month Vin would audiotape us talking of our feelings for each other, and the tape played as a voice-over for our walk on the beach. I would tell what I loved about Paul and he would do the same about me.

But before we could record the voice-overs, our path together took a completely unexpected turn.

THIRTEEN

FOURTEEN WEEKS since Paul died and I am falling in love with solitude . . . I can't get enough of it!

To be closer to the Edge meetings in Orange County, I accepted the standing invitation of the Probsteins to spend Tuesday nights at their vacation home on the beach in Laguna. It was a special place to me. Time always slowed for me there.

It was away from the busyness of the Inside Edge office, which Lexi and Lauren had cleverly moved into our home.

It was where I could spend hours listening to music. Letting my mind and body rest. Doing what I wanted, when I wanted. Healing.

And why not? I could take care of myself.

In the kitchen I found an "air" popcorn popper. I poured in some kernels and plugged it in, realizing only too late that it needed a lid. Lexi would have said, "Duh, Mom!" Which illustrated one of the great advantages of being alone. I could screw things up while I was making food just for myself. I could enjoy the daffy *I Love Lucy* scene that followed, as popping corn erupted all over the kitchen. I could say, "Who cares? Who's watching?" It was a wonderful mess and I laughed while cleaning it up.

I also used the time there becoming accustomed to being alone. As I did, I reflected on the romantic essence of the man who had been my soul mate—my husband, lover, and best friend. Doing that was easy here, where we had shared so much, even our twenty-fifth anniversary.

November 2, 1988

To commemorate our anniversary, we planned a small, private celebration. Bobbie and Larry graciously invited us to use the seaside condo in Laguna, since it was where, the year before, Paul and I had renewed our vows in front of family and friends.

But today, before our anniversary celebration could get underway in the evening, we had to take care of business. As usual, it started at our home, the same way so many of our days did: long before sunrise.

I awoke just before the alarm would have rung and I shut it off. My hand reached naturally across the covers to feel Paul's chest.

"Happy twenty-fifth, my love," I said.

He mumbled as he woke, "And they said it would never last . . ."

___

In the darkness of that anniversary morning, I heard Paul's shoes crunch Seymour's dry sycamore leaves blanketing our driveway. He carried the garment bag with the clothes for our celebration later on and put it in the trunk of our car. Minutes later, we were on our way.

Paul reached for my left hand as he always did and held it nestled on his thigh, his fingers feeling for and caressing my wedding ring. We stayed silent in the darkness of the car as we drove the sixty miles to Remick's Restaurant in Orange County. At that Edge meeting, and in the presence of a hundred or so of our friends and colleagues, we ate lightly, saving our appetites for the celebrations we had planned for the rest of the day. But it started there that morning, with champagne and flowers presented to us by the members.

"Twenty-five big ones!" one of our friends exclaimed. "What an accomplishment! What's your secret?"

Paul and I exchanged glances. People who regularly saw the spontaneous magic between us had asked that question for almost as long as we'd been together. We had no real answer. Our passion for each other had never cooled down and that's what made us special to others, and to each other. Though we spent almost every waking hour together, we never tired of each other's company.

From the Inside Edge meeting, we made our way across Newport Beach to the cliffs of Corona del Mar. Located midway between Los Angeles and San Diego, with a name that means "Crown of the Sea," Corona del Mar was a place I had always loved for its exceptional beauty. Widely known for its scenic bluffs that rise high from expanses of lovely white beaches, it overlooked Newport Harbor and provided a gorgeous view of the sailboats moving gracefully in and out. As always, Paul watched those boats, dreaming of the day he would own one.

Then we were off to our favorite Southwestern-style restaurant, where women patted *masa* dough into tortillas and placed them on a rotating griddle in the center of the room. The owners and staff knew us well, and Paul proudly spread the word of our celebration. At the end of the meal we were told that our lunch that day was a gift from the house, and we were presented with a small cake with a single candle as everyone circled the table and sang "Happy Anniversary."

Afterward, we drove down the coast through the artists' colony in beautiful and historic Laguna Beach, finally arriving at the condo. From its penthouse we had a full, unobstructed view of the beach, ocean, and Catalina Island. Larry and Bobbie had done a beautiful job of furnishing the place in tones that reflected the view from the terrace—the white sand and the blue sky.

In the bedroom I checked with Lexi by phone. She said that telegrams and calls of congratulations were coming in from all over the country. "I'm so proud of you two," she enthused. "You've really proven that dreams can come true. Have a wonderful evening!"

I found Paul standing at the railing of the terrace, looking down at the sunbathers on the beach. I linked my arm in his and rested my cheek on his shoulder.

"Just think. Everyone's looking for love," he said. "All of those people down there. They're all looking for love. And you and I . . . somehow we've been lucky enough to find it."

I nodded.

"Why do you think love is such a struggle for so many people?"

"I'm not sure," I answered. "I think it may be because everybody wants to have love, but not everybody is willing to give love."

Paul said, "They're probably afraid. Afraid that if they give love, they'll lose something. But, Kitten, after all this time, I love you even more. With all my heart I love you. And that's wonderful. The more I love you, the more love *I* feel."

"Me too," I said. "I think the way to have the love you want is to give the love you want. Needing it gets in the way. Be a lover— that's the secret!"

"It's a circle, isn't it? Letting it out, letting it flow, letting it come back."

He kissed me tenderly on the tip of my nose.

"Didn't we promise ourselves a nap right about now?" I asked. "You've been needing a lot of sleep lately, if you hadn't noticed."

Paul grinned and kissed me again. "A nap! What a good idea. A nap. I do need a nap." He took my arm and turned us toward the terrace door.

———

There was a reverence to our lovemaking that languid afternoon, a sacredness bestowed by years of memories. We fell asleep in each other's arms.

I awakened about an hour later. A lot of light was left, plenty of time before our dinner reservation.

For a while longer I snuggled into Paul, listening to his breathing, to his heartbeat, taking in his delicious masculine fragrance. I got up and kissed him on the forehead, then headed for the bathroom. "Come on, Sleepyhead," I called over my shoulder. "Time for champagne."

When I returned, he was still on his back, as if he hadn't moved at all. I touched him once, then again, and finally he stretched, groaned with the pleasure of it, and swung his feet onto the floor.

"Champagne time," I whispered. He sighed and shook his head as if to clear it, and then looked up at me and smiled. "What a great wake-up call."

———

Paul and I had many rituals, and sharing a bottle of champagne before an anniversary dinner was one of them. While I held crystal champagne flutes on the overstuffed white canvas sofa, Paul eased the cork out of the bottle. Together we lit a candle to our history.

The sun was low on the horizon and the evening onshore breeze was picking up. Paul filled the glasses and we toasted each other. For almost two hours we reviewed all of our years together, from the very first. We laughed a lot, cried a little, and felt very blessed.

Then came the question—always the same question. It was only a matter of which of us would ask it.

This time it was Paul. "What would you have done differently?"

I looked toward the sun as it started to slip behind the horizon.

"I wouldn't have been so afraid of change. I wouldn't have been so resistant to every new thing that came along."

Surprised, Paul said, "That's exactly what I came up with. Most of what I was afraid of never happened anyway. And the hard stuff only made us stronger, made us appreciate the good times more. Don't you think?"

"Oh, yes," I said. "But I can't help wondering why we made the hard times *so* hard when we were going through them. It's taken us so long to feel we can trust life."

"Isn't that strange? The hard times taught us that they didn't have to be so hard."

"Then that's our answer for this year," I said. "We'd have had more faith. From this vantage point we see that our path together has been perfect in its own way, forcing us to grow and set out on trails in new directions that we never would have explored otherwise."

"That's it, Kitten."

I nestled in the familiar warmth of the crook of his arm and we watched the sky darken. Then I had what I thought was a bright idea.

"After dinner, let's come back here and light another candle and talk about our goals and intentions for the next twenty-five years."

———

We dressed for dinner, grinning, sometimes making faces at each other in the mirror. Square-shouldered and slim, Paul looked especially handsome in his tux. His gorgeous head of brown hair hadn't thinned at all, and now the sides were streaked with silver. No wonder strangers stared at him, often asking, "Aren't you a movie star?"

Wearing black tie never bothered Paul. For him it was an opportunity to return to me the compliment I paid him when I dressed up. He believed that when I looked my very best, the least he could do was the same. That was true tonight especially, even though we were only going to a neighborhood restaurant. It was called Five Feet and was known for its mix of French and Chinese cuisines.

The flavors of the succulent pieces of whole fish floating on pungent black bean sauce reminded us of the first nights of our courtship as we dined aboard a gaily lighted floating restaurant in the small harbor of Aberdeen, near Hong Kong.

Paul took my hand, looked deeply at me, and said, "You're still the most beautiful girl in the world."

———

Later we returned to the sofa, which now was bathed in moonlight. Paul held a fresh candle for me to light.

We'd looked forward during dinner to this time for talking about dreams and setting goals. We always sparked each other that way, and our mutual enthusiasm was sometimes so contagious that neither of us would be able to sleep afterward. Now we looked expectantly at each other, waiting for the conversation to begin. Neither of us said a word.

How strange, I thought. *I can't think of a thing to say.* It gave me a chill—not the kind I would have wanted.

I silently asked myself something unthinkable, *Could it be that we're complete now? That this will be our last anniversary?* I shuddered at the thought, horrified at what it might mean.

We sat there a while longer but nothing came forth from either of us. It was odd and unsettling, and neither of us knew what was going on. We were both silent as we went to bed that night.

My father, Eugene Webb Jr., me—queen of the Beverly Hills Easter Parade—and my mother, Marguerite (Mimi) Rufi Webb, 1958.

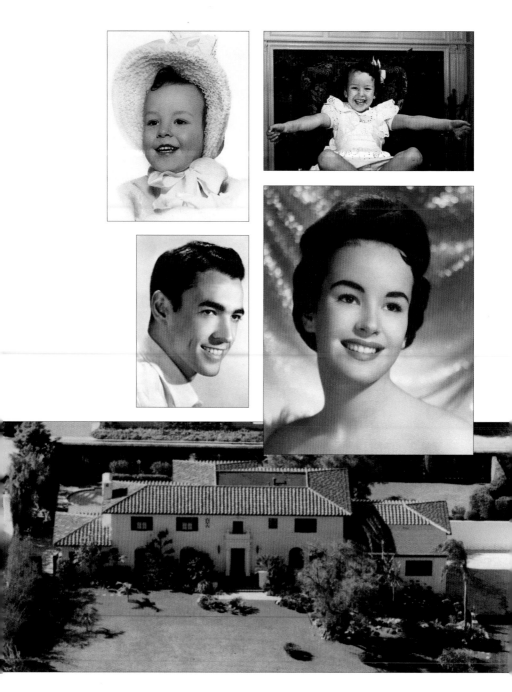

TOP LEFT: My baby portrait. *(Photo by Susan's Wilshire)*
TOP RIGHT: Me at five years old.
CENTER LEFT: My brother, Gene, a sophomore at UCLA, 1958. *(Photo by Autrey)*
CENTER RIGHT: A senior in high school, 1958. *(Photo by Autrey)*
BOTTOM: Our home at 9900 Sunset Boulevard, Beverly Hills, California, 1957.

TOP: Our tour group in Kyoto, Japan, October 1962, only a few weeks before I met Paul in Hong Kong. *(Photo by Kazuo Kokura, courtesy of Japan Travel Bureau)*

INSET: Paul when he was in the U.S. Army during the Korean war.

BOTTOM: Paul, a student at the American Academy of Dramatic Arts, circa 1945.

xcelsior Hotel
BEYROUTH · LIBAN

EXCELSIOR ★ PA

Miss Dian
34 Rue de Ɛ̇AT
Paris 8, Fr

BY AIR MAIL
PAR AVION

DIANA W WEBB

Le télégramme est identifié à l'aide des indications portées, dans l'ordre ci-dessous,
avant le texte du télégramme. L'heure de dépôt est indiquée par un nombre de quatre
chiffres.

ORIGINE	NUMÉRO	NOMBRE DE MOTS	DATE DE DÉPOT	HEURE DE DÉPOT	MENTIONS DE SERVICE
LAGOS	LT 3186	26	3	1257	

fantastoc letter stop love you terribly stop
be in Paris 2-3 Weeks please love
Paul

COMUNICACIONES MUNDIALES POR RADIO Y
TRANSRADIO ESPAÑOLA, S. A.
1064

TELEGRAMA
VIA TRANSRADIO

L695 tzb1215 aucklandnz 33 31 1553

lt miss diana webb castellana hilton paseo de la
castellana 57 madrid

hi sweetheart i love you
parnell apt 2 auckland 100 st
to rome writing
tiger

Some mementos from my meeting and courtship with Paul, including examples of his telegrams
and cartoon-illustrated letters.

BÁIYÁT OF
R KHAYYÁM

Treasury Series

62
D P W

I feel a great deal more
kindness for you than I
shall ever have time to
speak. And a single page
is little space for the
troops of gentle thoughts
that invest themselves,
on every hand, with affection
and chosen words

Approved for Posting in N.Z.
New Zealand Post Office Authority No 9
To open cut here
29 MY 63 4 PM
AUCKLAND EAST
N.Z.
Created AEROGRAMME
?WHEREDYAG
F. PAUL WEINETZ
100 ST. STEPHENS AVE APT 2
PRENELL ALCCKLAND N.Z.
SENDER'S NAME AND ADDRESS

TLP1378 TP
SINGAPORE 19 20

25 II 63. 12
OMONOIA
E — VOIE TELE FRAN

LT
DIANA WEBB 34 RUE DE CONSTANTINOPLE PARIS

KITTEN RECEIVED 8 LETTERS SENT 7 WILL YOU MARRY ME
PAUL

PARIS
PAR. &
AVION

F. Paul Weinetz
Excelsior Hotel
BEYROUTH · LIBAN
XCELSIOR * PALM-BEACH * LES HOTELS DE LA RIV
NOPLE
W. WEBB

Because Paul and I were in separate countries most of the year before we were married, we filled our
lonely hours by writing each other daily.

TOP: Paul kisses my mom, Mimi. *(Photo by Sergis Albert)*
BOTTOM: Our wedding, November 2, 1962. *(Photo by Sergis Albert)*

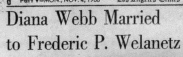

Diana Webb Married to Frederic P. Welanetz

Tall white tapers and white chrysanthemums decorated Beverly Vista Presbyterian Church for the marriage Saturday evening of Miss Diana Webb to Frederic Paul Welanetz.

Members of the families and close friends attended the ceremony and reception-dinner that followed at the Beverly Hills Club.

A second dinner-reception for 250 friends will be Nov. 22 in the Upper Bel-Air Bay Club.

Bride's Attire

The bride, daughter of Mr. and Mrs. Eugene Webb Jr. of Beverly Hills, was given in marriage by her father. She wore a long, white taffeta gown with lace and a pouf veil of tulle crowned with a tiara of crystals and pearls.

Mrs. Kurt Neumann Jr. attended the bride as matron of honor, and Miss Alice Blair was maid of honor and Misses Kay Hanley and Bobbi Rufi bridesmaids. All wore rose petal chiffon and carried one large pink cabbage rose.

Brother Best Man

Mr. Welanetz, son of Mr. and Mrs. Kirk Henry Welanetz of Ft. Lauderdale, Fla., was served by the bride's brother, Eugene Webb III, as best man, and Robert G. Rufi and Mr. Neumann Jr., ushers.

The bride was presented at the 1958 Coronet Debutante Ball. She is a Marlborough graduate and attended UCLA, where she was a member of Delta Delta Delta sorority.

After a honeymoon in

MRS. F. P. WELANETZ
Sergis Alberts photo

Carmel and the Hawaiian Islands, the couple will live in Hollywood.

Vive la différence!

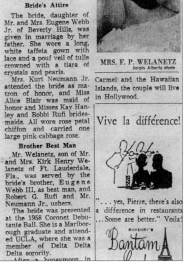

". . . yes, Pierre, there's also a difference in restaurants . . . Some are better." Voila!

McHENRY'S

Bantam

TOP: Our wedding reception on the day JFK was killed, November 22, 1963. *(Photo by Sergis Albert)*

BOTTOM LEFT: Wedding-day candids.

BOTTOM RIGHT: Our wedding announcement in the *Los Angeles Times*.

TOP LEFT: Paul on our honeymoon.

RIGHT: On our first wedding anniversary, 1964, we captured our high spirits on a strip of photos in a booth, four for a quarter.

CENTER LEFT: Papa and Lexi, December 1970.

BOTTOM LEFT: Our Christmas in Arrowhead, 1974. We made all the ornaments.

TOP RIGHT: Richard Simmons as the guest on our first taping of *The New Way Gourmet*, 1983.

INSET LEFT: Four of our books. (The von Welanetz Guide to Ethnic Ingredients *design by Warner Books;* The Pleasure of Your Company *design by Muni Lieblein;* L.A. Cuisine *design by Sussman/Prejza & Co., Luci Goodman;* Celebrations *photo by Keith Gaynes photography, design by Günther Stotz)*

INSET RIGHT: Our cooking school on the Sunset Strip, 1978.

BOTTOM: We begin our association with Robinson's department store, 1980. *(Publicity photo by Keith Gaynes)*

TOP: In 1976, when our cooking career took off with the publication of our first two books.

CENTER LEFT: Visitors to our train compartment en route from Moscow to Leningrad, May 1985. From left, Gerry Weaver, Mike Farrell, Gary Carter, Patricia Sun, me, Paul, Dennis Weaver, Shelley Fabares.

BOTTOM RIGHT: With author Alan Cohen in Leningrad, the day we gave the doll away on the subway, May 1985.

BOTTOM LEFT: The real Patch Adams, M.D., one of our group of citizen diplomats at the First International Peace Conference in the Soviet Union in May 1985. He wore a rubber nose and said he was practicing "nasal diplomacy." Robin Williams later portrayed him in the film, *Patch Adams*.

TOP LEFT: The Humanitarian Awards Breakfast celebrating the fifth anniversary of the Inside Edge, November 1990. I presented an award to Norman Cousins three weeks before he died.

TOP RIGHT: Inside Edge brochure.

CENTER: Standing ovation at the fifth anniversary of the Inside Edge. Visible in the audience are Louise Hay, Mark Victor Hansen, Lely Hayslip (author of *When Heaven and Earth Changed Places*), Boyd and Felice Willat, creators of Day Runner. *(Photo by Pamela Shandel)*

BOTTOM LEFT: In front of our Treehouse and Seymour the Sycamore, 1987. *(Photo by June Crockett)*

BOTTOM RIGHT: Paul at the helm for a sailing lesson, 1988.

TOP LEFT: Hosting a Gourmet Getaway aboard the Love Boat, 1984.

TOP RIGHT: Lexi and Paul, 1982.

CENTER: Paul on the day he bought his favorite purple robe in Big Sur, 1987.

BOTTOM: Our renewal-of-vows ceremony, August 1987.

TOP: Paul's memorial service, Good Friday, 1989.

BOTTOM: Paul, when we founded the Inside Edge, Fall 1985. This is my favorite photo of Paul because it captures both his strength and his gentleness.

TOP LEFT: Ted with his first wife, Sharon Wentworth, June 1965.

TOP RIGHT: Perfect partners—me and my best friend, Mary Olsen Kelly.

BOTTOM LEFT: Me and two of my closest male friends, Tim Piering (my bridge-jumping, bag-lady buddy) and photojournalist Tom Sewell, at an Inside Edge meeting, 1991.

BOTTOM RIGHT: Ted and I are dating, October 1989. *(Photo by Nomi Wagner Beane)*

TOP: Ted's and my wedding day, December 9, 1989. *(Photo by Jack Schneider)*

CENTER LEFT: My dearest friends at Ted's and my wedding. From left, Candace Wheeler, Patricia Sun, Mary Olsen Kelly (best friend and minister at the wedding), me, Mimi, Pamela Shandel, Sharon Lindsey, Lexi.

CENTER RIGHT: Ted with Aidan, our first granddaughter.

BOTTOM: Harvesting pumpkins at our ranch, 1999.

Lexi's wedding day, March 25, 2000. From left, Kathy, Ted, Lexi, Dave, me, and Christy. Paul was there in spirit. *(Photo by Jonathan Farrer Photography)*

INSET: Lexi and Ted, before the ceremony. *(Photo by Jonathan Farrer Photography)*

FOURTEEN

ONLY DAYS after our twenty-fifth anniversary celebration, Paul complained that his chest hurt.

For the entire quarter-century of our marriage, our doctor was Wilbur Schwartz, M.D., in Beverly Hills, and we gave but little thought to visiting him this time. Paul and I went to his office together. Dr. Schwartz listened, palpated, x-rayed, and left the office. A few minutes later he returned and held the large black-and-white x-ray up to the light.

"You have a spot on your lung, Paul," he said gently but straightforwardly, as if he knew bad news was bad news, however he pitched it. "It looks like pneumonia. It could also be a tumor."

The color drained from Paul's face.

I was jolted. *Oh God, no!* I thought. *A tumor? That's cancer. We just celebrated our anniversary. How can you talk about a tumor?* I remembered the teaching of my childhood and counseled myself, *Don't breathe, Diana. Don't feel. This can't be happening.*

"Go home, get into bed, and stay there. Come back in seven days and we'll have another look at you."

I knew Paul too well to believe the smile he put on for me in the car on the way home. But I knew he wanted me not to worry and I wasn't going to challenge the apprehensive look I saw in his eyes. I also knew *he* didn't want to worry. So we drove home without saying a word about Dr. Schwartz's speculations. It was, as I was later to recognize, my first real introduction to the tenuous, marginal world of *denial*. It's a child's tool, but very effective anytime. *If you pretend you don't see it, it's not there.*

Still, Paul wasn't in a mood to argue with the doctor's orders. When we got home he went straight to bed.

And slept. And slept . . .

I wouldn't allow myself even to think of the possibility of cancer and focused on keeping an upbeat attitude. I also remembered the years when we cavalierly smoked cigarettes—hundreds of them, thousands of them—when smoking was so fashionable and everyone did it. I wondered what all those cigarettes had done to Paul's lungs.

My journals from those first days—in their carefully dated and timed entries—say I felt like an impostor, pretending to be so strong, and that I was barely holding myself together.

Paul was in his own game of pretending, and he was especially grateful for all the attention I showered on him.

I went to the Edge meetings by myself, telling the members only that Paul had pneumonia. After two weeks of total bed rest, interrupted only by our brief trips to Dr. Schwartz's office for more medical tests, we learned that Paul's x-rays showed he was now worse, not better. Dr. Schwartz sent us to a lung specialist at nearby Cedars-Sinai Medical Center. There, Dr. Robert Wolfe looked over the x-rays, then spoke to us solemnly. "There is a fifty-fifty chance that the spot on your lung is a tumor."

Paul asked, his voice low, "What kind of tumor? The kind you could operate to remove?"

Dr. Wolfe reported that he could say nothing more, that he would just be guessing.

But in that instant I had a flash of intuitive understanding. *Oh . . . Paul's leaving . . . but I'm not.* The sudden knowing was emotionless at first. It was simply a statement. But as I realized what it implied, I quickly shoved it aside and convinced myself it was just a crazy, random idea, my mind playing a mean trick on me. A thought like that just couldn't be true. Of course not.

———

After making appointments for all the necessary tests, we got out of there. We waited for the elevator, crossed over to the garage, and began the trip home.

The world was the same world as before. The streets of Beverly Hills were already dotted with Christmas decorations— Thanksgiving was the following Thursday. All of Paul's tests were scheduled for the days before the holidays. Lexi would be home. How were we supposed to deal with any of it? We were in the center of the unthinkable.

Despite the oddly ominous moment on our anniversary a few weeks earlier, we'd both felt that a wonderful new stage of our lives was just beginning. The Inside Edge was in three cities and had the potential to become a nationwide success. Our television pilot, produced by Vin DiBona, was almost ready to make the rounds. Lexi was twenty years old, in her second year at the University of California at Santa Cruz—on her way into the life of a mature young woman. What would happen to all that now?

———

Lexi and I prepared Thanksgiving dinner together while Paul lay on the couch. He was very tired and I couldn't help but suspect that he really did have an illness that was draining his life away. He and I didn't want to spoil anyone's holidays so we had told no one what was actually happening, not even Lexi, who would leave in a few days to go back to school.

On November 28 we returned to Cedars for a bronchoscopy, an exploratory surgical procedure that would tell us exactly what was going on in Paul's chest. The nurse was so inept at inserting the IV that would sedate him, that by her fifth attempt it was all I could do to keep from screaming at her, shaking her. At last, however, it was in place properly and they wheeled Paul into the operating room. The doctor said the procedure wouldn't take long and suggested I wait in the lobby.

Time crawled. I had to stop myself from looking at my watch every minute. I glanced around, feeling a kinship with those others nearby, those old people and young people and people of so many different educational and social and economic backgrounds here in multicultural Los Angeles. Hospitals and medicine and illness were the great levelers. I marveled at how we were all, some of us by appointment, some of us surely unexpectedly, flung together into this waiting room of the Terrified and the Anxious and the Sad and the Hopeful. Were they waiting too for a life-or-death diagnosis? I tried to read the expressions on their faces, curious whether the lives of their loved ones also hung in the balance.

At last Dr. Wolfe appeared, his expression grim. He said Paul was in the recovery room, coming out from under the anesthesia.

"We'll have the definitive results tomorrow."

"What do you think it is?" I sounded like a child, helpless.

"I'll be able to talk to you both as soon as . . ." He studied me for a moment. "But you asked, and you deserve an answer. It's cancer, all right. It's all through the chest cavity, in the lymphatic fluid . . ."

"My God! What can you do?"

"We can try chemotherapy and radiation, but they're not cures. Not in his case."

"Meaning what? 'Not in his case.' What does that mean?"

"The location of the tumor makes it inoperable."

As if I were drowning, I was grasping at anything, any thought. I wondered whether there was a way to cancel out his words, like we were actors in a movie who had said our lines wrong and he could say his again.

"This doesn't fit my pictures," I mumbled.

The doctor's expression didn't change. He'd probably heard strange words like this a thousand times before from other distraught husbands and wives whose future he was seeing destroyed.

I wasn't making sense even to myself. I swallowed over and over. "And if the radiation and chemotherapy don't work?"

Dr. Wolfe looked me straight in the eye. "He's got only a few months at best."

I didn't know how to absorb this information. "Will he be in pain?"

"Not right away."

"Are you going to tell him when he comes out of surgery?"

"Let's wait until we have the biopsy report to be absolutely sure. There's no reason to throw this at him any sooner than necessary."

I nodded, appreciating the rationality of that. But I thought, *I've never hidden anything from Paul. How can I not tell him? I am being called upon to offer my very best, my highest self. Doesn't that include honesty?*

I decided the doctor was right. Of course he was. I should wait for the results before telling Paul. I couldn't bear the thought of telling him something so horrible if it might be wrong.

After the bronchoscopy, when Paul had recovered from the anesthetic, he wanted lunch at a restaurant by the Marina. We then drove to the jetty where Paul always loved to park and watch the sailboats moving in and out of the harbor. We were silent in the car and I wondered if his dream of having a boat one day was dying.

That evening, at home, we had a quiet dinner and listened, as we often did, to *La Boheme* while sitting on our couch in front of the fire. Paul's arm was around my shoulders. At the end of the opera, when the heroine dies, Paul and I were both in tears.

At 3:30 the next morning I couldn't sleep and made the following entry in my journal:

Paul and I sat together on the couch and talked about what he chooses to call "the worst-case scenario." I didn't tell him what the doctor had told me, but Paul seems to know. I told him that my deepest fear is that he will suffer. His deepest fear is that I will suffer, and that there may come a time when he won't be here as my protector. Even though we have become full partners, Paul has always been my protector, devoted to caring for me, our home, and Lexi.

In a very mysterious way it feels as if time has stopped. There is only the present moment, golden and precious like the winter sunshine. "God gave us tears for a reason," my friend Mary Erpelding once told me, and the memory of her words seemed to give me unconscious permission to let them flow. As Paul and I ate lunch today, our tears welled up in waves. Were they really washing away our fears that there will be precious few more warm and beautiful days like today?

Dr. Wolfe called in the early morning, asking us to come to his office the next afternoon.

Paul dozed beside me in bed. The weather was glorious—Southern California at its finest. Curiously, I felt more vividly alive than I had since his illness was diagnosed. I wanted only to surrender my will to Paul's needs and desires. Our intimacy felt deep enough to transcend any problem.

At unpredictable moments though, dread would sweep through me like a chilly wind and I would realize that our dream might be coming to an end. Everything could suddenly be over. *Everything.*

As my moods swung in great arcs, from hope to fear, Paul drew ever more inward. He had always been reflective anyway, but now I knew he was studying the whole matter of life and sudden death in his own mind, pondering it carefully.

How odd then, as evening came, that instead of either dread or solemn withdrawal, we both felt hopeful, even elated. *Surely,* I told myself, *we will find not only a cure, but also a renewal in the way we've been living our lives.* This elation, I was certain, had to be some kind of denial. But that meant denial was a *wonderful* and a *seductive* thing, a *kind* thing. How impossible that this chapter in our lives would not have a happy ending.

The next morning I wrote in my journal.

It felt like a normal morning here—me up first as usual, adding to the journal, upbeat, but as I brewed a special coffee for Paul when he awakened, I was aware I was riding an undercurrent of dread. The time could come when I would give anything to have a morning as normal as this one again. I love our life here, the work we do together, our grown daughter, our silly calico cat who basks in the sun and greets us on her back with her hind paws hooked behind her ears.

As we drove to Dr. Wolfe's office the next morning, Paul said, "Peggy Bassett . . . is my minister."

What an odd thing for him to say! Peggy was an Edge member and a dear friend. Then I realized. *Oh my God, he knows!* The feeling I wrote about in my journal had been right. I felt horrible, as though I had betrayed him. Why had I imagined I could keep it from him?

There was a long, long pause. I was suddenly full of fear, full of fear, full of so much fear. I dreaded to hear what he would say next.

"Do you think," Paul said evenly, "that she would conduct a service at Forest Lawn? The day we visited your father's grave and you talked to him—I liked that. I'd like to feel you could talk to me that way . . ."

I struggled to keep my voice calm. I said, "I'm sure Peggy would be honored to conduct a service. Forest Lawn is a beautiful place for a memorial gathering. But you always said you'd prefer cremation. That way I could keep your ashes with me . . . I could talk to you anytime . . ."

The hardest thing we could ever imagine saying to each other had just been said.

———

In his office, Dr. Wolfe announced the fact that stripped us of any possible hope and sealed Paul's fate. We asked if there was any reason at all for optimism. Dr. Wolfe said miracles sometimes happen and referred us to an oncologist who believed in them.

And so began our descent into darkness.

FIFTEEN

WHEN WE got home we headed straight for the couch, where we could hold each other tight.

"You've turned into a lady with such strength and calluses and grit! Now I need to ask you . . . to be cheerful for me. Can you do that?"

His eyes were pleading. I nodded abruptly, reflexively. I smiled and said yes, of course. I wanted to meet his needs. I wanted to fulfill his wishes. But I also recognized that my doing so would open a gulf between us. In asking me to be cheerful, which meant not burdening him with my fear and dread, he was asking that I close off my feelings from him. I would need to withhold and monitor and edit myself. I would have to don a mask.

He also asked that we not tell anyone yet, not even Lexi, until she came home from school for Christmas.

"People think I have pneumonia. Let's just leave it that way for a while."

From that moment, only in my journal could I be absolutely honest about the terror and anger, the sorrow and grief and what-if's already surging through me. In the first month, those what-if's whizzed by as if I were racing on a fast train through unfamiliar territory, past little towns, farm houses, cities. *What if the doctors are wrong? What if they're right but he suffers for years? What if his disease has been misdiagnosed and the chance to save him slips through our fingers?*

In the second month of his illness, I continued writing to Paul in my journal, writing all the things I could not say. *I want to rage at you and what is happening to us—one long scream that could kill you with its terror . . .*

I recorded all these thoughts in the hours and hours I had to myself while Paul slept. I didn't know what I was doing or why I was doing it, but in looking over all those words from the vantage point of later years, I can see what they accomplished. If the unexamined life is not worth living, then the examined life might be too intense to bear if one had to live behind a mask and be unable to place that intensity somewhere.

———————

On the day of the first radiation treatment I finally fell to pieces. I screamed and yelled and totally lost it when I was alone in my car on the way home from an Edge meeting, then wept while I waited for Paul at the hospital that afternoon. *At least with cancer as the enemy I will have you a little longer . . .*

More was happening that day than merely the first radiation treatment. Paul was also going to have a bone scan, to see if the cancer had spread. He felt good about beginning treatment, but the possibility of discovering metastasis brought home the immediacy and reality of what was happening.

That led to the first harsh words between Paul and me since the onset of his illness. Despite my wanting to honor his desire that no one be told he had cancer, I now begged him to let me confide in Lexi and my friend Mary. In my defensiveness and my own pain,

I told him sharply he wasn't the only one who needed support, that I needed the support of being able to talk with someone about it. He told me icily that he wanted his condition kept a secret, and he felt it wasn't much to ask. I agreed that I would talk to no one.

I hate that you are making me pretend it is all going to work out, that you will recover, and we will have our happy ending. I have no one at all to be real with now.

Then a few days later, Paul returned from a session with psychotherapist Dr. Lee Shulman, who had offered to help him deal with the emotions associated with the cancer treatment. Paul apologized to me for his insistence on privacy. "Lee told me you're going through as much as I am, and in some ways even more. He said you need to be able to grieve and talk about your feelings. I just didn't understand that. I'm truly sorry." I was deeply touched by his willingness to see my side of things.

"Let's wait the few weeks until Lexi comes home from school, so we can tell her first. Then you can tell anyone you want. How's that?"

There was only one person in Paul's inner circle and that was me. That's just how he was. Inward-turned, extremely private, with terrible pride. He was the love of my life, but his deeply personal nature didn't usually get tangled in or inhibit our relationship, so I didn't see it all that often. But now, in those extremely painful days when he was so ill, I saw them with great clarity. And I ached for him, wishing he could relax his defenses and just let people know him and love him.

―――――

At the same time Paul began his radiation treatment, a group of Edge members were holding strategy meetings to help us expand the Edge to other cities. Of course, none of them knew about Paul's true condition. Our television pilot was finished except for the voice-overs that would be heard as the still photographs were shown, the ones Sharon took of us on the beach. We felt hopeful enough about his cancer treatments when we went to the recording studio to tape the voice-overs that we decided not to tell Vin and Sharon yet about Paul's health problems.

We each wrote what we wanted to say about the other and stood together in a darkened sound booth. Paul asked me to record mine first.

". . . I think of Paul as a sailor, steady at the helm through calm seas and storms, my guide, my protector, my partner. For over twenty-five years he has been my snug harbor."

Paul's face was grave and he wouldn't look at me as he spoke. "Women have shaped my life, and the feminine force has been an irresistible and gentling influence on everything I now hold valuable. Until I met Diana I had the sense of being my own master, but she was to be my lifelong and final teacher. Her priceless lesson to me has been, simply stated, 'the more we share, the more we have.'

"I've imagined being on a stage alone and unexpectedly asked to comment on Diana. I would look down into the audience and find her large brown eyes, and say something I might have said a thousand times. 'It has been an honor and a daily privilege just to have loved her.'"

I shopped for Christmas, although my heart wasn't in it. The planning meetings for the Edge proceeded without Paul. We prepared for Lexi's homecoming and I prayed to find the right words to tell her at last about his situation.

Meanwhile, I drove him to the Cedars-Sinai Cancer Center and fought with all my might to do everything possible that could lead to a cure. Daily trips for radiation treatments, MRIs, doctors' appointments. Inviting people who we felt could advise us to our home to see Paul. All that while driving before dawn to Orange County and San Diego for the Inside Edge meetings, preserving my social face. I was getting exhausted. When it was too much I would escape for a few minutes in the car in the garage, or in my bathroom, and weep silently, privately.

I often had nightmares about falling asleep while driving and about the guilt I felt over not being the one who was facing death. I could share nothing but cheerfulness with Paul; still I would see the question behind his silent eyes, *Who are you to cry when your body is not letting you down, when you will continue to live?*

We'd always been so close, like one single soul. I'd always felt we could share anything. But our despair we could not share.

When Lexi returned home, Paul and I welcomed her with hugs that were tighter than usual. After the flurry of helping her carry in luggage, her aquarium, a dozen bags of Christmas packages to wrap, we asked her to sit with us on the couch.

Paul told her straightforwardly he had cancer. She was devastated. We all cried together, telling her we were seeing a specialist who felt there was hope that her dad would survive. She insisted she wanted to drop out for the rest of the semester to come home to be close to us. She said she'd go to work for the Inside Edge and help Lauren run the office. She volunteered to take Paul for his cancer treatments when I needed to attend Edge meetings.

Lexi was more lovely than ever, just beginning to attain her true beauty. She was smart and high-spirited and tough, just as she would have to be in the next few years. I was tough too, but I longed to be held at night as Paul had always held me. The next day, for the first time in weeks, he gathered me into his arms as he got into bed. "How's my baby? What can I do to take care of you?"

I burst into tears.

He added, "Why don't you call Mary tomorrow . . . and anyone else you need to talk to."

Shortly thereafter I did call Mary and Candace, sorry to tell them the news of someone they both loved, yet relieved I could finally talk about it.

After only two radiation treatments, Paul claimed he was feeling better and breathing easier, but at the same time he pulled a muscle in his rib cage while coughing. A few days later his first chemotherapy left him horribly nauseous, so he was dealing with that in addition to the pain from the torn muscle.

We were in the middle of the holiday party season and everyone at the Inside Edge wanted to know how Paul was recovering from his pneumonia. Uncomfortable with lying to the very people who looked to us to be exemplars of the life worth living, Paul began composing a letter to the Edge members, informing them that his diagnosis of pneumonia had led to the discovery of lung cancer. He asked them to support me at the meetings by not asking how he was doing or fussing over him, but by working to make the Edge ever better.

That seemed to take a lot of pressure off him. Or were the stronger pain pills just extremely effective, and giving him a narcotic high? He was very weak, yet he did not want us to drop our "normal" life to focus on him—not that I would have known what to do for him during one of his coughing spells or in general for his pain, except to push more pills on him.

Distraught one evening, I cried out to Spirit in my journal. *Why all this suffering?*

The answer woke me in the night. *How else would you ever be willing to let him go?*

_____

It's been said that ambivalence is the natural state of humanity. While I kept striving to find ways of keeping my hopes up, I could not help but see the alternate universe, the memorial service Paul wanted, his cremation—the whole nightmare of gloom.

We had Christmas. Lexi wrapped the presents and prepared turkey tacos on Christmas Eve, all the while reorganizing her life to be closer to Paul and me. She was in the process of withdrawing from UC Santa Cruz to enroll at a school close to home. I tried to be brave all the time, but sometimes tears would come out of nowhere, suddenly pouring down my cheeks. If it happened in a restaurant, Lexi was the one to rush me into the ladies' room and comfort me.

_____

Toward the end of January, Paul awoke to find clumps of hair on his pillow. He'd always had and been intensely proud of his beautiful brown hair, now threaded with strands of silver, an absolutely gorgeous mane.

Now he went to the cupboard where I kept the cape I draped around him for haircuts on our patio. He put it on, lowered himself into a chair, and said, "Pull it out. Pull it all out. And whatever won't come out, shave it off." He didn't say please. He wouldn't even look at me.

My throat closed and I kept swallowing over and over so I wouldn't cry. His eyes glazed over as he watched my reflection in the sliding glass door, watched me pull his hair out by handfuls.

I couldn't stop the silent tears that ran down my face as I hid a large handful of hair I would later set aside to put in an envelope.

Under the cape he was wearing the huge purple velour robe he loved, the one we bought at the Ventana Inn at Big Sur. The hammock where he'd spoken to me so lovingly in our television pilot was reflected behind us in the same sliding door. In that moment I knew that one day soon the only way I would be able to touch him would be to feel the contents of the envelope containing his hair and bury my face in the robe to inhale his fragrance as long as it lasted.

A bald Paul was somehow even more beautiful to me than he had been with hair. I told him that Yul Brynner had nothing on him. Through RaeAnn Levey, an Inside Edge member who worked for Disney Productions, I found him a purple velvet wizard hat with gold stars. He loved it.

One day while Paul was having his tests at Cedars, I tied helium balloons to the armrests of the wheelchair he used to navigate from one building to another. After the tests were over, I covered the top of his now bald head with kisses, leaving bright lipstick prints, and we were both laughing as I wheeled him into the elevator. By odd coincidence, one of our cooking students happened to be standing at the back of the elevator. Her shocked expression suddenly reminded me of how much our lives had changed.

———

Now, with so little time left as a wife, I wanted only to care for my husband, learning especially from our daughter's grit and determination and self-sacrifice how it could be done. And with so little time left as a family, we were more perfectly together than ever.

Paul was weathering his suffering with gallantry and no complaint, his legs aching at night, his head hurting by day. In spite of all the radiation and chemotherapy, in spite of the meditation, the prayers, and good wishes, the cancer had spread out of his lungs up to his brain and down to his hips. His hearing was deteriorating and his voice damaged; his mind was foggy from the treatments and the painkillers. All of this in fewer than four months after our twenty-fifth anniversary celebration, where we had been ominously quiet as we sought to share our hopes for the next twenty-five years.

I wrote, *I am learning that feelings are like a kaleidoscope. In one moment I feel indescribable horror at what we are going through. In the next, there is a burst of absolute joy to feel so much a part of the beauty and magnificence of life.*

And on another day, *It is only an illusion to think we can control our lives to any great extent. The most poignant times require surrender. What would it mean to say "yes" to this disease that is weakening Paul more every day? We all have a limited number of days here . . . are his almost up? What if our struggle is futile?*

Sometimes I wrote in my journal to Paul, telling him the things I could not say. *Cancer is kind because it gives us time with each other. It is even giving me time to wish you will die, because seeing you in such pain is more than I can bear.*

Focusing on just living each day, trying not to think too far ahead, we were also having moments of the most tender love, moments filled with a dark beauty, knowing we were both becoming something completely new. Such love would wash through me, such grace in those moments. They were what carried me through it. They made me feel connected to all people in pain all over the world, to every person who had ever been losing someone and was helpless to prevent it.

I remembered my thought that long-ago winter at Lake Arrowhead, when I was sure there must be moments when a caterpillar is distraught about becoming a butterfly. Yes. We were both surrendering to something new, and there was both anguish and joy in that. I felt alive, and human, as never before, and I never spoke of that to anyone.

Paul was still capable of loving me in a way that left me feeling appreciated, supported, and satisfied, and he had a gift of being able to look into the abyss selflessly, even presciently. We had many a moment that turned mysteriously magical . . .

It was then we had the brief conversation that, perhaps more than any other, was to alter my life radically and thus remain perfectly in my memory:

"*I don't want you to be alone!*"

"Then send me someone!"

"I will," he said. "I *will!*"

SIXTEEN

ON MY BIRTHDAY, March 4, Lexi shopped for Paul, who gave me a crystal paperweight in the shape of the earth. Following his suggestion that Lexi and I go to a movie, Lexi took me to see the Bette Midler film *Beaches*, about two lifelong friends, one of whom is dying.

I wouldn't have gone had I known what it was about. But the theme song, "The Wind Beneath My Wings," was haunting, and as the final credits rolled by, Lexi and I couldn't stop weeping. We sat there long after everyone had left the theatre.

> *It might have appeared to go unnoticed*
> *that I've got it all here in my heart.*
> *I want you to know I know the truth:*
> *I would be nothing without you.*
>
> *Did you ever know that you're my hero,*
> *and ev'rything I would like to be?*
>
> *I can fly higher than an eagle,*
> *'cause you are the wind beneath my wings.*

We bought a copy of the soundtrack in the theatre lobby. When we got home, I played the song for Paul. He loved it too, and I knew then it was the song I would choose for his memorial service.

Nine days later, Paul and I realized that the burdens of caring for him at home were becoming overwhelming, that he needed more care than Lexi and I could provide by ourselves. He decided the time had come to go to the hospital. It was a terrible concession, for we knew this was the journey to the place he would die. Still, a part of him was not quite ready to go. When I told him I would find a way to sleep in his room at the hospital, that was all he needed to hear.

As we were leaving, going out the front door, he looked to his left, to the place under Seymour where we'd buried Misty's ashes four years before. He reached out to pat the tree, and that was the final moment, he knew beyond argument or alternative—we both knew—he was leaving our home for the last time.

I drove him to the hospital. I checked him in and a nurse took him to his room, having told me that getting him settled would take some time. I used the opportunity to return home and pack a suit-case for myself.

During our six days there, I slept next to his bed on a reclining chair. I fussed over him, straightened his bedclothes, moved the pillows continually when he asked for help getting comfortable. When I couldn't hold back tears, I ducked into the bathroom to sob quietly, my mouth open, taking silent gulps of air. Afterward I slipped back to his bedside. He must have known but he never said a word.

Our friend Bobbie Probstein, who had been a professional photographer, came by the hospital, asking Paul's permission to take photographs of our hands together. She told him she intended to one day publish a book of photographs of people's hands. He nodded his permission—but his face was expressionless. I had no idea what he was thinking. But what he couldn't have known was that her photos would beautifully capture an extraordinary moment in our lives, a moment that yet remains one of my most precious memories.

As Bobbie set up her camera and lights that day, preparing to take a number of pictures of different poses, I memorized his hands—his strong and sculpted artist's hands, his skin and its subtle hues, the hair on his wrists. *I will not have this hand to hold.*

———

A certain grace came into me during those days in the hospital. I would suddenly find myself buoyed up and able to watch it all as a drama unfolding, again feel a sort of joy bubbling up from within me that had to do with feeling the essence of life itself. I could never speak of it to anyone because I was certain it would sound horribly insensitive, even insane. But I was discovering that the deep abiding faith I'd always professed to have, the faith that all of life has a goodness and a purpose, was being tested and was true for me.

———

On March 17, Paul stopped eating. It was St. Patrick's Day 1989, and his hospital breakfast tray was decorated with a green-and-white plastic shamrock. I will always associate Paul's last days there with someone's effort to bestow cheer on the patients.

Nevertheless, fingering that symbol of good luck, I thought about how luck (or *joss,* as Paul had often referred to it) had always been such a part of our lives together. I believed in luck and we'd been continually surprised by its timely appearance throughout our twenty-five years together. But Paul had believed it was *my* good luck, not his, and felt he could only share mine. He had believed *he* would never really be lucky because he thought he didn't deserve it. In his present situation, attached to a catheter and an IV drip, with no real hope for the future, he was sure of it.

I tried to interest Paul in his plate of smoked salmon, cream cheese, and a bagel, but he urged me to eat it instead. Complex and conflicting emotions were so clearly running through him. I watched him look dismayed that I could taste and appreciate the food. Nothing I did was right. He'd always condoned my actions so thoroughly, but now his illness had come between us. I was losing him and his approval even before he was gone.

That St. Patrick's afternoon in the hospital I had my lowest moment. I completely fell apart behind the screen in front of the bathroom as Lexi made an effort to say goodbye, telling Paul he'd been a wonderful father. I sobbed, *Why? Why?* I was doubled over, wracked with grief, my knees buckling. I sank slowly and silently to the cold floor.

He couldn't bear to see me suffer; he'd asked me to be cheerful for him. In this, my worst moment, I couldn't burden him with my grief, and I'd never felt more alone.

From those days in the hospital, I realized more vividly than ever that feelings, even such difficult feelings, are fleeting. They are like clouds that pass continually through the sky, blocking the sun, then clearing. The phone would ring suddenly, a friend offering comfort, and Paul's eyes would light up with laughter. Or our eyes would meet, and all the joy we'd shared would bloom again for a few moments. Or I'd have a flash of higher perspective, a view that revealed our destiny as much deeper than this drama in which we found ourselves actors. In my moments of darkest despair, I told myself over and over, *This too shall pass. This too shall pass.*

SEVENTEEN

Good Friday, March 24, 1989

AS OUR LIMOUSINE approached the tall, stone Church of the Recessional, its pristine beds of pansies and English primroses were bathed in Southern California's morning sun.

Named and modeled after the church in England where Rudyard Kipling worshiped and found inspiration for his immortal poem "The Recessional," it is one of the most famous final destinations in the world. My father's funeral had been held there long ago, with only a few in attendance, but this day it would hold hundreds at the memorial service for Paul von Welanetz.

As I entered the cool stone interior, my eyes fell on the words inscribed above the chancel:

> *Now abideth faith, hope, love, these three:*
> *and the greatest of these is love.*

> I CORINTHIANS 13:13

Lexi and I sat next to the aisle in the right front pew. I could hear rustling and subdued whispers behind me as the sanctuary filled. When at last I turned, I saw more than 350 people—standing room only. Cousins to whom I'd hardly spoken in the seventeen years since my father's funeral here, were seated in the left front as "family." But it was the Inside Edge members who overfilled the church. They were, as they well knew, Paul's and my "family of choice."

Peggy Bassett, statuesque in white clerical robes, entered the front of the church. She began the service.

"Paul knew at the end that the Intelligence that he was, was taking him to his next experience. When we were together in the hospital on Sunday night just for a brief moment of recognition, there was a knowingness about him . . . that he was greater than the body he was leaving."

———————

Was it only five nights ago that Peggy had come to see Paul? He'd been drifting in and out of a coma all day, and she comforted me by offering a metaphor of what happens in a coma as death approaches. She told me it was as if his soul were crossing to the other side of a wide river, looking around, then coming back into his body.

Peggy said to me, "With each trip, the river grows narrower, and when he's satisfied that it's safe, he'll let go."

For an hour or so there in the hospital, she and I stood silently in vigil. Then just before she left, Peggy looked deep into my eyes and said, "Paul has been completely devoted to you. Don't you think he might be waiting for your permission to leave?"

Yes, I thought. Paul would do that. I took his hand and stood by the bed for a long, long time. He was sedated and silent. I wanted to get in bed with him and hold him, but the tubes running into and out of his body made me afraid I would hurt him. But how could I have hurt him any more than he was hurting? I read later of a woman who got in the hospital bed with her dying mother and cradled her in her arms as she died. I've wished ever since that I'd done that for him.

Instead, I stood by the bed and surrendered. *Oh, dear Spirit. I am your hands and your feet. Show me what it is you want me to do.*

Eventually I began to speak. "I'm here, my love. I know you can hear me. I love you more than anything in the world. You've always been my hero. And now we both know it is time for you to go. I want you to know it is okay with me for you to leave. I am so, so grateful to you. Thank you for coming to be with me. Thank you for all the love and joy we've shared. Thank you for Lexi. Thank you for all the years of the sweetest love anyone will ever know. You've always been my shining mirror, showing me the best of who I am. You awakened me and supported me with your love every day we were together. You've been a wonderful husband and father—the most perfect husband anyone could ever wish for."

Tears flowed down my cheeks as I remembered how protective Paul had always been. I'd felt I was the luckiest woman alive.

I swallowed hard and continued, my voice shaking. "You can go now. I am safe and you are safe. For reasons we simply can't understand, your work here is done. I promise you that Lexi and I will be all right. I'll always love you and we'll always be together in our hearts."

Say "I promise."

I heard his voice in my mind, and I smiled at one of his favorite phrases.

"I promise," I answered, then repeated my litany of reassurance over and over until I gradually felt complete in giving him permission to go.

I kissed him before I stepped away from his bedside. "Peggy says that death is perfectly safe, as easy as waking up from a dream. It's time to surrender to it. Just let go, my love."

——————

On the night of Sunday, March 19, out of habit, I changed into my nightgown and sat in the nearby chair with my journal. But instead of writing about the events of the day, I found myself writing, *Why have I prepared for bed? I won't be sleeping here tonight.*

Within minutes my ears told me something was different. *What's happened?* Paul's labored breathing had stopped.

"Paul?"

I moved quickly to his side.

"Sweetheart, have you gone so quickly?"

I touched my cheek to his, kissed him for the last time.

After a few moments, I rang for the nurse. When she arrived, I said—for some strange reason using the same words my father's nurse had used seventeen years before—"I believe my husband has just expired."

TWO VIEWS OF THE SAME SHIP

I'm standing upon the beach line.
A ship at my side spreads her white
sails to the morning breeze—
and starts for the blue ocean.
She is an object of beauty and
strength.

And we stand and watch her
until, at length, she hangs
like a speck of white cloud,

just where the sea and the sky
come down to mingle with each other.

Then someone at our side says,
"There, she's gone."
"Gone where?"
Gone from our sight, that is all.

She is just as large in mast
and is just as able to bear
her load of living freight to
the place of destination.
Her diminished size is in us
not in her—

And just at the moment when
someone at our side says,
"There, she's gone,"
there are other eyes watching
her coming—
And other voices ready to
take up the glad shout,
"Here she comes!"

And that is dying.

AN ADAPTATION
FROM JEWISH FOLKLORE

All at once, I had things to do. As I packed our things, Paul's
and mine, into my small suitcase, I felt an urge to talk to him, to tell
him over and over again how I loved him. As I did so, I imagined I

could feel his sense of lightness and joy in being free of his body, free of pain. It was almost as though I could feel him soaring. Surely I was imagining it.

A magical quality infused the clear and silent night as I stepped out of the hospital for the last time. Above I saw a full moon and vivid stars. On the ground a gusting wind whipped my skirt as I made my way out to the hospital parking structure. As cold as the air was, I lowered the windows of the car and let the air blow over me. Time seemed to have stopped and I was fully aware of every tiny movement, noticing the dashboard, my denim dress I had worn for days, the deserted freeway.

I could not have imagined such an ending to our love story all those years ago in the hills above Hong Kong. We'd been children—all lovers are children, I realized. But it was done now. Done.

——— ∞ ———

Peggy continued speaking to the hundreds in the sanctuary.

"When Paul was a child, when he was born into this plane of existence, his family admired him as a little child. He grew into a young man for all his friends and acquaintances to admire. Then he grew into a mature human being. No one cried for the baby when he grew into a young man, and no one cried for the young man when he grew into a mature human being.

"The same thing has happened now—Paul has just taken another step. The only thing that's different is that this time we cannot see his body. We cannot see him with our physical eyes. But we do have a different viewing point. We can see with our inner eye—that Paul, the soul that he is, just outgrew this body and outgrew these experiences. He has something else to do on another plane."

Peggy then invited those gathered to share stories about Paul.

Until she had begun speaking, the mood in the building was quiet and somber, but as she talked, the collective feeling lightened. And now, as one person after another stood to recall stories of Paul von Welanetz—stories of his charm, style, gentleness, and intelligence, often recounted with a large measure of humor—the stone walls there seemed to come alive, echoing with the hum of warm memories and laughter.

His friend Steve remembered inviting Paul to go surf fishing early one morning in Malibu. Paul had arrived dressed elegantly in white shorts and jacket, with a cooler containing warm sweet rolls and a big thermos full of coffee. Paul caught two little fish but took the hooks out and put them back into the sea. Paul the great hunter. In white. For surf fishing.

Dr. Barbara De Angelis said, "I was always so aware of his intelligence . . . the deep thought behind his every word. . . ."

Margaret Wright, manager of the San Diego branch of our business, said, "I can't help but feel that Paul is here, and as usual he is counting the house. He always loved standing room only. . . ."

Mary Olsen, who had flown in from Hawaii for the service, said, "Paul made standing still look like a work of art! He danced like the hero of every woman's fantasy, sweeping Diana across the floor in a lovely and elegant waltz, their bodies in perfect alignment, while we all watched in awe. Cinderella and Prince Charming would have to step aside if Diana and Paul waltzed by, because they were the stars of a real-life fairy tale."

And then, many minutes afterward, when the last person had spoken, Peggy continued, "I think, as we are celebrating this life we've known as Paul von Welanetz, that he's blessing us all wherever he is. I wouldn't be surprised if he is in this room, without form."

Oh, yes, I thought. *He's here. Free of pain at last, and appreciating every moment.*

————

Later, outdoors in the courtyard overlooking all of downtown Los Angeles, people streamed past for over an hour, greeting Lexi and me. I was afloat in a river of comfort filled with hugs and good wishes.

An Edge member had arrived at the church towing a trailer filled to overflowing with hundreds of helium balloons, which she passed out as Lexi and I spoke to the last of the well-wishers. The crowd lingered on the lawn so all of us could, following the suggestion of another member, set our balloons free together. Lexi and I now moved into the crowd, hands reaching out to other hands, and someone began to sing the David Pomeranz song "It's in Every One of Us."

As the multicolored balloons floated away, becoming dots against the clouds, a blue one lingered behind, bobbing and dancing in the breeze. "It's Paul," someone said, "waving goodbye."

Not goodbye, I heard him say in my heart, *waving hello, as I waved to you on the boat that afternoon in Hong Kong, from high atop Victoria Peak.*

————

Two years before Paul died, a man, his eighteen- and nineteen-year-old daughters, and a gathering of friends released bright-colored helium balloons from a hilltop home in Southern California. They followed the shrinking, multicolored dots with their eyes and hearts. The balloons climbed into the sky then disappeared into the distance, carried by a soft breeze from the Pacific Ocean just a mile away. Ted Wentworth, who was about to turn forty-nine, had just lost his wife, Sharon, after her prolonged battle with breast cancer.

PART TWO

Ted

EIGHTEEN

From the Journals of Ted Wentworth

SINCE SHARON DIED *I wake up in the morning and stare in disbelief at the four walls. The most delicate parts of my heart have gone with her.*

Along with being lonely, I feel guilty. Sharon died a millimeter at a time over a four-year period. She knew I was going to live, that I was going to have a new life and she wasn't. She knew she wouldn't see Christy and Kathy get married, nor would she see our grandchildren—and I would. I saw all of that in her eyes during the many quiet moments between us.

After she died, more guilt stared me down. Guilt for feeling relieved because I got to stay when she couldn't. Big guilt over not being able to give her the gift of life she wanted so badly. Guilt about how gracious she was about all of it. Guilt in feeling relieved the agony of the day-to-day struggle was over—at least I think it is. And guilt because . . . it's just endless.

I know I don't want to go through life with a cold, empty seat on the bench next to me. Sharon told me several times during her long illness that she wanted me to be happy and to go on. Even with that encouragement it's very difficult to face the possibility of "dating" again, especially in midlife and after so many years of marriage. Our generation regards dating as something that kids do. But self-pity isn't my style. I've always been a self-starter, and I know persistence is a virtue. What works is to pick myself up, dust myself off, and go back and overcome what threw me.

Ted Wentworth recalls having bought books on grief, studying the different stages described by death-and-dying researcher Elisabeth Kübler-Ross, and monitoring himself as he went through them—through the denial, anger, bargaining, depression, lethargy.

He was careful not to make any big decisions for a year. A year or so after Sharon died, he reached a level of acceptance, when, except during holidays and their anniversaries, the reality of his loss had found a place in his life. He didn't hate it anymore. He didn't fight it anymore. But he realized the time had come to move on.

He wanted a partner in his life, a woman he could love and give to, someone with whom he could continue to explore and expand his own capacity to love. To have that, he decided, he needed a strategy.

From the Journals of Ted Wentworth

How I care is who I am. It won't work to go shopping for someone to love me. That would turn me into a taker, and that isn't what I'm about. I want a woman to experience my caring as a deep, meaningful, sensitive gift, so safe that her heart can open and return an expanding love to me. I know it's my role to initiate that cycle—that will be my key to success.

I'm working on myself, to become the best me I can be so I'll attract just the right woman. Reminds me of the old Frank Sinatra song "The Tender Trap." It's about the sudden surprises of being in love, of being caught up in everything love and marriage brings. I want those feelings for my new lady and me. And I'm going to do everything I can to attract them. I suppose you could say I'm building a better spouse trap—yes! That's it. A better spouse trap!

I'm methodical about this. Every woman I interview or date is either my goal or the lesson I need to learn to reach my goal. The sooner I learn my lessons, the sooner I'll find her. I'm telling everyone I know that I'm looking for Ms. Right-for-Me and that I welcome their suggestions of likely candidates.

I tell them "no thanks" when they try to fix me up with someone too young. I don't want a trophy. I want someone who grew up as I did in the early days of rock'n'roll, who can remember roller-skate keys, drive-ins, chocolate cigarettes, and spooning cream off the top of milk that came in glass bottles.

Before long, Ted was deep into the process of methodically interviewing as many eligible women as he could find for the position of New Wife/Best Friend.

What he termed an interview was a quick breakfast, or a drink after work. An interview wasn't a date, but a way to find out if he wanted to get to know a woman. A date was when he and the woman were actually developing a relationship.

At the start of his search, friends assured him that it would be easy, that the women of the world were waiting eagerly for such a superb catch. A handsome, well-dressed, middle-aged attorney with his own law firm and a successful thirty-year career; father of two grown daughters; and the owner of a home with a view. He had it all, they said. He could expect candidates with casseroles in hand to form a line at his front door.

From the Journals of Ted Wentworth

I'm focused in my search. I'm checking out church groups and every lead I get. I know she's out there somewhere and I'm determined to find her. Some days I have both a lunch date and a dinner date. I've been on so many dates that I'm having a hard time remembering details about them all—where they went to school, their children's and pets' names, so I asked a friend who designs computer programs to come up with some software for me to keep track of all these wonderful women. My daughters call it my "black book," and tease me when I come home after each adventure, go straight to the computer, and enter the data.

One year passed, then two. Ted's daughters grew worried. They decided to talk with him about it.

"How's it going, Dad?"

"Not so great. Everyone thinks I'm just hard to please. If a woman isn't accomplished at anything, or talks badly of her children or family, I know right away she's just not the one. I'm meeting women as fast as I can."

"You don't have to try so hard, Dad! Just be patient and she'll show up right in front of you."

"I don't agree! She won't show up unless I show up. Meanwhile, I'm busy learning. Every woman I meet brings me closer to finding *her*."

———⊶⊷———

Two months after Paul died, Mary called from Hawaii to tell me she and Don Kelly were engaged. It was wonderful news, of course, but I knew she'd stay in Hawaii and I'd really miss having her nearby. She added that soon they were going to Tahiti to buy black pearls for Don's jewelry stores, and said the beach house they shared on the island of Kauai would be available for a week. Would I like to have it during that time?

I didn't need to be asked twice. I finished preparing the calendar for the next two months' speakers at the Edge and made arrangements for Lexi and Lauren to handle everything else.

And within a few weeks, I was starting a vacation in paradise. All by myself. At the airport in Los Angeles, I was surrounded by the usual crowd of travelers, including couples and families who were excited about the trips they were about to take. For twenty-five years I had felt the same way, since vacations meant companionship, romance, and family time for me too. But not this one. All through the flight I felt unsettling currents of grief, pain, and general unease. I deliberately allowed myself to feel them, which meant I continually reeled with sadness at what both Lexi and I had lost.

Mary and Don greeted me at the little airport in southeast Kauai and had just enough time to show me around before they were on their way to Tahiti. And there I was—alone in their modern wood-and-glass home on the beach.

I slept that first night in their king-sized bed surrounded by mosquito netting, listening to the waves nearby and rereading Anne Morrow Lindbergh's *Gift from the Sea*—the book Paul had given me in Mexico. At sunrise I acquainted myself with the surroundings, marveling at the pastel colors of the Kauai beach, lavender and pink and aqua glistening on gentle waves that washed over the sand.

I spent most of that first day walking on the beach, feeling the beauty of the environment mix with unexpected assaults of sadness, making entries in my journal, and talking with Paul. Once that morning I heard, *Thank you, thank you for your love and courage and cheerfulness. Thank you for being so in service and tending to my every need. I wish I had hidden a thousand love notes for you to find. Fortunately, I can send them from here, and you are sensitive to them.*

A few days later my emotional turmoil began to subside in response to the island's beauty and tranquility. The weather in Kauai was moody and so was I. Moments of relative calm sometimes appeared when the pain slid away, and I could sometimes perceive other aspects of my life—the future, my interests, my desires, my goals. As the days passed, the intervals when I felt rested and ready for something new came more frequently.

I asked Paul in my journal one afternoon, *What shall I do, what is my next step?*

He answered: *Write our love story . . . as you look through our memories together, a pattern will gradually emerge, as a photographic image begins to develop in a darkroom. What you begin seeing will become much clearer with time.*

Initially that idea brought me neither comfort nor inspiration, for writing about what still seemed so vivid was not comfortable at all. *Write our love story? As though it's a thing of the past?* To do so, I'd need to let go of it somehow and I wasn't ready to do that.

But as I continued allowing the island to heal me, the idea began to feel right, as right as the idea of writing a cookbook had seemed when it came to me in Mexico, almost twenty years earlier. In fact, it now seemed the thing to do.

I began making notes. I had no specific goal other than feeling close to Paul and allowing my painful emotions a place to be expressed. Little did I know, though, how well Paul had foreseen what would happen, that those journal entries—capturing the intense reality of our times together, my memories of that year we'd lived in Mexico, and our winter in Lake Arrowhead—would one day become the first half of this book.

Those times of turmoil were the most important times we had together. If you can see and accept that, you will open to the chaos of change so it can reveal to you the truth of who you are. Embrace change! Comfort is seductive, but too much of it is your enemy—don't get stuck seeking comfort! Seek radical aliveness! Fly into action when you catch an idea.

How things began to change! "Oh God," I thought, "this is bliss. I love this book, our book, and the feelings that are stirring in me, the waves crashing, the wind howling."

As the days passed, I practiced yoga and listened to music and walked on the beach, following my slightest whim, whatever appealed to me in the moment. And the most astonishing thing happened: I fell in love with solitude, something I had never known in my adult life.

My body, to which I'd paid little attention since Paul had gotten ill, began to come alive again. Who was I physically, I wondered? One night I went swimming alone in the surf—my first time in the water since I arrived—and it was one of the most intensely sensual experiences of my life.

But sensuality aroused yearns for companionship. That night I longed for Paul's physical presence.

I spoke aloud, "I miss the warmth and closeness of you in bed with me. You can be so completely present in my mind. Isn't there any way you can come to me physically?"

That evening he answered through our journaling: *Yes. Feel me wrapped around you in an invisible hug. We are woven together now, two silken strands, inseparable.*

———

But something new began to happen. The arousal of my feelings on that most sensual of islands would begin to have consequences.

As much as I loved my newfound solitude, and as close as Paul still felt to me, the sense of his closeness and the memory of his presence no longer were enough to send away the yearnings that were awakening in me as I strolled that romantic beach. Other stirrings began rippling in my awareness. Would he really send someone, as he said he would? He was irreplaceable, of course. And I couldn't imagine being with another man again. Nonetheless I found myself wondering: is another man out there in my future, somewhere? And if there were, how would I ever know him?

The next day, as I walked the beach for the last time, I picked up a plumeria blossom that had fallen in the path in front of me. Holding it gently, I lifted my thoughts and spoke to the future that awaited me. "Whoever you are," I said, speaking softly, "wherever you are, whenever you begin looking for me, let this flower lead your way."

I walked into the gentle surf and sent the flower out to sea. I returned home, feeling to my surprise that I had opened a new part of my heart.

From the Journals of Ted Wentworth

It's been nearly two years. I was so sure I'd find her by now. I decided I had to do something to formally release the past, so I took a bag of roses from Sharon's garden to Catalina this weekend. After breakfast, I hopped in a dinghy and motored west until I found a secluded cove off a point where rocks jut into the sea.

Setting the motor to drive in circles, I scattered the roses behind the boat, creating a blanket of blossoms. I turned off the engine in the center of the flowers and sat quietly, holding the urn with Sharon's ashes on my lap. Waves slapped gently against the sides of the boat as I removed the lid from the urn and poured her pale ashes into the dark green water.

Goodbye, my love . . . *I told her all the things I'd loved about our marriage, that I would always love her, and that I needed her help in finding someone to love.*

Just as I was about to start the motor again, I heard the low lamenting cry of a seagull. Looking up, I saw two gulls approaching. The calling one swooped low toward the boat, circling it over and over, nearly brushing me with its wing and

surrounding me with a keening cry of kow-kow-kow. The other flew silent circles
high above, as if waiting.

   I watched in wonder. I felt sure that Sharon, who had such an affinity for birds,
was saying goodbye. The gull looked at me closely on its last circle before rising to join
the other, and then the two birds flew in tandem away from the cove and out to sea.

⸏⸎⸏

Returning home after that idyllic week, I began to spend more and
more time alone, arranging my schedule to have every Tuesday
evening by myself at the Probsteins' condo.

   I hadn't had the opportunity to spend much time alone in
twenty-five years. In a marriage, particularly when there's a child,
true solitude is rare. Now I relished this solo time, knowing I
wouldn't be interrupted. I could spend hours there looking out to
sea or listening to music or simply dreaming. Time slowed. I wanted
only solitude . . . and popcorn.

   In fact, I was becoming a popcorn addict, eating *only* popcorn
unless I forgot to eat altogether. I was losing weight and looked very,
very slim.

   That evening, listening to music, I felt the urge to get up and
start moving—*dancing*. I was wearing a nightgown I loved, and I
whirled and spun and drifted to the music for a long time. The telephone rang.

   It was Lexi.

   "What are you doing?"

   "I'm dancing in my nightgown to Barbra Streisand while the sun
goes down."

   "I'm glad I'm not there!" This meant, I suppose, it would be just
too weird to see her mother dancing around in her nightgown.

"I'm glad too," I said, "because I couldn't do it with anybody else here!"

———

I continued to savor my solitude. As the days passed, I spent my time doing whatever interested me, feeling Paul still with me, even if not so frequently as I felt him in the beginning.

———

Men. Men began to be more forward in their interest in me. I still hesitated to ask Paul about them in my journal or to discuss them with him. Doing so would have felt disloyal.

I did encounter one man, an old friend who, I learned quickly enough, was *not* Paul's choice. I agreed to meet him at a restaurant, quite certain from our phone conversation he wanted to have an affair with me. I was mildly interested in the idea myself. When I parked my car there, heading in, I realized it wasn't close enough to the wall. So without getting back into the car completely, and with my left foot still on the garage floor, I turned the engine on again—and accelerated too quickly. The car lurched forward into the wall then bounced backward, not once, but three times, slamming the open door painfully against my leg.

I finally turned the engine off, pulled in my leg, and just sat there, scolding myself for handling the car so foolishly. I also wondered if there was a deeper meaning to what had just happened.

I didn't have to wait long for the answer. It seemed pretty clear: an affair with this man would be like driving into a wall—it would go nowhere, bounce me around, and I would get hurt! I limped into the restaurant, enjoyed a pleasant lunch, and was polite but very, very firm. The gentleman understood he and I would be friends, but never more.

———

In the meantime, business matters needed to be handled, as usual. The producer of our TV pilot, Vin DiBona, thought I could still host the show he had in mind if I were paired with another man. Vin thought a certain well-known television actor might be right. Vin, the actor, and I had several meetings, and even pitched the show to Disney Productions and others, but without Paul and our easy repartee, the spark was missing. No one was interested. I wasn't even sure I was interested.

From the Journals of Ted Wentworth

Ran into my old buddy Ron Dick today. Haven't seen him in a long time. Told him about my quest, and my frustration that it's taking so long.

He said it's hard to find someone again, that the girls and I are still healing.

I said I don't believe that. It's been two years. Sharon always said she didn't want me to be alone.

That inspired him. He said I ought to join him for breakfast tomorrow morning at a thing called the Inside Edge. It's a bunch of high-energy early-risers. They meet at Remick's Restaurant at 6:30 A.M. Some very attractive women are there, he said.

I told him I'll show up.

The next morning, circuitous pathways that until then had wound mysteriously beyond the borders of time and space converged. Out there among those pathways, the subtle turns of chance and the unstoppable designs of destiny came together.

Ted Wentworth met Ron Dick in front of the two-story, New Orleans-style Remick's Restaurant, ready for Ted's introduction to a curious group of people who belonged to something called the Inside Edge.

As Ted walked through the entrance he felt a chill . . .

"Ron, she's here! I can feel it," he whispered.

"Great! Get ready to ask someone to dinner!"

"No . . . there's something odd about this. Normally, you know, I'd do that, but I have a feeling I've got to be very careful. I can't make that kind of move. It sounds crazy but, whichever one she is, she has to come to me in her own timing."

As I hosted the Orange County chapter meeting that morning in May, I was feeling really balanced for the first time since Paul died. The week in Kauai is what had done it for me.

I knew the audience well—friends and supporters who had been through the last nine months with me and were eager to find out how I was faring. But knowing that people can feel awkward around someone so recently bereaved, I wanted to put them at ease. I described how beautiful and restful Kauai had been, adding, "I'm enjoying my solitude so much, in fact, that the first man who looks at me with the idea of a live-in relationship may just become the victim of an ax murder!"

They responded with shocked laughter and applause.

After the meeting, as I mingled with the group, a playful voice behind me asked, "Will you live with *me?*"

I spun around and looked into the bright blue eyes of a man I'd never seen before—a guest, a newcomer. I raised my hand and waved it as if I held an ax, and he ducked away. I learned later that this man, a widower, told his daughter when he arrived home that as he entered Remick's, he had the oddest sensation the new wife he'd been looking for was inside.

For me, however, after the moment of our meeting I thought no more about him.

NINETEEN

I BEGAN trying out new hairstyles and wardrobe choices, finding the experimentation fun. Because Paul had been so visual, I'd delegated most appearance decisions to him. He noticed everything about me, even if I changed my fingernail polish, and he had a strong preference regarding which hairdo and lipstick color I chose.

Now I was eager to try new looks and discover what *I* liked. So I abandoned the sprayed and sideswept style I'd worn for years, got a perm, and cut my hair in a sort of waif look. Instead of the classic tailored clothes Paul favored, I bought several very, very feminine outfits.

Judging by the raised eyebrows my outfits elicited at Edge meetings, I realized that some of my experiments were less successful than others—or, depending on who was doing the eyebrow raising, more successful.

One day after the San Diego meeting, Lexi and I met Margaret Wright, the chapter manager, at an elegant restaurant called Mr. A's at the top of a skyscraper in San Diego. A man in his late thirties entered the elevator as we stepped out and gave me the eye, obviously approving. Lexi and Margaret both commented on it, and I sat up straighter through lunch, delighted to know that at forty-eight I was still attractive—at least, to the discerning few.

On Mother's Day, Lexi gave me a gift certificate for Victoria's Secret. "Use it to buy some sexy lingerie, Mom."

"Not yet, sweetheart. Maybe someday . . ."

———

Because I still felt Paul's protective presence, I usually wasn't lonely. And I often lunched with my men friends from the Inside Edge. Still, after a few months I found myself wondering what it would be like to go out on a date, a real date. I remembered Paul's promise to send someone. I had recognized Paul the minute I saw him. Would that happen again?

———

One evening, just after I checked into my room in the hotel in La Jolla where the San Diego chapter held its meetings, my phone rang. One of the Edge members invited me to dinner that evening. I thought he probably wanted to talk about something having to do with Edge business, but was surprised to realize over dinner this man seemed to be romantically inclined. *Oh dear, I'm not interested in him at all in that way. What do I do now?*

———

When Shellie Fraddin gave a talk the next morning to the Edge on the subject of flirting, I realized I hadn't thought about it in years. For those who were not clear about the matter, Shellie explained flirting is simply being friendly in a way that tells the other person you're available.

Am I available? Am I really? I suddenly found myself embarrassed even to be thinking that. Or flirting.

Then she said, "Now everybody please stand up and look around. Pick someone of the opposite sex and walk up to that person and say something as outrageous as you dare."

I spotted an old friend, an attractive man I knew was safely in a relationship. Blushing madly, I blurted, "Hey, Bill! I think you're really hot!"

He hugged me and tried his line on me. "Hey, Diana! You have a really great body!"

We laughed out loud at the boldness of what we'd said, and with that simple exercise, the idea of flirting became funny and much, much easier for me.

At the Edge meeting the following week, I saw the man with the bright blue eyes again. He was wearing a new-member tag now, not a guest tag. His name, I saw, was Ted Wentworth.

Since an important part of my job was welcoming new people, I approached him, smiled, and said, "Hello! You're a new member . . . Welcome!" We chatted for a few minutes. Before I moved on, I invited him to sit at my table at the following week's meeting so I could learn more about him and introduce him to some other members. I was just being friendly, doing my job.

But by the next week, our previous encounter had slipped my mind. Following the meeting, I noticed him again as though for the first time and said the same thing I'd said the previous week, "Hello! You're a new member . . . Welcome!"

An amused look crossed his face. "Yes. Don't you remember we spoke last week? You even invited me to sit at your table."

Flustered, I mumbled, "Oh. Well, why didn't you? There was an extra seat."

"Because, Diana, you're really *very* unapproachable."

I was dumbfounded, and a little defensive. "Really? I don't believe anyone else thinks so."

He grinned, "I know! It's my problem! I'm working on it." That said, he turned on his heel and walked away.

What a strange man, I thought, completely missing his irony.

———

Ted Wentworth had definitely made an impression on me at our third encounter, and when he didn't show up at the next week's breakfast meeting I became concerned—strictly for business reasons, I told myself. He might actually have been offended enough to cancel his membership!

After the meeting I looked through the Edge records to find Ted's phone number. I learned he was an attorney, with an office in Newport Beach, and telephoned his office to tell him he'd been missed. He told me he'd had an early court appearance, and then in a friendly way asked how long it had been since my husband died. For the next fifteen minutes we talked about the big thing we had in common: having lost our spouses to cancer. His wife had died two years earlier. He asked if I'd gone through the Kübler-Ross stages of grief.

"Bargaining, denial, anger, depression, and lethargy. Denial is the hardest one to spot."

It was something for me to think about.

———

The following week, standing at the door welcoming members, I watched Ted Wentworth approach. I smiled and said, "I've been thinking about what you said. I really don't think I'm in denial."

"Hah!" he said emphatically, looking amused, as he marched past me into the ballroom. He never came near me or spoke to me the rest of that morning. *The man is strange*, I thought. I resolved to keep my distance.

Weeks later, on a Saturday, the Inside Edge Annual Picnic was to be held. The afternoon before, as I wrote in my journal, I was sure I heard Paul say, *Buy a squirt gun!*

"You're kidding!" I said aloud.

No, I'm not kidding. I was right about the dining table, wasn't I?

I couldn't argue with that, so I drove to a toy store and chose a silly squirt gun that looked like a hot dog in a bun. I thought, *This will liven up the party.*

A crowd of three or four hundred people began pouring through the entrance to an Orange County park just before noon, as our staff and I finished putting up booths and games. Members and their families spread picnic blankets on the grass and settled in under the trees that rimmed the circumference. A lively volleyball game was in progress.

Pulling out my hot-dog-in-a-bun water weapon, I playfully squirted a number of people when they weren't looking. But their reaction wasn't as playful as I expected. *Maybe I really am unapproachable*, I thought.

As if on cue, I saw Ted Wentworth, the widower who, right after my recent ax-murder threat in front of the whole Orange County chapter, had asked me to live with him. He looked very cute—a bit like Robin Williams in shorts and a baseball cap. I ducked behind a tree, and as he walked past I squirted him too—but his reaction was the opposite of the others.

"Oh . . . *really?*" he said when he spotted me. "We'll see about *that!*"

Frightened by his mock-vengeful look, I sprinted away. Ted gave chase and we streaked past all the picnickers, past all the games, before he caught up with me. Then he wrestled the gun out of my hand and squirted me back, right in the face!

So much for being breakable. I was in shock. Mouth open, I stared at him, speechless.

Ted just grinned. Then, looking momentarily chagrined at the damage he'd done to my mascara, he said, "Aw, I'm sorry, pretty lady. Here, come with me."

He led me by the arm to a nearby water fountain, where he set about refilling my squirt gun. Handing it back, he cheerfully asked, "So, are you going to have dinner with me?"

TWENTY

I HADN'T the slightest romantic interest in Ted Wentworth. He was cute, but I was thinking only that this would be a step in learning the logistics of midlife dating.

In the middle of the next week, on July 19, I was scheduled to give an evening talk to the Writer's Edge, one of the "sub-Edges" of the Orange County chapter of the Inside Edge. So I suggested to Ted that he and I could meet for dinner beforehand. He'd been so unpredictable I wanted to make sure I'd provided myself with a way to flee. I thought we'd just have a short evening together, then join the others. We arranged to meet at 5:00 at a restaurant he suggested.

We discovered very quickly when we talked during dinner, however, that we had more in common than having lost our spouses to cancer. Lexi was nearly the same age as Ted's daughters Christy and Kathy. We had both studied meditation in the early '70s and still shared enthusiasm for it, as well as for psychology and many of the same books. He was so full of different interests and so fascinating that I was a bit disappointed our time together went so quickly. Not for a moment had I wanted to escape.

I wasn't surprised when Ted called me the next day to set up another date the following week. In fact, I was delighted, and this time our phone conversation continued where we'd left off. Thereafter he called nearly every day. But we lived sixty miles apart and spending time together was going to be difficult. He lived in the ocean-side community of Corona del Mar, in Orange County, a part of Newport Beach that Paul and I had always loved. I still lived on the west side of Los Angeles, in Pacific Palisades. Thus did our friendship, at least in the beginning, deepen more over the telephone than in person.

Ted told me of his thirty-year career as a medical and human rights attorney, and of his passion for ranching and boating. I quickly realized he was passionate about every facet of his life.

I told him I was glad to learn of the wide range of his interests, and to discover what a steady, reliable man he was. I said our conversations now felt comfortable and safe.

"*Safe?*" he asked. "Why is safety an issue? Safe from what?"

I answered—truthfully—that his antic, rapid-fire sense of humor initially caused me to put up my guard. "Paul was quiet, modulated, and poetic. He always reminded me of Sean Connery," I said. "But *you* remind me of Robin Williams! You're totally unpredictable."

"Ah, yes," he said, not displeased at the comparison. "I've always looked at life through an entirely different slat in the fence . . ."

Of course, that was it. I'd always been sure *I* had a good sense of humor—don't all people think they have a great sense of humor and superb taste in clothes?—but talking to Ted was teaching me I was often humor-impaired. And even if I was sometimes mildly amusing, *he* was a great, merry, rolling-along, madcap, chortling, chuckling, nonstop generator of mirth and downright knee-slapping fun. Looking through a different slat in the fence indeed.

Okay, as he had said, I probably *was* quite unapproachable. Formidable. Maybe aloof? Regarding myself as "significant"? But he loved to poke fun at me, and feeling significant around him was impossible. He had a natural merriment that seemed to emerge from being an amused witness to himself and his own actions, with an accompanying sense that being human was itself absurd. In one conversation he said, "God is a comedian playing before an audience that's afraid to laugh."

For our second date a week later, Ted invited me to his home for dinner. As an author of cookbooks, I was rarely invited for anyone's home cooking, and I was intrigued with this man who could not be intimidated. Actually, considering my uncertainty about the dating game, I was the one feeling intimidated.

I didn't really remember much about dating or about single men in general. How was I to act? What would I say? I wasn't exactly a teenager who could ask pertly, "What's your sign?" Further, despite the five or six telephone conversations we'd had since our first date, my imagination failed me when I thought about being in his home, or any man's home. Not having dated in three decades, I wasn't even sure how a single man lived.

I followed Ted's precise directions to the very top of Spyglass Hill in the high, rolling terrain of Corona del Mar. He was waiting for me outside his single-story, hilltop, Mediterranean home. Stepping out of my car, I saw beds of vivid, multicolored impatiens next to a protective peach-colored exterior wall and a heavy, white wrought-iron gate. Leading me through the gate, he took me on a tour of the lush interior garden, which was skirted by a pale-peach stone patio. There were hanging baskets of fuchsias and large white pots with every imaginable kind and color of roses.

I was amazed.

"When Sharon was ill, I needed a project to just lose myself in." He explained that he had the pale-peach sandstone rocks quarried and trucked in from Sedona, Arizona. "Making this garden beautiful so she could enjoy it from the window kept me busy for months."

I understood.

He led us around the side of the house through an arch covered with wisteria, stepping on stones that were nearly covered by a green, luscious ground cover called baby tears. We went to the patio in back and I realized the house was perched on the edge of a canyon overlooking all of the Los Angeles basin. It was lovely.

Ted barbecued fish on the patio, served it with a baked potato, and forgot the rolls in the oven. After dinner he suggested a walk around nearby Balboa Island. "Would you like to go by car or on my motorcycle?"

I was mildly dazed at the alternative, but also intrigued. I hadn't been on a motorcycle since Paul and I were first married, and when I answered "motorcycle," his eyes lit up. Later I learned the choice he'd offered me was one of his "girlfriend tests." Choosing the car earned a low grade. Choosing the motorcycle earned a high one. I'd passed the test.

Paul had taught me how to be a good rider, how to hold on and lean with the driver into the turns, so I got on the rear seat of Ted's sleek, maroon Honda Gold Wing, put my arms around his waist, and rested my cheek against his back. Off we went, my new curly hair flying in the wind that whipped past us as we rode. Later he told me a woman communicated a lot by the way she held onto him. I asked him what I'd communicated. He dismissed me with a glance that seemed to say, "Oh, you want to know too much too soon."

Ten minutes later, Ted parked the motorcycle near the bridge that led to Balboa Island. We walked across and for the next two hours were in a world of enchantment. When I was a teenager, I used to visit a friend there, and the island had changed little: charming little stores on Marine Avenue and ice cream shops selling chocolate-dipped frozen bananas as well as Balboa Bars (chocolate-covered ice cream bars encrusted with your choice of assorted nuts and candies).

I spotted the old familiar Ferris wheel across the bay and told Ted I just had to ride, so Ted took my hand to help me onto the ferry for the ride to Balboa Peninsula and the Fun Zone. He didn't let go of my hand even during a walk along the oceanfront back to the ferry and the two-mile walk around the rest of the island. Holding his huge, weathered hand was for me the strangest feeling after so many years of holding Paul's smooth artist's hands . . .

———

A few days after our walk I wrote in my journal:

What contagious energy he has! I had been exhausted this afternoon, but when he phoned I felt revitalized. We talk for what seems like hours, about everything, like two giddy teenagers. Now we've decided to spend most of Saturday together and I am excited and a bit frightened. Ted tells me, "Reach out to me as much as you want to. I will only encourage you to reach out even more."

———

I felt a gathering of butterflies around my heart as I drove up Spyglass Hill to his house on Saturday morning to spend a whole day with him. I told myself if I could go rappelling off a bridge, I could certainly risk seeing where this might be going.

"I want to spend some quality time with you," he had said, and I agreed. He took my hand. "Come with me." Then he led me to his flower-filled back patio. In the far distance, fifty miles to the north, the famous Hollywood sign was a dot high in the range of hills bordering the Movie Capital.

Ted offered me a chair facing the view, got us some sodas, and pulled a chair up nearby. He talked enthusiastically, gesturing animatedly. He told me stories from his life, personal and professional. He ended with a long tale of a crazy investment he'd made in Hawaii years earlier. I loved watching his face and was impressed that he could share both the good and the foolish about himself.

Eventually he said, "What would you like to do now? We have some options. We can drive to Laguna and walk around and look at art galleries. I can take you for a ride in my airplane. Or we can cruise around the bay in my boat." This man was full of surprises and I was not just a bit in awe of the lifestyle he'd created for himself and that he seemed so eager to share.

"Are you joking? Do you really have an airplane?"

He gave me a silly grin.

"And you fly it yourself?"

"No," he said. "Not usually. I'm still taking lessons. But if you want to go, I think I can remember enough to fly it by myself today."

By that time I didn't know if he was certifiably mad. Did he really intend to take me up in a plane he barely knew how to fly?

I tried to articulate my concern in a way that wouldn't insult him. "Will it be safe?" I asked.

"You never know in those things," he responded, smiling sweetly.

Seeing the doubt on my face, he stopped teasing and set me at ease by describing how he'd decided to take flying lessons seventeen years earlier. While his law partners had been enjoying two-martini lunches, Ted headed to the airport for years of bag lunches and flight instruction that didn't let up until he was an instrument-rated pilot. Since then he had criss-crossed the United States, including Alaska, many times and had even flown his wife, Sharon, to the Bahamas on four occasions for cancer treatments.

We drove—in his car this time—to a private entrance at nearby John Wayne Airport and then along rows of small private planes tied down to the tarmac. We pulled up under the wings of a brightly painted, single-engine plane Ted identified as a Cessna Turbo 210.

Ted helped me into the plane, checked it over thoroughly, adjusted my seat belt, and closed the door. As he started the engine I watched the black, three-bladed propeller turn into a blur. Less than a year earlier, before Paul became ill, he and I had taken a flying lesson and dreamed of learning to pilot our own plane. As I recalled that fact, the events of the present moment suddenly seemed almost mystically uncanny. *Paul might choose someone like this for me,* I thought.

Within minutes we were watching the surf of Newport Beach pass below us as we headed over the ocean for Catalina Island. Ted inserted an audiotape called "Deep Breakfast" and the headphones came alive with haunting, heart-lifting music that seemed to keep time with the cadences of our adventure.

I was thrilled by the fairy-tale quality of our flight that day. We watched the island grow closer and larger as we cruised above the deep blue Catalina channel. It was dotted with sailboats and the long wakes of powerboats. Thirteen miles long and just two miles wide at its midpoint, Catalina was lightly populated. Its circumference was indented with little coves, some with a hundred boats at anchor and some with only one or two. We turned left and flew toward the middle of the island, where, coming into view, I saw a ribbon of pavement atop a mesa bordered by a few buildings.

"Catalina Island Airport," Ted said through the intercom, pointing at the strip of pavement ahead. It had only been a fifteen-minute, over-water flight, and we were now in an entirely different world.

Ted taxied to where we could tie down with some other small planes. He led me into a nearby building where he paid the landing fee, then we walked into the spacious patio of the airport restaurant. Deciding against the buffalo burgers suggested on the menu (the island was known for its overpopulation of buffalo), we ordered a salad, iced tea, and what Ted said were the best chocolate-chip cookies anywhere, all of which was served outdoors on a tiled patio, beneath an umbrella. The setting reminded me of a lanai in coastal Mexico. Hummingbirds were everywhere checking out the hibiscus flowers and hovering around the diners. Ted said he loved to study and learn about birds. He told me about the habits of the hummingbirds—they were called "Anna's hummingbirds," he said.

"It may sound strange to you, but just after Sharon died, something really uncanny happened. I was eating breakfast and a little sparrow on the patio tapped repeatedly on the sliding glass door. It returned day after day to tap, at the same time, for weeks." He told me he was sure that Sharon had influenced the bird. He added that her nickname in college was 'Bird' and she had a special affinity for them.

I told him then about feeling Paul's presence almost constantly just after he died. I was relieved to be able to talk freely about it to someone who seemed to understand me fully. I said, "It's strange, but being able to talk to you about Paul relaxes me. It takes some kind of strain off. And it makes me feel closer to *you*."

"In what way?"

"In a warm and fuzzy way."

The next day Ted sent me eighteen long-stemmed red roses with a card that said, "Dear Warm, watch the buds. Like a friendship, each opens a petal at a time." He signed it "Fuzzy."

Ted also telephoned me several times over the next few days and we talked for hours. Our comfort with each other was growing quickly. I was speechless when he suggested we take his yacht to Catalina the following weekend. He didn't fail to notice the change in my mood.

"Tell me what you're feeling," he said.

His dazzling lifestyle, his take-charge personality was all so new. Suddenly, all of the old intimidation and wariness came back. When men and women are together, regardless of how the friendship is going, regardless of whether the players are in midlife or adolescence, questions about physical intimacy always identify the point at which a major change is on the way. When you're with someone who is clearly uninteresting, the choice is so simple. But with someone you care about . . .

I addressed the matter directly. "I'm feeling a little frightened. Our friendship seems to be moving awfully quickly into something more. I really love spending time with you, and I'm not sure I'm ready for us to spend a whole weekend together." I waited through several uneasy moments of silence, then added, "Can you understand that?"

"Of course, I can," he said. "I don't mean to rush you."

When we hung up, I was pretty sure no damage had been done. But I'd been true to myself, which was the most important thing to me. I knew that many women would not have failed to go with this man on his yacht. A weekend on the yacht would probably have been their *goal.*

I wondered if I'd hear from him again.

I found out soon enough.

TWENTY-ONE

OVER THE NEXT two months we spent so much time on the phone that Ted offered to split my phone bill with me. Though I was busy running all three chapters of the Edge and Ted was trying one of the biggest cases of his career, we talked several times daily. He had good business judgment and I enjoyed bouncing some of my ideas for the Edge off him, valuing his opinions.

One Saturday he surprised me by asking me to come with him to see a fifty-foot yacht like the one he was having built, asking me to suggest any changes in the layout of the galley—the yacht term for the kitchen—so he could tell the builders before it was too late. He wondered if the counters needed to be a little higher because I was so tall.

"Because of the way things are going between us, I want to be sure you and the yacht are a good fit."

I admit I felt thrilled to be included so completely in his life . . . but a bit like Cinderella dusting herself off one moment and, in the next, finding herself at the ball. Afterward, Ted took me to dinner and the theatre with his daughters before they headed back to college.

My friends were hearing about Ted now and making sure they got a chance to meet him. Candace had heard me referring to him as a teddy bear and wasn't exactly certain what I meant. But after she sat next to him at a meeting she said, "He's much more than a teddy bear. He's as solid as a rock, and *very* sexy."

Tim was concerned, telling me I was acting fourteen years old. "Let it stand the test of time," he cautioned. Other friends warned me about letting the relationship become a sexual one too soon, reminding me that sex changes everything.

Lexi was beginning to worry too. "Who is this guy and where is this going, Mom?"

I told her, "I realize I'm acting a little giddy from all the attention, but I do know what I'm doing. Please trust me."

In the meantime, I was discovering how extraordinarily intuitive Ted was. Paul had seemed sometimes to read my mind, but perhaps that was because we were often having the same thoughts.

I sensed, though, that he would choose to send someone who was so keenly perceptive. It was an ability I was particularly able to appreciate because of my own intuitive sense. But while I tended to see far-reaching patterns in people and events, Ted seemed especially attuned to physical sensations.

While writing at my computer one evening at home, I had a sudden, sharp stomach pain. It didn't last long, and as it subsided I attributed it to have eaten too much popcorn. I forgot about it until fifteen minutes later, when the telephone rang.

"What was that pain?"

"What pain?"

"The one in your lower abdomen."

"Oh . . . ! How did you know about *that?*"

He told me he had been out walking around Balboa Island, felt an ache, and realized it wasn't his own. He had a notion it was mine, and so he called.

I was amazed, for I'd never heard of anyone having an ability like that. I asked him if he felt such things all the time.

His voice took on a soft intensity. "Oh, no. If I did, I'd constantly be feeling everyone else's aches and pains. But it comes in handy in my practice."

"How do you do it?"

"What I do isn't some kind of psychic trick or special talent. It's just an ability to quiet my mind and be aware of what's underneath. It's all very natural and effortless, and it depends on how and where I direct my attention. The spiritual universe, the *real* universe, is nowhere near as limited as the everyday world of material things. It's a place of consciousness and energy, of freedom and flow, where knowing and feeling are constantly alive and interpenetrating each other.

"Not only that," he added, "*all* people are extremely sensitive to such things. They just don't know it. We all have the ability to feel exquisite things beyond the boundaries of our physical senses."

"If you can sense pain, can you sense other problems as well?" I asked.

"Sure. It's really all the same stuff. Wherever I move my attention, the awareness follows." He told me that when he was with other people, he would sometimes even become aware that they had undiagnosed or misdiagnosed medical problems. "That's handy in my law practice," he said wryly. "It can save me a lot of time figuring out what's really going on."

255

He also noted that he would often feel the presence of other people in him—their spirit or energy—especially if someone happened to be thinking about him at the moment or was trying to communicate with him. "When they're directing their attention to me, I feel it."

He said that love is fundamental to the whole process. Not the kind of love that comes as intense feelings or is needy, but pure love that's just a quiet awareness of being. "I never become aware of another person without loving that person in the process. That's because we all exist in a universal field—a field of love—a love that's in everyone, that *is* everyone. It extends beyond all boundaries and makes all things possible. Loving isn't really something you do. It's something you are. You discover it as yourself and as everything around you."

I was moved by the beauty and the passion of his understanding, especially because it all seemed more than just ideas to him. It seemed to represent how he lived, and I felt so fortunate that I had attracted such a man into my life.

———

The next day, when Candace was helping me do some redecorating at home, I told her about Ted's spiritual philosophies and his ability to feel what was going on with me.

"That's all fine," she said with a grin, "but didn't you tell me he sometimes doesn't even notice what you're wearing?"

I laughed. "I'm willing to wait on that one. He'll get the idea eventually. I'll just remind him now and then." But in the meantime, I thought, he was a man with a beautiful mind, with a hugely loving heart, and that was quite enough for me.

Still, his psychic sensitivity was intriguing, and later in the day, after Candace had left, I had an idea. I mentally sent him a message to telephone me. Within minutes the phone rang.

What? he said.

Hmmm, I thought, after we'd laughed together and hung up. *That worked. Let's see if he gets this!* So I sent him a mental image that I'd like some roses.

When no flowers arrived that day, a Thursday, I didn't give the matter much thought. But the day after *that,* my first at Ted's ranch in Temecula, about ninety miles from Los Angeles, I had a big surprise.

Our relationship was deepening and I could clearly see where it was going. So could Ted, though he was comfortable letting me move at my own pace. Since the almost-yachting weekend, I had realized Ted was becoming the most important man in my life. My nesting instincts were warming as I learned to trust him more and more.

He had been saying he wanted to show me his ranch. I told him gently that my unease about the yachting weekend had passed, and that a weekend at his ranch sounded great, but I wasn't sure where it might lead, if anywhere. I asked him if he would nevertheless be interested in my presence at the ranch.

"The greatest gift you offer me is your presence," he responded. "How can you imagine that your just being there with me will not be enough?"

Any charming man could have said it, but my experience with Ted had shown me he meant it. I looked forward to our weekend at his ranch with a growing love in my heart.

———

It was a hot August afternoon. Ted was at the wheel, the back of his Range Rover brimming with weekend luggage, sacks of vegetables, and warm loaves of fresh bread from a farmers' market we discovered along the way. Exiting the freeway, we turned right on Rancho California Road and climbed westward along a winding highway into the rolling hills.

"If we're lucky, we'll see a tarantula!" Ted said expectantly. His twinkling eyes met mine. "This is the time of year the poor guys go a-courtin'."

At my horrified look, he continued, "Aw, Diana, I've never met the ones from Beverly Hills, but these guys have heart."

A few miles up the hill he turned left onto a narrow, paved road that meandered past a white-fenced yard where three goats cooled themselves in a small patch of shade beneath a willow tree. We continued past five-, ten-, and twenty-acre estates, ranch houses, and persimmon and citrus groves.

By a giant oak tree, the pavement ended. Bumping along a washboard-surfaced dirt road, we soon arrived at a fork. The left branch led us beneath a narrow tunnel of sycamore trees framing a dirt bridge that spanned a small creek. The creek had obviously flooded the winter before. Coasting to a stop in the center of the bridge, Ted turned off the engine.

"Listen . . . the sounds of the creek, the birds, the insects . . . and listen to the silence behind it all."

I heard a hum of insects and a soft breeze through the sycamore leaves, and the welcome fragrance of vegetation. After a minute, the creek croaked.

"That's the local frog. I call him Caruso. He's happy I've brought you here!"

258

The unspoiled beauty of the spot, the sunlight and shadows playing through the trees . . . it all captivated me. This was a new world for me. I'd had few country experiences, and now I encountered surprises at every turn. Among the twisted logs on a curve upstream, the city girl spotted a three-foot patch of greenery.

"Isn't that watercress?"

Ted nodded.

I asked, "Is it safe to eat? I could make us some lovely soup."

Ted opened the Range Rover's door, removed his shoes and socks and tossed them in the back, then waded into the creek. He carefully severed two huge bunches from their roots with his pocketknife.

"This is safe to eat when the water is fresh and moving. But most people don't realize they should leave the roots, so it can keep growing."

That man—now standing knee-deep in a stream, baseball cap askew, radiating aliveness—was not only gathering bouquets of watercress for me, but he had also been placing at my feet a multitude of new adventures. What a welcome new friend he was in my world, one that only a few months ago seemed to hold such little promise.

Half a mile farther, Ted pointed out a white pole protruding from the base of an oak tree. "That marks the north boundary of Eagle's Ridge Ranch." My eyes traveled beyond the pole and across a gully overgrown with graceful California oaks, then on to rolling hills intersected with narrow farm roads and dotted with young avocado and grapefruit trees.

The vehicle topped a hill and Ted turned right into a gravel driveway. Espaliered red rose bushes spilled over split-rail fences as we drove to the highest point. How different it looked from the picture

I'd painted in my mind of a working ranch, which I'd assumed would consist of precise rows of trees on flat dusty land, like the countless such groves lining California highways between Santa Barbara and San Diego. As we rounded the final upward curve, I suddenly saw the vastness of the 360-degree view and gasped at the beauty of it.

Ted parked in front of a modest, single-story ranch house. The wood and etched-glass door beckoned invitingly.

In the entry hall inside the house, I saw two huge bouquets of flowers. One, with a mixture of summer flowers, had a note welcoming me to Eagle's Ridge Ranch. The other was a vase of long-stemmed roses.

Ted said, "I saw no point in responding to your request for roses yesterday. You wouldn't have enjoyed them for more than a few hours that way. Now you've got them for the whole weekend."

I was astonished. Had I really ordered roses psychically?

He showed me around, hanging my clothes in the closet next to his. The furnishings were perfect. He'd hired a former girlfriend, an interior designer, to decorate it in the best Southwestern style, in shades of ivory, dark gray-violet, and dusty rose. I couldn't imagine changing a thing.

Ted eagerly took my hand and led me through a sliding glass door to the petunia-bordered lawn in back. Approaching the far end of the lawn, I saw we were atop the very highest hill in the surrounding area, overlooking rolling valleys and meadows, small ranches, and, in the far distance, a silvery strip of Pacific Ocean. Ted's backyard had a near 360-degree view that extended from the 12,000-foot snow-covered San Jacinto Mountains forty miles to the east, to Camp Pendleton and the sea thirty miles to the west.

Leading me further around the perimeter, he drew my attention to an orchard just below the house, consisting of perhaps three dozen fruit trees.

"Something is in season all year 'round," he said proudly. The sunlight and stillness of the moment warmed us like a benediction. I knew I was feeling something I couldn't explain; the place had a haunting familiarity. It was calling me to be something new, and at the same time calling me home.

That evening, together, we watched the sun set from two rope-and-wood slat swings hanging beneath the eaves of the patio roof. Strains of Zamfir, a pan flute virtuoso, wafted from the music system in the house and Ted whistled along in perfect harmony.

His eyes met mine and he looked quizzical. "Do you suppose . . . ?" he asked. I knew he was asking if I might be his destiny—the one he'd been seeking for so long.

I wrote in my journal that evening: *The beauty of being with Ted is far beyond my expectations. We are deliciously tuned into each other, and I sometimes wonder if Paul and Sharon aren't influencing our coming together from the other side.*

TWENTY-TWO

THE NEXT DAY, on the dirt road leading to town, Ted suddenly braked the car to a dusty halt.

"What's wrong?" I asked.

"Come with me! I've found someone you have to meet."

I got out of the car and ran toward the front to see Ted sitting on his haunches, his hand flat on the ground, palm up, in front of a tarantula.

I screamed as I backed away.

"Oh, don't be silly!" he said softly, not taking his eyes off the spider. "He's a wonderful guy. Come here—give me your hand."

"No!"

"Look, Diana! They never bite unless they feel threatened." The huge black furry spider touched Ted's hand with his two front feet. Now, having tested the safety of what he'd come upon, the spider seemed to decide crawling ahead was worth the risk. He moved slowly ahead until his entire body was atop Ted's flattened palm.

"Look how sweet he is. The gentlest, sweetest thing," Ted said softly.

I approached warily.

"Give me your hand, Diana. I promise it's safe." With trepidation, my heart pounding, I finally—reluctantly—offered my hand, but only after nearly pulling it away several times.

"Just put your hand down on the warm dirt next to mine." The tarantula began to move toward me and I watched in awe and dread.

"You may be who he's looking for. See the hooks on his legs? He's about eight years old and searching for a girlfriend!"

The instant I felt the soft legs touch my skin, my heart melted and I found the creature suddenly beautiful.

Enthralled, I asked the huge soft spider, "Hey, how did you guys get such a bad reputation?"

Ted Wentworth and I became lovers. And as a lover, Ted was wonderful . . . patient, sensitive, joyous. He made me feel treasured. The rest of my life was on hold now, including the book I was writing—this book—while I focused on the increasing depth of our relationship.

The more I saw of Ted, the more I loved and appreciated him. I watched him in court, with his friends from all over the state, and at Eagle's Ridge—the ranch. Ted employed three men full-time to tend the newly planted trees. Besides 10,000 Haas avocado and Coastal Ruby grapefruit trees, the orchard below the house had peaches, nectarines, red flame table grapes, tangerines, blood oranges, pomegranates, persimmons, apples, and two kinds of figs for family use.

The dirt roads that wove around the hillsides were bordered with thousands of palm trees planted at angles so their slightly curved trunks would be interesting to look at when they were sold and replanted by landscapers. The 108 cultivated acres were spotted with young trees that looked from a distance as though they were spread like icing along the top of a half-mile-long ridge, with the cozy and comfortable ranch house at the center.

I was in love with the ranch and with Ted's concept of stewardship. He killed nothing, going to the trouble of relocating rattlers and researching ways to harmlessly discourage the gophers and coyotes, whose offspring teethed on the miles of soft, black plastic irrigation pipes.

Galumph, galumph, galumph. My eyes flew open, my heart was pounding. I could see only the silhouette of the bedpost in the moonlit bedroom of Ted's home in Corona del Mar. What had awakened me? I heard Ted's even breathing. He was asleep with both arms wrapped around me holding us together like two spoons.

Then again, the soft *galumph, galumph, galumph* of kitten-like feet scampering on the carpet followed by cellophane crinkling in the corner.

Ted, suddenly awake too, said, "What was *that?*"

"I don't know, but it's not a mouse. Something bigger . . . much bigger . . ."

The crinkling had to be coming from the bags of peanuts and birdseed Ted keeps next to the sliding glass patio doors for feeding the finches, doves, and scrub jays who show up outdoors every morning. But whatever was visiting that night was an uninvited *indoor* guest.

Ted slid out of bed. I watched the outline of his nude form as he disappeared down the hall, returned with a sticky rodent trap, and placed it next to the bag of nuts. He was soon back under the soft covers and we drifted off to sleep again.

Flop-flop, flop-flop, was the new sound that woke us. We'd captured something and Ted bounded out of bed. I retreated further under the covers, clinging to remnants of warmth and coziness.

"Don't you want to see it?"

"Are you kidding? It's two in the morning!"

"Oh, come on. He's really something special—a beautiful Norwegian rat!"

I peeked out to see an immense silver rat staring wildly at me; his body, not counting the tail, was at least twelve inches long. With his right side firmly embedded in the trap's clear yellow glue, he wasn't at all happy.

I squealed and scooted even further under the covers.

I heard a clattering from the kitchen. Moments later the front door banged shut, the electric garage door opened, and a car drove off. *What can he be doing?* I wondered before drifting back to sleep.

The next thing I knew, Ted was sliding back into bed with me.

"Did you kill it?" I asked, cringing at the thought.

"Of course not! You know I never kill anything! I grabbed him by the nape of the neck and poured vegetable oil over him to get him unstuck from the glue board. After I pulled him off the trap, there we were, looking at one another. I realized I didn't want him anywhere around here, so we jumped in the car."

"Without your clothes on?"

"Yep. I looked down and realized I had that problem too, but with a rat in my hand, getting dressed wasn't one of my options!"

"Where did you go?"

He laughed. "I drove with my left hand on the steering wheel down the hill to the house of a psychologist I know. I dropped him off on her lawn."

"Why there?"

"He seemed *awfully* happy to be there! And, I figured with what she charges, she could donate a little time to handle his post-traumatic stress disorder."

This new man of mine was going to take some getting used to . . .

———

We began to spend every weekend together, alternating between going to the ranch, flying somewhere in his plane, or cruising to Catalina Island on his boat and mooring in Emerald Bay. Having hours and even days of extended, intimate companionship carried us to a deeper level of involvement, in which we would see new and unfamiliar aspects of each other's lives. In our case, it also led to one of our first major confrontations.

One Saturday morning, at a hotel in Santa Barbara, we rose before dawn in order to get an early start for the airport where we'd left Ted's plane. We planned to fly to Columbia, a tiny, historically preserved town on old Route 49 in the California Gold Country, where we would have lunch and attend the annual Fiddle and Banjo Contest before returning to Los Angeles that evening for a formal dinner party.

Ted wore blue jeans and cowboy boots, a get-up he described as "two hundred pounds of rompin', stompin' California romance." He was leaning against the bathroom door, talking with me as I put on my makeup—the first time he'd seen me doing that. In those days it was fashionable (or at least *I* thought it was) to wear false eyelashes for the dressy kind of occasion we'd be attending that evening. As I got ready, Ted was in high spirits, delivering a passionate lecture on the nature of love.

Then the moment came for me to put on those eyelashes. I felt shy about doing it in front of him and wondered if I should tell him I needed to close the door for some privacy. Deciding that would seem rude, I proceeded wordlessly with my task, holding the little strip of lashes in my hand and pulling off the old glue with my fingers—something I'd done hundreds of times. While I listened intently to the point he was making, I took a tiny tube of glue, squeezed a thin line of it along the lash, leaned close to the mirror, and laid it on my lid, pressing it as close as possible to my natural lashes.

As I did so, I remained fascinated by what Ted was telling me. This was an area in which he had done a lot of thinking and had considerable experience. *"Eros,"* he was saying, "the stage of 'falling in love,' is exciting and beautiful while it lasts. But the next stage, *agape,* is even greater. In *agape* we find a subtle love, as sweet as *eros* is powerful. Many people, however, mistake *eros* for true love . . ."

Then he fell silent. The whole bathroom was suddenly drenched in silence. Right in the middle of his sentence, deep in his impassioned discussion about love, Ted simply stopped talking. He wasn't standing in the doorway any longer either.

I was *mortified!* I was sure I knew why he'd fallen silent and left. I had clearly crossed some invisible line by putting on my eyelashes while he was watching. Lipstick would have been okay. Mascara, likewise. But false eyelashes—no. I had totally turned him off.

I felt like a fool. I was embarrassed. I'd always heard that certain layers of the feminine mystery mustn't be disclosed to a man, but I'd never hidden anything from Paul and, in this new situation, I was taking the same attitude toward Ted. It was clearly a mistake though. He'd seen me at my unglamorous, phony worst, and didn't like it *at all.*

I wondered if an apology would fix things. But an apology for what? I shouldn't have to apologize for my feelings about how to look my best at a social occasion, should I? I shouldn't have to defend my concept of *femininity*, should I? I had a right to wear false eyelashes if I wanted to, didn't I? In fact, I could do *whatever* I wanted to, couldn't I?

But that wasn't the point, was it? The point was, regardless of how right or wrong I felt I was, I had unthinkingly driven this wonderful man out of the bathroom, perhaps even out of the hotel bedroom, maybe out of all future bedrooms, and most probably my life.

Hoping not to look like a foolish, desperate adolescent, I pretended composure and went into the bedroom to make things better. He gave me a blank look, an absolutely uncomprehending stare. It wasn't judgmental or critical. It was just empty. As far as he was concerned, I wasn't even in the room. He was obviously turned off and trying to figure out how to tell me he was through with our relationship and so disappointed in the overly made-up creature I had turned out to be.

I said nothing. He said nothing. We continued packing. I wondered what he might be thinking but just couldn't break the awful silence. He didn't even try. How could I have been such a fool as to put on those eyelashes in front of him? Was our whole wonderful relationship going to be sacrificed over *makeup?*

We checked out of the hotel and drove to the airport, most of the way through heavy fog, neither of us speaking a syllable.

When we were almost there, Ted finally spoke. "I'm sorry, Diana. I guess I overreacted back there."

Tears of relief sprang to my eyes, as my feelings of being exposed, vulnerable, and rejected were soothed. I waited for him to stop the car to give me a hug, a kiss, and plenty of reassurance, but he didn't. I couldn't think of anything to say, so I stayed quiet for the rest of the drive. He did too.

At the airport I busied myself loading my luggage in the back of the plane. I reminded myself of KC, now Lexi's cat, who, after she does anything awkward or uncool, proceeds to groom herself and lick her fur nonchalantly as if it never happened. But this extraordinarily uncool disaster *had* happened, and now—as I thought about it—the whole situation was starting to annoy me.

"Well, so much for intimacy!" I snapped as I climbed into the copilot's seat.

Ted said nothing as he readied the plane for what he said would be a tricky takeoff through low-lying clouds. "This stuff is two thousand feet thick. I need to be very focused on getting us through it."

What was *that* all about, I wondered. He'd been silent for half an hour for no good reason, and now that he had something to say, it was about *clouds?*

I pretended to be unaffected by the embarrassment, disappointment, distrust, and irritation I was feeling. And Ted, other than his occasional terse conversations over the radio with the air traffic controllers, said nothing. I was silently practicing the conversations I would have with various people about why Ted and I had broken up.

We took off through dense overcast and soon burst into full sunlight and clear blue skies. But my mood remained dark as I waited for him to bring up the subject we weren't talking about.

We flew on for another few minutes, when he said, "I guess you're wondering what happened back there."

I took a deep breath and pondered the obvious. "I'm pretty clear about what happened. We found out you don't like certain parts of who I really am."

"What?"

"I do what I do, and I like it."

"Diana, I wasn't being critical of you. Did you think I was being critical?"

"What would you call it when you just stop talking and disappear and then won't talk to me?"

"Look, I'm not sure I have words to explain it, but I'll try. And see if you can hear this from my viewpoint. There I was, in the doorway to the bathroom, looking at the woman I love. I was *feeling* that love, passionately describing it in terms of the difference between *eros* and *agape*—between infatuation and that sweet, deep, abiding affection that comes only with time, which is the feeling I've started having lately . . . *with you.* Being with you has begun to feel so comfortable, so much like *home.*

"Then you did something I hadn't seen you do before—I suppose it could have been anything at all—but it was with that false eyelash. And I was shocked. Sharon hardly wore any makeup at all, and when I watched you there in the bathroom, I was hit very hard by the reality of what's going on with us. I suddenly remembered that you *aren't* the woman I loved and lived with for so long. You're someone completely new, and regardless of how deeply and sweetly I feel my love for you, we have a long way to go before we'll develop what comes with being together for years, before we have a real history together."

All at once I wasn't so mad at him anymore.

He said, "Can you see how shocked I was to recognize that? To see the reality of our relationship, that you actually are someone completely different? *That's* why I was so quiet. I had to have a talk with myself. But I certainly wasn't being critical of you."

"I thought you didn't like me anymore."

He gave me one of his patented sweet looks, mixed with a trace of impish humor. I smiled at him and felt my heart go soft.

He gently took my hand and we flew on in silence, both of us lost in our own thoughts. Until finally he looked at me, stone-faced, and said over the noise of the engine, "It looked like a caterpillar."

I came out of my reverie. "What?"

"The eyelash thing. It looked like a caterpillar when I first saw it. That was the other part of the shock."

I heard myself make a little laughing noise but tried to conceal it so Ted wouldn't feel embarrassed. "A *caterpillar?*" I asked.

"Yeah. There I am having a conversation with the woman I love, and while we're talking she lifts a little dead black caterpillar out of a case and calmly starts pulling its legs off. And then, even worse, she squeezes something white onto the caterpillar . . . and sticks it in her *eye!* I mean, I knew what it was, but the way I saw it right then—it was a caterpillar."

It was the most ridiculous confession I'd ever heard in my life.

Oh, I just *hate* the feeling of having to laugh when I'm angry, but I couldn't help it. I burst into laughter. Moments later we were both wiping tears of hilarity from our cheeks.

Abruptly, I realized how dear and sweet he was, and how kind he was to make me laugh at what had been a horribly awkward situation.

"Ted," I yelled. "I love you so much. Don't you ever do that to me again."

"I love you too. Do what?"

"Refuse to talk to me like that. When you don't talk, I don't know what's going on with you."

"It was awful," he said. "I didn't know what to say. That's why I didn't say anything. I didn't mean anything by it. I was just so startled."

"Like I told you," I shouted, "so much for intimacy . . ."

It was a saying we would remember for years. We started laughing all over again.

And so I forgot about the dismal speeches I'd no longer have to make to my friends and I decided I wasn't such a miserable fool after all. But I also decided I'd think about whether to continue living in the world of false eyelashes. Yes, my life was truly changing.

The caterpillar episode reminded us dramatically that we weren't each other's former spouses and that our relationship was different.

With Ted, I was always aware of our separateness. Conflict could level us both, making us head for our separate corners. However, in order to build an honest relationship, we couldn't remain there. We would eventually have to come before each other with open hearts, as equal human beings, playing no roles, seeking neither to dominate nor to submit. We would have to discover the balance between us.

But when there was no conflict, when we were just living our lives, we did fall naturally into the roles in which we felt the most comfortable.

Ted, for instance, was a take-charge sort of person. I had understood that clearly from the first moments we were together. But I had not seen how he was in other parts of his life. Soon I was to find out, when he invited me to come to court while he was making final arguments before a judge and jury in a trial.

I discovered that the take-charge Ted of my personal experience was also take-charge Ted of the courtroom. I was dazzled by his persuasiveness and self-assurance as well as by his warm, engaging manner, which enthralled everyone, even the opposing attorneys. Nor did he forget I was present and I reveled in the loving glances he sent my way as he returned to his seat. Ted was clearly a master of every moment. I could feel that Paul had carefully chosen this vital and protective man, knowing I'd be in safe hands, and that he approved of him.

He executed our weekend plans with a similar sense of mastery and flair. I loved following his lead, for I had realized that because of his great energy, sensitivity, and intelligence, I could completely surrender my heart to him.

In making a plan, he thought of touches that made experiences even more memorable. One weekend, approaching Sedona, Arizona, as we flew at 180 miles per hour above rugged terrain toward our destination—an airport atop a distant mesa—he descended near the desert floor, flying between towering monuments of red rocks sculpted for millennia by wind and sand. Gently then he'd banked the little plane so it soared among the clusters of red stone towers. Through the headset we listened to gloriously haunting music that seemed orchestrated especially to accompany our graceful rolling flight alongside the giant carvings of ancient rock. It was a symphony in music and stone that this man in my life, an artist of the most wonderful kind, had brought together just for me.

One weekend in Garberville in northern California, while staying at the lovely Benbow Inn, we waded into a stream to study the polliwogs and ended up having a spectacular water fight. Over dinner that night we first began discussing the idea of marriage. From polliwogs to . . . the M-word, as Ted called it. Yes, I had fallen in love. And so quickly!

The following weekend in Temecula we were walking toward Bistro Ferrari, one of Ted's favorite restaurants there, where he was eager for me to taste their coq au vin, chicken braised in red wine. A puzzled look came over his face, and suddenly he tossed some pocket change on the sidewalk.

"Why did you do that?" I asked, surprised.

"I don't know! I had a strange desire to throw money away."

I stopped breathing. Ted didn't know—*he had no idea*—of Paul's habit of dropping coins to send luck to others. For me the very air was electric; time had stopped.

So I told him, "Paul always lit up when he found money in the street. He thought it was an omen of good luck. He loved tossing a coin or two on the sidewalk for others to find."

Ted didn't say anything. He seemed troubled, distracted. We entered the restaurant and were shown to our table. Studying the menu was already superfluous: coq au vin for two. I sat back, waiting.

Ted leaned forward, intense, agitated. "Was Paul very square-shouldered?"

"Yes. And he always sat very straight."

"Did he eat like this?"

I watched *these* hands, relatively new to my life, do something I'd watched Paul's hands do for a quarter of a century. Holding his fork in his left hand in the European manner he pushed food onto the back of it with his knife.

"Yes."

The silence resumed. Ted's eyes grew round. *"He's in me, Diana!"*

I was too astonished to say anything.

We continued eating in silence. Ted buttered half his roll and handed it to me. He responded to my raised eyebrows. "What?"

"I've never seen you do that before."

"I've never *done* that before. Don't tell me Paul did it too!"

"Yes, always." He began to use his knife to form the pat of butter on his bread plate into a shape, a heart shape. We stared at each other for a long time.

Then I asked, "Are you all right?"

Ted swallowed. "I'm fine . . ." Then he brightened. "And under the circumstances . . . I don't mind sharing my body with him so he can have a more physical experience."

I was completely stunned. I'd of course become familiar with feeling Paul's presence in our journal conversations, but to have him here physically, even if it wasn't his own body, was startling.

"What does it feel like to you to have him . . . *in* you?"

"I felt him sit inside me, but his position was straighter and bonier. The way he held his fork and put food in his mouth was different than the way I do it. I thought, *This has to be Paul.*"

Ted's feeling of Paul being with him continues to this day, especially when Ted and I are doing something Paul liked, such as dancing, or boating, or riding a motorcycle.

I marveled at how gracious Ted was about the idea of Paul being around, yet as time passed he began to wonder why, sensitive and intuitive as he was, he had never felt Sharon's presence or sensed any communication from her—except a few times through a bird. So one night, just as we were getting into bed, he sent out a silent request for her to come to him in his dreams. He said nothing to me about it until later.

In the middle of the night, he was sleeping with his back to me. I was in a deep sleep. Later he told me he suddenly woke and his eyes flew open as he felt me sit up in bed. The hairs on his arms stood up because he knew it wasn't me beside him, but Sharon. He waited without breathing to see what would happen. Moments later, he felt a tap on his shoulder and heard a voice, "I will always love you . . . and I will never leave you." With that, I lay back down. He was awake for a long time, marveling at the perfect message she'd sent.

The next morning Ted asked if I remembered sitting up in bed and tapping him on the shoulder.

"No . . . well, *maybe* I did . . . you know how it is when you're asleep and things happen . . ."

TWENTY-THREE

LATE IN OCTOBER, Lexi was surprised to receive a call from Ted asking to meet her privately for lunch. She had grown to like him during evenings we'd spent together and marveled at how he always seemed to know the right thing to say to make her feel comfortable with him.

Ted took his time in getting to the point and they talked about many things while they ate. Then the moment came.

"It must be hard to watch your mom and me getting so close when your dad has been gone less than eight months."

"In some ways it is hard . . . but I like seeing you together. You seem to understand so much about what she's gone through. I love how you can talk about both of them—Sharon and my dad—and not be jealous." She studied him carefully. "You know, Teddy, you're so different than my dad was. You make her laugh so much."

"I'm so grateful you feel that way," he told her. He acknowledged having dated a lot of women over the past two years, but said this relationship was different. "Your mom and I have been moving very fast. I've never before felt so safe or gone so deep with anyone. She has an infinite capacity for partnership, doesn't she?" Lexi nodded, happy with his assessment. "I feel like she has no hard edges for me to bump into—I can just let go of any fear or hesitation."

"Are you trying to tell me you're in love with her?"

"Even more than that. Maybe I'm pushing my luck, Lex, but I came to you today to ask for your blessing. I'm getting ready to ask your mom to marry me. It's awfully soon, I know, but it feels so right, and I think we're both ready . . ."

Lexi closed her eyes and smiled. "Wow . . ."

He added that he'd asked the same thing of Christy and Kathy, his daughters, when they'd been home the previous weekend. "They both say they'll be relieved to get me off the street," he reported.

Lexi had to smile. "I think you're wonderful, Teddy, and I'm really, really happy for you both."

"Don't tell her, okay? I'm taking her somewhere special on Friday night."

———— ∞ ————

Ted and I were spending every moment we could together, and the forthcoming weekend was to be one almost like any other—flying somewhere romantic. This time the plan was to go to Carmel again for good food, great lovemaking, and walks in the woods to bird-watch. Always doing something interesting, Ted was incapable of doing "nothing."

"Nothing" always had to be "something," so even walks in the woods took on the educational aspect of identifying and listing the birds we came upon. Carmel had become a romantic location for us too, as it had been for Paul and me.

I parked my car at Santa Monica Airport and watched Ted bring the 210 in from Orange County. I hurried to the open door and hopped aboard with my garment bag containing the "something special to wear to dinner" he'd asked me to bring. He revved the engine and we were rolling toward the city end of the runway for an over-the-ocean takeoff. Suddenly he braked, apologized, looked in my eyes, and gave me a quick kiss hello.

Soon we were flying over the ocean, at eye-level with my mother's and stepfather's home on a bluff in Malibu. I had telephoned Mimi to be on the lookout, and when she appeared on the patio, Ted rocked the wings in salute. He liked my mother, and she was delighted with him.

In another few minutes, Ted announced we were clear of the high-traffic zone, which meant we could relax a little. I produced a basket lined with a blue-and-white cloth that held a late lunch of chicken sandwiches and fresh fruit.

Before long I realized we weren't on our regular route along the coastline, headed for Carmel, but had worked our way inland. I might have known. If there was anything consistent about this man, it was his unpredictability. An hour later I watched him curiously as we circled and landed at a tiny airport in the western foothills of the Sierra Nevada range. The sign on the roof of the operations office read "Mariposa." I had no idea where Mariposa was.

I had a sudden fantasy that he'd planned a surprise wedding. I wouldn't put it past him! He'd told me to bring something special to wear, and I had, but it wasn't what I'd want to get married in! And what about our families? Oh dear. No, wait. We *couldn't* get married. We didn't have a marriage license.

Ted tied the plane down, asked me to wait beside it, and returned in a few minutes behind the wheel of a rental car. Soon we were off for an hour's drive along a winding road lined with trees and glowing with the vivid reds and golds of autumn—into Yosemite National Park.

It was October 24. Ted had reserved a room at the historic Ahwahnee Hotel, and for the next several hours we explored the grounds before dressing for dinner. I took a long time getting ready, putting on a romantic, ruffled, white organza blouse and a black crepe skirt from Paris. Our eyes met in the bathroom mirror causing us to break out into shy smiles, though I wasn't exactly sure why.

The maître d' met us at the doors of the huge, cathedral-like dining room. He showed us to the special table Ted had reserved, a single table, the only table at the base of an immense, twenty-foot arched window with a spectacular view of the hotel grounds and the forest and dark, gray granite cliffs beyond. I felt like a queen being led to her throne.

I couldn't help marveling at the setting. It was beyond romantic; it was a masterpiece. We ordered dinner and Ted insisted on four courses, saying he wanted dinner to last a long time.

Ted reached for my hand. "Diana, what I love about our relationship is . . ." He stopped. The waiter arrived with the first course. He began again, picking up where he'd left off. What followed through three more courses was a whole discourse on exactly what he loved about the way we had come together, who we were together, and what we could become together. He had prepared this speech like a closing argument. I was thrilled.

When the desserts were in front of us, he took my hands and looked into my eyes. "So . . . will you marry me?"

I was flooded with a sense of the absolute rightness of what was happening, just as twenty-six years earlier I'd known marrying Paul was exactly the right thing to do.

"I would love to marry you!"

Tears were gleaming in Ted's eyes. He grinned broadly and said, "We can go ring shopping together. Choosing a ring was a decision I didn't feel I had the right to make by myself."

Back in our room after dinner we telephoned the three girls and the two moms. Everybody was happy hearing the news they had been expecting anyway. And later that night, laughing at something together, a memory a quarter-century old was set off for the first time ever: I'd had my head on Paul's chest on our honeymoon, watching the Ed Sullivan show, and suddenly dissolved into hysteria over a fantastically funny dog act. The memory rose like a bubble to the surface of my consciousness and I burst into tears. Ted held me, saying, "As you open yourself to our relationship, you open yourself to all your feelings . . ."

I was with the right man. Again.

Thank you, God. And thank you, Paul. *You sent someone who is so different from you. And, of course, you would do that. You knew I wouldn't want a rerun. You knew the second feature had to be completely different. Not another* Love Story. *You must have thought, Hmmm, why not a romantic comedy?*

A month later, for our first Thanksgiving together, Ted and I were to host both families, including our mothers, my stepdad, and all three daughters, for a traditional feast of roast turkey at the ranch. Just a year before, Paul and I had received his fatal diagnosis, and on this, my favorite of holidays, he was never far from my thoughts. Nor was Sharon far from Ted's.

Because we had only used the ranch house on weekends, I wasn't sure the lovely and spacious country kitchen was stocked with the equipment I would need to prepare turkey with all the trimmings.

Concerned about forgetting something, I spent hours on the two preceding weekends making scrupulous lists of every ingredient and piece of kitchen equipment I would require. We devised a complex plan that included getting Ted's daughters home from separate schools and having them drive separately with more of our equipment to meet us at the ranch in time for dinner on Wednesday night. Lexi would drive separately from Los Angeles. Ted and I knew we had to leave early to allow for heavy traffic.

Despite all my lists, as we packed the car on the Wednesday before the holiday, I said to Ted, "I'm worried about forgetting something . . . something really big."

Traffic was bumper-to-bumper at sundown as we inched our way down the freeway on our way out of town, toward the ranch. An hour and a half later we'd gone only ten miles. Suddenly Ted turned on the directional signal and started edging to the right to exit the freeway.

His face was ashen.

"What's wrong?"

"We forgot something."

"What?"

"It's really big, Diana. It's really, *really* big! We have to go back!"

I was growing more alarmed by the moment. What in the world could have been so important? In my mind I checked and rechecked my lists. "What did we forget?"

"My mother!"

"Your *mother*? My God, I had no idea she was coming with *us*."

In the evening's half-light I could see Ted beginning to smile.

———

I'd already talked to Alice and liked her. Ted had called me weeks before from his car phone to introduce me to his mom, who had been sitting beside him. I'd naturally wanted to make a good impression and was relieved and delighted when we hit it off famously right away. She asked me to call her Mom. Before we hung up, she said, "Just a little suggestion, dear. Ted's been telling me he'd rather you didn't wear those long, flowing nightgowns. Why don't you just keep the nightie under your pillow in case of fire . . ." That was when I learned where Ted had gotten his sense of humor.

Now going to get Alice meant we would be really late and surely miss dinner with the three girls, who were by now already waiting at the ranch. I was disappointed and didn't want to complain, but I underestimated Ted's flair for solving problems.

"Don't worry, Diana. We'll just go to Plan B!" The next hour had a certain Keystone Kops craziness. Traffic in the direction we'd been headed was hardly moving. But traffic going in the opposite direction wasn't nearly as heavy. So we turned around and went back to Newport Beach. We picked up Alice, her luggage, and the candied yams she'd made, then headed for John Wayne Airport and the Cessna. Ted's plan was becoming clear. If we couldn't get there in time by driving, we'd fly! We loaded everything—all of my cooking equipment, an extra oven, a food processor, and bags and bags of groceries—into the plane's luggage compartment and the backseat. We could barely get the doors closed after we cozied Alice into the backseat and convinced her to hold the pan of yams on her lap.

And off we went, soaring high above the long, long lines of headlights on the freeways below, and we were over the airport in Temecula twenty minutes later. On the approach the plane hit turbulence and there was a yelp from the backseat. The sticky juice from the yams was now all over Alice's skirt.

Our three girls were waiting at the airport with two cars for all our gear. Alice was an incredibly good sport about it all. She said she wasn't uncomfortable and wouldn't mind going straight to the restaurant as she was, yam juice and all. But there, at our table, the unthinkable happened—the waitress reached across Ted to refill a glass with ice water, momentarily looked away, and poured it right into Alice's lap!

"Bull's-eye!" Alice yelled, and then, with a lapful of freezing water and ice cubes, laughed until tears ran down her cheeks. Yes, it was clear how Ted had first learned to see through a different slat in the fence.

Thanksgiving Day started off perfectly, with a phone call from Mary in Hawaii. Exactly one year ago she and Don had met, and on this anniversary day of their meeting, they would be getting married. But she of course was not the only one with wedding news. I told her Ted and I were going to be married soon. She was overjoyed. Then she made a remark that's since become famous—in my mind, if nowhere else—though it's the sort of thing only a best friend can say: "Wow! You certainly have a short shelf-life!"

Mary was right. Maybe some women would have needed a ten-year break from marriage before they'd be ready to do it again. But in my case, with the pathways of fate being whatever they were and with the fact of my having met a perfect man less than a year after my other perfect man had gone to a greater life somewhere, I could only feel enormously fortunate. I don't think spending many years between marriages would have been the best for me. *This* was the best for me. I was getting to love again.

"It just feels so right. I can't wait for you to meet him!" I said.

"It won't be long—we're coming to see you on our honeymoon. We'll be there in a few weeks."

———

Ted had a large round tabletop made of plywood to fit over the dining table at the ranch so we could seat all sixteen people. I had rented a huge peach-colored tablecloth and our daughters decorated the house with peach- and rose-hued persimmon leaves, miniature pumpkins, and colorful ears of Indian corn we'd bought at a farmers' market the weekend before.

I rose before dawn to prepare every traditional Thanksgiving dish I knew. The menu would be enhanced by a Wentworth family favorite, *Alice's Yummy Yams*, a decadent recipe made with several sticks of butter, a whole box of brown sugar, and a bottle of maple syrup.

At the table we spontaneously began what would become a family tradition. Ted and I took turns welcoming each family member and telling them individually what we loved and appreciated about them. Without prompting, the others followed suit. By the time we were finished, there was such a feeling of open-heartedness and joy in the room we wondered why we hadn't thought to be married in the midst of such a great and meaningful family celebration.

———

Ted and I had made the announcement to our families, and now the time had arrived to tell the people I had always regarded as my extended family, the members of the Inside Edge.

The host that morning at the Beverly Hills chapter of the Edge composed a limerick to announce our engagement to the group. Ted and I went up on the stage and he spoke briefly, then Lexi stepped forward from the audience to join us. She spoke emotionally to the audience, "I want you to know how truly happy I am." She told them she'd gotten to spend a lot of time with Ted and that she was looking forward to what a loving and benevolent teacher Ted was going to be for her.

Even though these wonderful people were a bit stunned—as I still was—at the speed of it all, they welcomed Ted and hugged us both.

When we discussed a date for our wedding, Ted reminded me that as a trial lawyer the only time of year he could ever depend on getting time off for a honeymoon was during the Christmas holidays when court business was at an ebb. I'd wanted to wait until March, a full year after Paul's death, but knowing how thoroughly Paul approved of this union, I decided to honor Ted's schedule. We invited Lexi, Christy, and Kathy to join us on a ten-day Caribbean cruise during the holidays, so they would be with us for our wedding on the ship.

Getting our marriage license at the courthouse was easy, but I soon found that getting married on a ship was a whole lot more complicated than commonly thought. For one thing, cruise ship captains no longer perform wedding ceremonies for passengers. For another, foreign ports have complicated laws governing marriages.

On the Tuesday night before the recent newlyweds, Mary and Don Kelly, were to arrive, I told Ted I was growing discouraged about our prospects of getting married on the holiday cruise. As we wondered what to do, I suddenly remembered something. "Mary has a ministerial license! We could get married this weekend!"

"Really? You don't need any more preparation time than that?" Before I could change my mind, he said, "I'll call Kathy and Christy and see if they can fly home from college by then!"

We planned a very small wedding, because that is what Ted and I both preferred. Even though I'm an expert at organizing parties, I didn't want to be working on my wedding day. I didn't want to even be thinking of the countless details involved in a big party. I wanted a small wedding with only my very nearest and dearest present, so more of me could be there.

From then on, it was all simple and wonderful.

On December 9, 1989, Ted's friend piloted Ted's new boat, *Salute*, in Newport Harbor, holding it into the wind in the turning basin by the Lido Bridge just west of Balboa Island. I sensed that Paul, too, was at the helm that day—grinning at the attainment of his dreams, of knowing I would be cared for, and having a magnificent yacht at his command. Mary Kelly had brought wedding leis for Ted and me to wear as she performed our marriage service in front of both families and a few close friends on the aft deck while the sun went down.

At our request, Mary invited the presence of Paul and Sharon to participate in the ceremony. Not a soul doubted they were there, silently applauding, wishing us joy.

TWENTY-FOUR

AFTER WE'D been married about six months, Ted and I simultaneously felt the time had come to sell Paul's and my home in Pacific Palisades. It was a terrific notion, except . . .

"Mom, I'm living here and this is our office! *Your* office."

Lexi had a point. She'd lived there for thirteen years, since the age of seven, which meant it was the most permanent home she'd ever had. And indeed, the office for the Inside Edge was in the loft.

"Besides," she said, "don't forget that you and Dad promised you'd give me five years' notice before we moved again."

"Good try," I replied, "but don't *you* forget that we gave you notice the day we moved in."

I heard her grumbling playfully into the phone.

"Sweetie," I said, "it's an emotional situation for both of us. I know that. But life's a lot different now and there are other things we need to think about."

"Such as?"

"The Southern California real estate market. Real estate values are sky-high, the highest they've ever been in this area. Selling the house now would be a smart financial move. Intuitively, Ted and I feel it's the right time."

Lexi, ever the realist, became serious, thoughtful. "That's hard to argue with, Mom."

"I know this is sudden for you, so I thought I'd give you some of the money from your dad's mortgage insurance to help you move into a new place. Would that be good?"

"Sure it would," she said, "even though this isn't so much about money. It's about leaving the past behind, and that's hard. But sure. It's okay with me. And I'll be grateful for your help."

I was proud of her—our little girl, grown up.

The house not only sold quickly, but our intuition was also validated in a way that neither of us could possibly have anticipated. Just one week after escrow on the house closed, the Gulf War erupted and real estate prices in the area plummeted.

Meanwhile, Lexi and her friends had helped us pack everything up, and soon we were ready to let the house go.

I decided to spend one last night alone there to say goodbye to it, to thank it for protecting our family both physically and financially. Lexi had already moved her cat, KC, and all the furniture to her new home, and Paul's and my bed was the only piece left. All my mementos had been packed except what we'd called our "proud wall": framed book jackets from our six books, a color photograph of us with our crew on the set of our television show on our last day of taping, and a *Los Angeles Times* article citing praise for the Inside Edge as "a watering hole for the soul" and "the next evolutionary step in networking."

The sky was darkening outside the window of the office/loft as I tenderly removed those final items, letting the memories of each one flood through me before wrapping them for storage.

The weather that night grew eerie—fierce winds and lightning storms, but no rain at all. Windows rattled as I made my way through the house, sitting on the floor in each room, purposefully sorting through the recollections it held for me. I had to fight the denial and the dread. To keep myself present and to access the feelings, I asked aloud, over and over, "Remind me now! What else happened in this room?"

I let the poignancy of it all flow through my body, feeling it all as fully as I was able. Along with the memories, I was filled with gratitude for every minute of it all, and thankful to my body for its part in letting me feel. Finally, exhausted, I fell asleep, only to be wakened over and over by claps of thunder and bright flashes of lightning.

When I looked at the clock it was 3:45 A.M., time to rise and go to the Inside Edge. After closing the front door for the last time, I slipped the key for the new owner under a stone at the base of Seymour, our sycamore tree, protector of our home and of Misty's ashes which were buried below its sheltering limbs. I wrapped my arms around the tree and said goodbye.

———

I realized that there was one more completion for me to make—the fifth anniversary of the Inside Edge was only a few months away. A year and a half earlier, Paul and I had looked ahead to the fifth anniversary and contemplated a gala celebration. I decided we could still do it. And to that end, I engaged Paul in a journal dialogue.

Diana: So, what kind of party will it be?

Paul: A gala! Except it will be a breakfast instead of a dinner dance. How about a black-tie breakfast?

Diana: Great! What if we acknowledge inspiring, forward-thinking people who have contributed significantly to the world? People who have had a positive impact and who reflect the ideals we at the Edge collectively admire and support? Who are those people?

And thus it was that an awards breakfast in the Crystal Ballroom of the Beverly Hills Hotel, a black-tie breakfast, was held on Tuesday, November 3, 1990, at 7:00 A.M., one day after what would have been Paul's and my twenty-sixth wedding anniversary.

Five hundred reservations came in. It must have been a strange sight to see our members and guests arriving from all over Southern California in black tie and evening attire—at dawn. It all reminded me wistfully of those very first Edge meetings, when Paul and I had been so thrilled with the excitement of the preparatory activity. But even more was going on now, with five performers waiting to rehearse onstage, thirty volunteer staff in position, television news cameras and crews in place for the awards presentations.

After the ceremony got underway, there was a video segment Tom Sewell and Sharon Lindsey had edited, which included clips of Paul and highlights of the five years of the Edge. My friend Mary, the host for the morning, invited me to the stage.

I spoke briefly about Paul and how I was sure he was present, able to feel their love and appreciation of his legacy. I said, "Paul and I saw the Inside Edge as a garden and ourselves as its stewards. We chose the locale, drew the boundaries, and made it a nourishing place to grow. But the garden seeded itself with the people who were attracted to it. Our job was to let its natural beauty unfold and to tend it so nothing would harm it. We felt honored to be able to do that."

After summarizing some of the highpoints of the Edge's many activities, I concluded by noting that it was time now to celebrate the success of what we had all created together. I declared that the specific purpose of the morning's breakfast was to recognize, in a formal way, significant contributions made by outstanding individuals who had helped people stretch beyond their concepts of what is possible—for themselves and for humanity.

Edge members presented awards to Norman Cousins, author of *Anatomy of an Illness* and twenty-four other books; Andy and Katie Lipkis, founders of TreePeople; John Vasconcellos, creator of California's Task Force on Self-Esteem and Personal and Social Responsibility, who was then serving his twelfth term in the California Legislature; actor Dennis Weaver, and many others. Each recipient came to the stage to receive a crystal globe and to make a brief acceptance speech.

I felt Paul loving every moment, especially when Boyd Willat introduced and acknowledged Rama Vernon, founder/director of the Center for Soviet-American Dialogue and one of the coordinators of the First International Peace Congress which Paul and I had attended in Russia in 1985—the adventure that changed our lives.

In the previous five years, Rama, the mother of five children and grandmother of two, had journeyed to the Soviet Union a total of thirty-eight times and taken over seven hundred American citizens to meet with Soviets, opening up communication between private citizens and government officials. She told us, "The people who went [to Russia] at the height of the Cold War had the courage to cross barbed-wire borders to enter a place that represented the unknown on our planet at that time. They faced their fears to help make the breakthrough that Gorbachev's advisors described to me in Moscow in the following words: 'It is the people you have brought into our country who have made the major contribution to *perestroika* and have helped to free our people.'"

As the gala concluded, we all stood while Stephen Longfellow Fiske performed his song "Earth Anthem," sung to the melody of "The Star Spangled Banner"—

Oh say, can we see,
By the one light in all,
Our earth to embrace
At the call of all nations?
Where our children can play
In a world without war,
Where we stand hand in hand
In the grace of creation . . .

For two more years after the fifth-anniversary celebration, I continued to run the Inside Edge. I always tried to wake up a few minutes before the alarm rang so it wouldn't disturb Ted, but he still knew I was leaving and he missed me.

Eventually, his sense of unease grew, as he became worried about the effects of the early mornings and my running the Edge alone. In truth, I was weary and wanted to stop, but I knew I would be disappointing hundreds of people who regarded the Edge as home, and whenever I thought of shutting it down I just couldn't do it. The idea had been a gift, and I had promised Spirit I would give it my all. Even as I considered my alternatives, I still saw the ripple effects of the Edge in action as the lives of so many people continued to be positively impacted.

Finally, though, a time came when I confided to a few of its most supportive members—Michael Coleman, Joe Broderick, Margaret Wright, Bobbie, Larry, and Tim—that I just didn't feel I could do it anymore.

What happened then was wonderful, as a group of some forty Edge enthusiasts gathered together to pledge support in the form of their money and time. One positive consequence of their participation was that the Edge changed its form, becoming a not-for-profit educational foundation. Two of the chapters closed after a few years, but the Orange County chapter, run by a board of directors, still thrives, only a mile from where Ted and I live. I love to visit it sometimes in person (or on the Web at insideedge.org) to hear such speakers as Thomas Moore, Julia Cameron, Gary Zukav, and Ram Dass. As I look around the room during its meetings, I feel satisfied that so many lives continue to be touched by it.

————

After my retirement from the Edge, I began fully recognizing that for the first time in many years I didn't have to work for a living. I experimented with being a lady of leisure. With more time for journal writing than ever before, I explored who I was and what I was becoming, now that my identity wasn't a function of the work I did—now that I was no longer Ms. Inside Edge, Ms. Cooking Lady, or Ms. Cookbook Writer.

What I discovered was that I'd created the busy persona of an entrepreneurial woman and was so identified with the role that I didn't know how to just *be*. I felt adrift, without purpose, without a real reason for getting up each morning. The only way out of those uncomfortable feelings, I realized, was to experience them, live them, move through them, and see what was on the other side. I decided to do so in the most open and vulnerable way I could—by entering, like a caterpillar beginning its transformation, into a place of complete surrender. I said, *I surrender. What is it, dear God, you want me to do?* I resolved to wait for as long as it would take.

When, after a long time, I began to emerge from my solitude, my new skin felt very tender. I told myself I hadn't formed yet into what I would become, that I must be patient. But I soon realized the need to surrender would never end. There is always more to let go of and forgive myself for and open up to as I grow. There is never an end to evolving.

———

I enrolled in a few art classes and did some travel writing. But I still felt a nagging sort of drive within me, a drive I couldn't quite identify, a kind of soul hunger that wanted . . . I didn't know what.

When I told my friend and minister, Peggy Bassett, how I was feeling, she asked me a key question: "Diana, are you driven . . . or drawn?" Her question gave me food for thought and it released me from the distressing sense that I was being pushed and shoved against my will. The idea of being *drawn* was somehow more comfortable. Yes, I *did* feel I was being drawn, but wanted to know by what, when I would get where I was going, and why I'd be there. I realized I needed to surrender even more.

Occasionally, I remembered Papa's oft-repeated phrase, "You'll never have to work for a living," and recalled the easygoing, chocolate-eating, party-going, talking-on-the-phone-to-my-friends life to which I had always thought he was referring. With more clarity than ever before I knew I hadn't the slightest interest in such a life. I loved to work, to express myself, to give of what I had and who I was.

I told Ted that I felt at loose ends now that I wasn't working regularly and that I longed to discover what else was in me so I could give even more.

He said, "You *do* have a job now, and that is to follow your heart." His insight was startling to me and I loved it, for it brought me a feeling of comfort in the middle of my discomfort. I understood for the first time that searching and opening to change and being willing to do something new was itself a valid and useful thing to undertake—a worthwhile job to have. I even thought that Papa, if he could have heard, would have approved.

So I began writing this book in earnest, and also found myself writing short essays on my life with Ted, and stories of people I loved.

"I don't know where this is going," I lamented regularly. "I'm writing all these pieces, but I don't know why. I think they should have some sort of purpose . . ."

"You'll see, Diana," Ted replied one time. "Sometimes there is nothing to do but boogie in the void. Haven't we learned that the purpose of all we do becomes visible soon enough?"

———

The day before Thanksgiving 1994, as I was packing up all the food we'd take to the ranch for our annual family Thanksgiving gathering, the phone rang. I was surprised to hear it was two old friends from the Edge, Jack Canfield and Mark Victor Hansen.

They got to the point immediately, speaking with their customary excitement and energy. "What are you doing right now, Diana? Can you be here in fifteen minutes?" They were at a nearby hotel, meeting with their publisher about the need for an addition to their "Chicken Soup" book series. They wanted to create a *Chicken Soup for the Soul* cookbook. I felt a buzz of excitement.

When we met a few minutes later, Jack and Mark told me that because "chicken soup" was in the title of their book series, people often looked for their books in the cooking sections of bookstores.

Mark said, "So we want to give them something to find when they're there!" We all talked about it and decided it wouldn't be a book of chicken soup recipes but a book with the kinds of heart-warming, inspiring stories for which the two bestselling *Chicken Soup for the Soul* books were already known. This particular title would feature stories involving food and showing how food had been a vehicle for drawing people together.

Within an hour after my phone rang, I was on my way back home with an agreement to work with Jack and Mark to put together the book in time for publication in the fall of 1995. I was *ecstatic!* Ted was right—nearly every essay I had already written fit perfectly into the book.

More than eleven years have passed since I married Ted. (He claims to be my *late* husband, insisting that Paul was my *early* husband.) I love being married to a man who shares so much with me, including the experience of having lost a spouse. We cherish being able to talk, without editing, about Paul and Sharon whenever a memory, happy or sad, breaks through to the surface. We know we don't feel less love for each other because we still feel so much love for them.

And, yes, Paul still shows up. Not long ago, in New Orleans, Ted and I walked the streets of the French Quarter. Friends had told us about a tearoom where psychics read tea leaves and we decided to peek inside. A woman there beckoned us to a table and I didn't hesitate to sit down.

The first thing she said was, "A tall elegant man wearing a safari jacket is standing behind you. He's offering you a very unusual bouquet. It's a Victorian nosegay, with satin ribbons and love knots on the ends." I could hardly believe it. She was, of course, describing the bouquet Paul had specially made for me on our first New Year's Eve.

After I married Ted, I noticed Paul's presence wasn't as intense or as constantly protective as it had been before, and I'd been thinking my not feeling him around so much was probably fine. After all, I was doing wonderfully in my new life and I felt he must have his own progress to make where he was now. Yet I still missed him, particularly on certain occasions. As anyone who has lost a beloved spouse will tell you, anniversaries and holidays of any kind are the hardest times to be without that partner. On those days, emotionally disabling grief may rise without warning—or other powerful, unexpected feelings and experiences.

Like Valentine's Day 1991. The skies were gray and it was raining as I drove down Spyglass Hill, listening to a station on the radio. My eyes fell on the car clock—12:34. I remembered Paul's superstition that when one looks at the clock and finds the numbers all lined up, it's a sign of good luck. Since he'd been gone, he frequently announced his presence by shifting my glance to the numbers.

Suddenly, I was startled to hear these words spilling into the car: "This next song is a Valentine from Paul von Welanetz to his wife, Diana. Happy Valentine's Day!"

Oh, I knew the words hadn't come from a disk jockey but from my heart and from somewhere beyond time. A melody began, an unfamiliar, romantic melody that immediately brought tears to my eyes. It was a Richard Marx song I'd never heard before, so I pulled to the side of the road and listened to the words all the way through.

> *Wherever you go*
> *Whatever you do*
> *I will be right here waiting for you.*

I was sure, deep in my heart, Paul had sent me a Valentine.

———————

One of the eeriest indications of Paul's presence happened a year or so after Ted and I were married. It was the result of the great personality difference between my two men. Paul, with his artist's soul, was intensely visual. He would notice if I changed my nail polish. And Ted, who is a mystic at heart, doesn't know I wear any.

So imagine my surprise one day, when we walked into a department store and Ted stopped suddenly and stared at a jewelry counter a few feet away.

"Diana! Those earrings!"

"What earrings?"

"Those daisy earrings!"

I saw a large display of single and double daisy earrings on the counter.

"What about them?"

"Paul wants you to have those daisy earrings!"

My breath caught in my throat and I stood very still. "Which ones?"

"The single white daisies with the yellow centers."

Dim bells of memory rang in my heart. Those earrings were identical to the pair Paul had bought for me when we were first married, over twenty-five years ago. They were his favorites, the ones he repaired over and over until they just fell apart. I hadn't even thought about them for years, and Ted had no way at all of knowing they ever existed.

Episodes like this are deeply comforting, and every one of them heartens me, adding to my deep conviction that the love we've shared is never lost.

I found a deeper understanding of that conviction one afternoon in a shopping mall. I stood with several others next to a kiosk display of graphic art, images made of thousands of tiny, multicolored, computer-generated dots. I asked the people what they were staring at.

A man said, "If you look long enough, your eyes relax and you can see a three-dimensional figure behind the colors on the surface." I stared in the way I thought they were staring, did so for a long time, and saw nothing.

Paul would have been fascinated with this, I thought. Then I heard his voice coaching me encouragingly, patiently, as he loved to do. *"It's like raindrops on a window, Kitten. You can focus on the raindrops on the surface, or relax your vision to see past them to a whole different view beyond."*

I strained my eyes, struggling to see, trying to make something of the apparently random dots. Then, unexpectedly, I saw my own reflection looking back at me from the glass covering the pictures. In that moment some subtle perceptual sense in my brain shifted and I saw *beyond* the dots. As though it were a slowly developing photograph, the previously random patterns suddenly turned into a three-dimensional picture of two dolphins. It was an astonishing revelation, like some form of magic, with order coming gradually out of chaos.

As soon as I saw the dolphins, I concentrated my focus, sure they *weren't really there*, but not wanting them to disappear. To my surprise, I saw them even more vividly, more clearly. With practice, I found I could see the hidden images in each picture almost immediately.

I didn't know then that I would eventually use a similar technique to integrate my many mementos into a coherent view of my life. From the old red-velvet Valentine box to the faded pages of my wedding album; from the color snapshot of Paul at the helm of a sailboat to another photo in which I am holding our baby, Lexi, and wearing the daisy earrings he loved—I looked at them all and thought back over the days of our love, the times of our passion, the shining moments when the world was ours.

Sorting through those memories then took on a greater significance as I began to surrender to the mystery of it all and *see beyond* the photographs and the mementos, into their larger meaning. I saw with different eyes, through the softened focus of an altered perspective—one of understanding and wisdom. I could see past the worldly drama and behold the beauty of a larger pattern, the wonder of a grand design. In it was a clear transcendent truth, *this* truth: that shared love spins eternal shimmering threads, interconnecting everyone, and that *love, and love alone, endures.*

Such sudden clarity was almost unbearably poignant, too beautiful, and I was reminded of the words of Edna St. Vincent Millay:

> *Oh God, I cried, no dark disguise*
> *Can e'er hereafter hide from me*
> *Thy radiant identity*

TWENTY-FIVE

OUR FAMILIES continue to bring us our greatest joy. I've delighted in throwing myself into supportive roles as wife, mother, and stepmother.

Ted's younger daughter, Kathy, married Court from Boston, whom she met soon after we married. They dated for six years, all during the time Kathy was earning her M.A. in psychology and Court was attending law school and passing the California Bar.

Ted's older daughter, Christy, earned her law degree as well, and also married a lawyer, Jeff.

To top off the joy of our expanding family, in 1999 Ted's daughters gave us our first grandchildren, two beautiful girls—Kathy and Court's daughter, Aidan, and Christy and Jeff's daughter, Lauren.

Lexi and I were determined to stay close, and we did. Every Tuesday I drove to Los Angeles to have lunch, catch up with her life, and hear news about KC, Lexi's (now twenty-one-year-old) calico cat.

She left her work at the Inside Edge to finish college, as she promised her dad she would, earning a bachelor's degree in broadcasting. After graduation she pursued various jobs in that field, but they led only to dead ends. A few years later, her maturing preferences led her to recognize that she really wanted to become a clinical psychologist, and she eventually earned an M.A. and a Psy.D. Ted and I both applauded her success all the way through her state board licensing exams.

We now call her Dr. Lexi.

As both Court and Jeff had done with Ted before they proposed to his daughters, Dave came to Ted and me in October 1998 with some understandable minor nervousness and a major question.

I had known Dave for a number of years, since he and Lexi dated briefly in the early 1990s. But they had gone their separate ways for some seven years—until recently, when they discovered each other again and began dating once more.

Thus, Dave appeared before Ted and me one evening with a simple request: for Lexi's hand in marriage. I knew Dave expected a quick and positive answer, since he knew we liked him, but I wasn't about to let him off so easy with my only child.

"Tell me what your life is going to be like, Dave. How do you see your future with Lexi?" I asked.

Dave spoke earnestly of his hopes and dreams for the future, his business goals, his desire for a long, loving marriage.

"Now, Dave," I said somberly, "this is important. Tell me what you love most about Lexi."

He looked puzzled as he thought. "There isn't a thing I *don't* love about Lexi."

And so Dave passed this mother's test.

March 25, 2000

Lexi and her bridesmaids dressed for her wedding in our suite at the Beverly Hills Hotel, a spot she and I chose because of its shared memories in her life and mine. A large bouquet of white daisies was on her dressing table in honor of her dad.

During the flurry of joyous activity, Ted sat quietly in a chair by the window, contemplating a photograph of Paul. I knew Ted was inviting Paul to join him in walking Lexi down the aisle. Watching him do this, I felt incalculable gratitude for my great good fortune at having such an extraordinary and sensitive man as Ted in my life. What other man would have considered being so thoughtful, so unselfish, so giving of himself at a time like this?

Now the doors in the back of the church swung open to frame Lexi, a romantic vision in her white bridal gown and veil, holding Ted's arm firmly. Both were beaming as they proceeded slowly toward the front where Mary Kelly and Dave's pastor shared ministerial duties.

"Who gives this woman in marriage?"

Ted replied solemnly, "Her mother . . . her father . . . and I."

On the night Paul died, Lexi had sobbed in my arms that her father wouldn't be present at her wedding to give her away. But she couldn't have known, could she? She couldn't have known then the miraculous truth. That he *was* there. He really was.

Their vows complete, Lexi and Dave kissed and walked out of the church to an exuberant country-western rendition of "Amazing Grace."

Indeed, I thought to myself, *a touch of heavenly grace has been with us here today.* And then I added, *Perhaps even more than just a touch . . .*

—◦◦◦—

It is evening now at our ranch—Ted's and mine. I'm a different woman than I was eleven years ago—stronger on the inside, softer on the outside. I thought when I retired and turned the Inside Edge over to its members to run that I'd just take it easy after so many years of work. I'd catch up on my reading, just relax. But Ted didn't think much of that idea.

"As long as you're with me, sweet lady, you aren't going to have much time for third-person experiences! You're going to be experiencing things first-person!"

He was right, and I loved it! I loved the immediacy he sought from life and I loved his including me in it.

Just this morning, I slipped out of bed before dawn to get a glass of water, eager to return and get back under the warm covers again. But in the minute or so I was gone, Ted had made up the bed—bedspread, pillows, and all.

He stood beside the bed, an impish look on his face. "Ready to pick tangerines for breakfast?" he asked as I came through the door. No breakfast in bed these days. He wouldn't dream of picking fruit from our orchard and bringing it to me. "It's *your* ranch, Diana! You have to go out there, feel the mist in the air, smell the trees in bloom, and bite into icy fruit, fresh from the tree!"

———

This afternoon he called me to come and sit in the swing on our patio and watch him fly huge, six-foot-wide toy gliders from the lawn out over the valley below. While they had no engines, they did have battery-powered remote controls, and Ted was able to maneuver them expertly as they caught the rising thermals and soared into the far distance.

"Look!" he yelled. "That raven thinks the glider is another bird—he's flying close to check it out!"

Later, settling into the swing beside me, he took my hand. "It's better than we imagined, isn't it?"

"Yes," I responded. "And we hardly ever get what we expect, o we?" It was something Ted and I both understood so well, tha che unstoppable designs of destiny can change everything in an i tant. But that fact didn't trouble me anymore, because I'd learned much about trusting the kinds of counteroffers that life brings

We sat silently for a few moments watching two ra ns swoop and curve in a complicated, playful dance. Soon one flew above, the other below. Then the lower one suddenly flipped upside down, its feet grabbing the feet of the other bird while they spiraled downward several hundred feet before separating and gliding off along the ridge together.

As sundown approached, Ted suggested going for a ride in the little green flatbed the workmen use to get around in and to haul equipment on the ranch.

"I want to check the set of new fruit on the avocado trees. The men say we've lost a lot of our crop in the recent heat."

We maneuvered along the twisting roads on the backside of the ranch, intent as we stared into branches, reassuring ourselves we still had fruit. Ted brought the machine to a halt and hopped out to cut some tight bands loose from the trunks of several grapefruit trees. The bands had been placed there to brace the trees against large, adjacent stakes, but now bound them too tightly, suffocating their growth.

"Hey, we're missing the sunset," I said.

"We'll see it around the next corner," he assured me, and we arrived just in time to see the last wedge of brilliant red-orange disappear. I thanked him with a touch of my hand.

Ted headed uphill, rounded a rising curve, and pointed the green machine again in the direction of the sun, which from this higher vantage point seemed miraculously to be setting again, showing an even larger wedge than we'd seen a few minutes before. We smiled at each other. Once more we watched it sink slowly below the horizon.

"Now, watch this! My girls loved it too!" Ted raced up the last steep hill toward the house. "You'll see three sunsets tonight!" From the edge of the rose garden next to the house we watched yet another sunset, again in its final moments.

I sighed, satisfied. "Well, that's it. No more hills to climb."

He looked at me. "Don't say that, Diana. We'll always have wonderful sunsets, wherever we are together! There are always more hills to climb."

You waited until you were alone.
Death is a private thing.
You knew your last act
was to a different audience.

As it entered you—
oh how you must have danced!
curving toward God,
elegant and alone.

Dear one, what is it like?
Tell us! What is death?

Birth,
you say, your voice swathed in wings.
I am born in the endless beginning.
I am not. I am.

You start turning into us,
we who love you.
You weep in our sadness,
you laugh when we do,
you greet each moment fresh,
When we do.

So may your gift of loving enter our own
and be with us that way, forever.

ELIAS AMIDON

GRATITUDES

IN THE ELEVEN YEARS I have walked the adventure of writing this book, there have been many who have served as guides. They deserve more than words of thankfulness.

An endless and overflowing stash of rich dark chocolate to Ted. More than anyone, you empower and inspire me every day. You are my hero.

A forever-best-friend hug to Mary Olsen Kelly for coming up with the perfect title and therefore the right scene with which I began telling my story. You read and reread every draft, continually cheering me on. Without you I would never have finished. And thank you, Don Kelly, for sharing Mary and so much of yourself with Ted and me.

A reverent bow to one of my most cherished male friends, free-lance editor John Niendorff. You did so much to help me develop the structure for the story line. You listened deeply to my every emotion and felt each one as your own. I loved the creative hours we spent together.

Sprays of purple orchids to my treasured friend and colleague Bobbie Probstein for being there through so many times, both sweet and sad. I appreciate your early editing suggestions, your countless readings of the pages, and the sepia photographs of Paul's and my hands. You are an angel in my life.

Bouquets of red roses to my extraordinary agent and dear friend Carole Bidnick for your having captured my artistic vision, and for your dedication and expertise in agenting and marketing. Thank you Patti Breitman for introducing me to Carole and to the talented Connie Hatch. And thank you Jeremy Tarcher, friend and publisher of five of Paul's and my earlier books, for recommending to Carole that Renaissance Books would be just the right home for this one.

A lifetime supply of frosted, heart-shaped, *Send Me Someone* shortbread cookies to all at Renaissance Books, who took the story to heart and nurtured it into final, final form: my publisher Bill Hartley, his wife and most extraordinary copyeditor Anni Hartley, acquisitions editor Richard F. X. O'Connor, my delightful editor Amanda Pisani, designers Lisa Lenthall and Susan Shankin, head of promotion Mike Dougherty, publicists Jens Hussey and Kathryn Mills, as well as Arthur Morey, Joe McNeely, and the enthusiastic sales team at St. Martin's Press.

Advance applause to Arielle Ford and the Ford Group, who, along with the promotion team at Renaissance, will carry my dream to its highest potential.

Mahalo and pikake leis to John and Shannon Tullius, founders of the Maui Writers Conference, and to the conference presenters who guided and encouraged me—especially John Saul and Mike Sack, Richard Paul Evans, and Terry Brooks.

Sterling silver soup spoons to my coauthors at Chicken Soup for the Soul Enterprises, especially Jack Canfield, Patty Aubery, Mark Victor Hansen, Patty Hansen, Hanoch and Meladee McCarty, and Dan Millman. I am so honored to be part of the most loved and largest-selling book series in history.

A standing ovation with cheers and loon calls to all the members of the Inside Edge, past and present, just for showing up.

A necklace of stars to June Crockett, who helped me gather and create a collage of my mementos to decorate the box in which I submitted the manuscript. What a light you are.

Victorian nosegays to my circle of readers (in alphabetical order): Sally Albers, Jean Ardell, Gwyn Blanton, Gail Boyd, Patti Breitman, Beth Broderick, Kathy Bryant, June Crockett, Barbara Curtis, Christine Dahm, Gale Evans, Judy Foley, Susi Fuller, Sharon Glommen, Susie Gross, Judith Handelsman, Floren Harper, Candi Piech Hart, Arlene Hodges, Susan Jeffers, Theresa Kaplan, Mike Krpan, Mary LaRue, Joan Linder, Jodi Olsen, Tim Piering, Linda Rosetta, Pat Rypinski, Tom Sewell, Alice Simmons, Judi Skalsky, Amy Thyr, Rama Vernon, Jo Vogelbacher, and Candace Wheeler.

A ribbon around the first copy off the press for my precious daughter, Lexi. I am lost for words to describe all your contributions. You are strong and beautiful and wise. I love you with a heart and a half.

Warm fuzzies to my stepdaughter Christy for thoughtful and expert editing suggestions. You were great.

A special hug and an unlimited number of favorite recipes to my stepdaughter Kathy, her husband Court, and their daughters Aidan and Caitlin—for your compassion and laughter and for including us in your lives. You inspire Ted and me every day.

Bouquets of love to my darling mother Mimi who taught me to create beauty. You encouraged me always, and I'm sorry you didn't live quite long enough to hold this book in your loving hands. And a big thank you to my precious stepfather, Jack Schneider. I love you both.

And, finally, thank you, Papa. I now know you did your best.

ACKNOWLEDGMENT FOR PERMISSIONS

Excerpt from *Life Prayers*, edited by Elizabeth Roberts and Elias Amidon, copyright © 1996 by Elias Amidon, published by HarperSanFrancisco. All rights reserved by the author.

Excerpt from "Names Are Ships," by Don Blanding from *Vagabond's House*, copyright © 1928 by Don Blanding, copyright renewed 1956 by Don Blanding. Published by Dodd, Mead & Co. Used by permission.

Excerpt from "Stopping by Woods on a Snowy Evening," by Robert Frost from *The Poetry of Robert Frost*, edited by Edward Connery Lathem, copyright © 1923, © 1969 by Henry Holt & Co., copyright © 1951 by Robert Frost. Reprinted by permission of Henry Holt & Co., LLC.

"The Well of Grief," from *Where Many Rivers Meet*, by David Whyte, copyright © 1990 by Many Rivers Press. Reprinted by permission.

"Wind Beneath My Wings," by Larry Henley and Jeff Silbar, copyright © 1982 Warner House of Music & WB Gold Music Corp. All rights reserved. Used by permission. Warner Bros. Publications U.S. Inc., Miami, FL 33014.

"Right Here Waiting," by Richard Marx, copyright © 1989 Chi-Boy Music (ASCAP). Rights outside North America administered by WB Music Corp.

All rights reserved. Used by permission. Warner Bros. Publications U.S. Inc., Miami, FL 33014.

"Renascence," by Edna St. Vincent Millay, copyright © 1912, 1940. From *Collected Poems* of Edna St. Vincent Millay, HarperCollins.

ABOUT THE AUTHOR

DIANA VON WELANETZ WENTWORTH has enjoyed a celebrated career as an author of award-winning cookbooks and as a
popular public speaker and television host.

Her books include the *Chicken Soup for the Soul Cookbook* with Jack
Canfield and Mark Victor Hansen (Health Communications, Inc.,
1993), which has sold nearly half a million copies to date in seven
languages. Along with Dan Millman she is currently co-authoring
Chicken Soup for Body and Soul, featuring 101 stories that inspire readers
to attain their physical goals.

With her late husband, Paul von Welanetz, Diana wrote and
published six cookbooks, including *The Pleasure of Your Company*
(Atheneum, 1976), winner of the French Tastemaker "Cookbook of
the Year" award, and *The von Welanetz Guide to Ethnic Ingredients* (J. P.
Tarcher, 1983), considered the classic reference for international
ingredients. Diana and Paul also hosted their own long-running daily
television series, *The New Way Gourmet,* broadcast to millions of viewers internationally on the cable Health and the Lifetime networks.

In 1985 the von Welanetzes launched a visionary new enterprise
called the Inside Edge. At weekly breakfast meetings throughout

Southern California, individual chapters of the Inside Edge provided a high-energy environment in which members heard prominent speakers present forward-thinking ideas about expanding human potential. (To receive information via the Internet on the Inside Edge Foundation for Education in Irvine, California, please visit the Web site at Insideedge.org.)

Diana lives in Southern California and has been married for eleven years to Ted Wentworth. Both are featured in *Who's Who in America*.

DATE DUE

ISSCW B
        V945

VON WELANETZ WENTWORTH,D.
  SEND ME SOMEONE : A
TRUE STORY OF LOVE HERE
AND HEREAFTER

ISSCW   B
         V945

HOUSTON PUBLIC LIBRARY
CENTRAL LIBRARY